KUTAKOV
Japanese Foreign Policy

Leonid N. Kutakov

Japanese Foreign Policy

on the Eve of

the Pacific War

A Soviet View

by

Leonid N. Kutakov

Edited with a Foreword by
GEORGE ALEXANDER LENSEN

THE DIPLOMATIC PRESS
TALLAHASSEE, FLORIDA

PUBLISHED BY

THE DIPLOMATIC PRESS, INC.

1102 Betton Road

Tallahassee, Florida 32303

Library of Congress Catalog Card No. 77–186316

ISBN 910512–15–9

PRINTED AND BOUND IN THE UNITED STATES

Rose Printing Company, Inc., Tallahassee

Foreword

During the Second World War the origins of the conflict had seemed clear to every American: Germany, Italy and Japan had set out to conquer the world and had given the other powers no choice but to fight for survival. They had embarked on their "naked aggression" without justifiable cause and were solely responsible for the war and the "crimes against humanity."

After the Second World War the origins of the conflict were obscured by the "revisionist" thesis that President Franklin D. Roosevelt had courted war with Japan in order to maneuver the unwilling American people into the European fray. With the outbreak of the Cold War the responsibility for the Second World War was clouded further by the equation on the part of some publicists of the Soviet Union, America's recent comrade-in-arms, with Nazi Germany and the allegation that Joseph Stalin would have made common cause with Adolf Hitler, if the latter had not attacked him unexpectedly. The absolution of Japan has continued along with the indictment of American and Russian policy by revisionists of the right and left, Japan being depicted as a victim of her struggle against both international Communism and American economic imperialism.

If historians studied the origins of wars merely to apportion blame, one might well say "Let bygones be bygones," but their analyses of policies which failed to deter hostilities must be considered if we are not to repeat the same mistakes. The views of foreign scholars are of particular importance, because foreign relations consist of actions and reactions, conceived less on the basis of facts and actual motives than of images and suspected aims, so that, for example, the United States will act toward the U.S.S.R. in response to what she *thinks* Russian ambitions are and the Soviet Union in turn will formulate policies on the grounds of her conception of American designs.

The fact that there are lessons to be learned from the past does not mean, of course, that the right conclusions are always drawn or the correct parallels applied; sometimes mistakes are overcorrected. America's overinvolvement in world affairs after the Second World War was the result in part of the conviction that her underinvolvement in years past had contributed to the failure of the League of Nations to maintain peace. The fear that the countries of Asia would fall like a row of dominoes if the spread of Communism were not contained by force of arms from the outset, was rooted in the memory of Munich, when appeasement had allowed Germany to expand step by step.

If Americans who are now in their 40's and 50's are suffering from a Munich complex, so are their Soviet contemporaries, with this difference: the Russians, who had favored a strong, united stand against German aggression at the time of Munich, are convinced that Western appeasement of the Axis powers must have had an ulterior motive, namely that Great Britain and the United States sought to encourage Germany and Japan to attack the U.S.S.R. in order to rid the capitalist world of Communism. Tempting as it may be to dismiss this charge, the fact remains that the Russians are at least as suspicious of the Americans and the English as the latter of them. While the Soviet and American governments have worked hard in recent years to prevent a confrontation, as the stakes are too high in the age of the hydrogen bomb for either power to gamble on a policy of Russian roulette or poker bluff, the dreadful possibility remains that the conviction shared by both countries as the result of the Munich trauma that a timely show of force will prevent war might lead them into a situation where they could maneuver themselves into a collision in an attempt to avoid one. And they would do so, ironically, out of fear and self-defense rather than aggression, failing to see how their actions looked to each other.

In his analysis of Japanese, German, English, Soviet and American foreign policies on the eve of the Pacific War, Dr. Leonid Nikolaevich Kutakov acquaints us with the Soviet point of view. Whether or not we accept his interpretation of history, we must familiarize ourselves with it, for it, rather than our conception of East Asian international relations, underlies the thinking of Soviet policy makers.

Dr. Kutakov is widely known in diplomatic as well as academic circles. A graduate of the Moscow Institute of History, Philosophy and Literature and a veteran of the Red Army, in which he held the rank of captain, he served as chief of the Historical Diplomatic Division of the Soviet Ministry of Foreign Affairs (1946–51), prorector of the Moscow State Institute of International Relations (1952–55), adviser to the director of the Peking Institute of Diplomacy of the Ministry of Foreign Affairs of the Chinese People's Republic (1955–57), counselor of the Soviet embassy in Japan (1959–60), deputy director of the Moscow State Institute of International Relations (1963–65), and senior coun-

selor for political questions of the Permanent Mission
of the U.S.S.R. to the United Nations with the rank of
ambassador extraordinary and plenipotentiary (1965–
68) before attaining his present position of under-
secretary-general for political and Security Council affairs of the United Nations. He is the author of *The
History of International Relations of Modern Times,
1918–1945; The Portsmouth Peace Treaty; History of
Soviet-Japanese Diplomatic Relations; Foreign Policy
and Diplomacy of Japan;* and *Essays on the Newest History of Japan.* The first of these titles was published in
Peking in Chinese, the others in Moscow in Russian. A
Japanese edition of his history of Soviet-Japanese relations has also appeared. He coauthored with Dr.
Israelyan *Diplomacy of Aggressors: The Italo-German-
Japanese Bloc, Its Creation and Fall* and wrote chapters
for such multi-volume Soviet works as *History of Diplomacy, History of the International Relations and
Foreign Policy of the U.S.S.R.* and *World History.* In
writing his books, Dr. Kutakov had access to the archives
of the Soviet Ministry of Foreign Affairs and of the
Ministry of Foreign Affairs of the People's Republic
of China.

To make the present work meaningful to American
readers I have taken wide liberties with the manuscript
in preparing it for publication. Not only have I supplied the full names, customary English spellings, and
identifications for the many Chinese, Japanese and Western figures mentioned, but have pruned the text to half
its size, deleting material already well known to American readers and cooling the rhetoric. Dr. Kutakov remains the author, for the views are his, not mine. We
have made no attempt to reconcile our ideological differences. He is solely responsible for the interpreta-

tions offered in this book, I for the style of their presentation.

Thanks are due to Professor James William Morley of Columbia University, who first suggested that I publish the manuscript, and to Professor John G. Stoessinger of the City University of New York at Hunter College for his encouragement of the collaborative effort.

GEORGE ALEXANDER LENSEN

Tallahassee, Florida
January 1, 1972

Contents

1

Japan and Germany:
The Policy of Alliance

The formation of the German-Japanese military-political alliance, which hastened the outbreak of the Second World War, was facilitated by the anti-Soviet policy of the United States, Great Britain and France, which were loath to accept the Soviet proposals for collective security and hoped that Germany and Japan might be turned against the U.S.S.R. and the national liberation movement of the peoples of Asia.

The Soviet Government had made a number of proposals to curb and isolate aggression. Putting forward the idea of creating a system of collective security, the Soviet State had proceeded from the principle of the indivisibility of the world, from the contention that any war, even a small one started by an aggressor in a remote corner of the earth, was fraught with danger for all peace-loving states.

In 1933 the Soviet Union had proposed to the League of Nations a declaration on the definition of "aggression"

1

and "aggressor," but the proposal had been rejected under pressure from Great Britain and France.

In 1937, at the Brussels conference, convened to discuss the situation in the Far East, the Soviet delegation had demanded application of Article 16 of the Charter of the League of Nations and adoption of collective measures against Japanese aggression. However, the British, French and American delegates had refused to consider active opposition to Japan in the hope that the latter might be turned against the Soviet Union. Similarly the governments of the United States, Great Britain and France hoped that by appeasing Hitler in the West, they might deflect him eastward against the U.S.S.R. Had the Western powers supported the Soviet proposal for the creation of a system of collective security and taken a strong stand against Japanese and German expansion, the aggressive Axis might never have been formed and the Second World War might have been prevented.

Lack of English, French and American opposition to the reintroduction of military conscription in Germany and to the remilitarizaton of the Rhine Zone had emboldened Hitler to embark on an aggressive foreign policy, making common cause with other powers that were discontented with the system of international relations established by the Versailles and Washington conferences.

As the signing of a political agreement with Italy in October 1936 had not removed the contradictions between Germany and Italy, which were striving for hegemony over the Danube basin and for control over Austria, and as there had been little help that Germany could expect from the weak Italian fascist state in the event of hostilities with Great Britain and France, Germany had decided to ally herself with Japan, whose military and civilian ultranationalists seemed capable of providing her with strong military support against the Soviet Union and the United States, as well as Great Britain and France.

An alliance with Japan appealed to Germany because it would allow her to threaten Great Britain with war not only in the North and in the Mediterranean, but also in the Far East. At the same time, Germany calculated, such an alliance could be effected without opposition from Great Britain, France and the United States by cloaking it in the flag of anti-Communism. The ruling circles of Japan, meanwhile, saw in an alliance with Germany substantial assistance for their aggressive policy against the U.S.S.R., Great Britain and the United States.

The Japanese tried to gain control over the Mongolian People's Republic. When the Mongolian government did not bow to diplomatic pressure and military threats, the Kwantung Army resorted to arms. But the Mongolian troops repulsed the Japanese-Manchurian attack in the autumn of 1935 and again in early 1936. On March 1, 1936, Joseph Stalin told the American journalist Roy Howard, "In case Japan should attack the Mongolian People's Republic and endanger her independence, we will have to help the Mongolian People's Republic."[1] Eleven days later, on March 12, the Soviet Union concluded a mutual assistance pact with the Mongolian People's Republic.

As Japanese provocations on the Soviet-Manchurian frontier were rebuffed with equal determination by the U.S.S.R., whose international position was being consolidated by mutual assistance pacts with France and Czechoslovakia, Japan desired a powerful ally capable of pinning down the bulk of Soviet forces in Europe and

[1] *Pravda,* March 5, 1936

thus leaving the Russian Far East exposed to military inroads.

In the spring of 1935,[2] Friedrich Gaus, a high-ranking official of the German Ministry for Foreign Affairs, visited Colonel Oshima Hiroshi, the Japanese military attaché in Berlin, and, claiming to act on behalf of Joachim von Ribbentrop, sounded him out on the possibility of concluding some "defense alliance" between Germany and Japan against the U.S.S.R.[3] Gaus approached Oshima rather than the ambassador because the attaché, like many Japanese militarists, was known to be a fervent admirer of Hitler and of fascism.

In response to Oshima's report, the Japanese General Staff replied that it wished to know more about the German proposal and would send a special representative to delve into details. Early in December, Colonel Wakamatsu Tadaichi, an official of the German section of the Japanese General Staff, arrived in Berlin to confer about the matter.

The accession of the Hirota Government in March 1936 expedited the progress of the negotiations. Despite the fact that the Putsch engineered by the "young officers' group" in February 1936 had ended in failure, the fascist ultranationalists had retained their influence on Japanese foreign policy. In spring Viscount Mushakoji Kintomo, the Japanese ambassador in Berlin, entered the negotiations and conducted them together with Oshima. The German side was represented by Ribbentrop. By the middle of 1936 the Nazi government had prepared a

[2] In his testimony at the Tokyo War Crimes Trial, Oshima stated that the meeting took place in May or June.

[3] Foreign Policy Archives of the Ministry for Foreign Affairs of the U.S.S.R., hereafter cited as "Soviet Archives", collection 436b (Documents of the International Military Tribunal for the Far East plus preparatory material of the Soviet Prosecution), file 13, p. 122.

draft agreement, replete with secret addenda. To fore-
stall objections on the part of the Western Powers, the
treaty was labeled as an "Anti-Comintern Pact." Indeed, Mushakoji actually suggested to the British Government later that it join in the treaty and thereby con-
firm its purely anti-Soviet character.[4]

In mid-1936 the merits of the proposed Anti-
Comintern Pact were debated in Tokyo. In a paper prepared for the Privy Council, the Japanese Ministry for
Foreign Affairs analyzed the causes that had prompted
Japan to effect a rapprochement with Germany and
formalize it in a special agreement. Noting that the international position of the Soviet Union had been consolidated, as seen in the conclusion of treaties of mutual
assistance with France, Czechoslovakia and the Mongolian People's Republic, the Foreign Office stated that
"in order to secure the existence of Japan and to conduct
policy in peace on the continent it is absolutely necessary
to join forces with another power," allegedly, "to contain the Soviet Union." Germany, the report stated, was
the most obvious ally, "because both Japan and Germany
hold identical positions with regard to the international
situation."[5]

Yet the Foreign Office realized that there was a significant difference in the respective positions of Germany
and Japan vis-à-vis the U.S.S.R.: "Japan borders on the
Soviet Union and has many concessions on the territory
of the latter. Besides there are still many controversial
questions pending solution." One was the question of the
fisheries convention. The rights of the Japanese to fish
in Soviet waters were regulated by the convention con-

---

[4] Great Britain, Foreign Office, *Documents on British Foreign Policy,
1919–1939,* hereafter cited as "DBFP", vol. VIII (London, 1955), No. 473.
[5] Soviet Archives, 43b, file 57, p. 59.

cluded for an eight-year period in 1928 in accordance with Article III of the Basic (Peking) Convention of 1925. The Japanese industrialists were very much interested in concluding a new convention.

The Foreign Office felt that Japan was not prepared for a "big war" against the U.S.S.R. and warned that "it is necessary to proceed from the understanding that the coalition should not bring about a war against the Soviet Union."[6] It drew attention furthermore to a possible reaction of the Western Powers to a rapprochement between Germany and Japan. It proposed, therefore, that Japan improve her international situation by building friendly relations with Great Britain or at least by avoiding clashes with her because Great Britain "has interests and great influence the world over."[7] Sensing correctly the dual position of Great Britain with regard to Japanese policy in the Far East, the Foreign office recommended "to act with great caution" in relation to Germany and "not to irritate Great Britain." It recommended that the government weigh relations with the U.S.S.R. and Great Britain "before realizing the coalition with Germany."[8] It proposed a number of amendments to the German draft in order to conceal the essence of the agreement.

The first article stipulated that neither Japan nor Germany would undertake measures that might put the Soviet Union in an advantageous position. The Japanese proposed to amend the German draft by substituting "a third power" for "the Soviet Union" and by stipulating that "such measures shall be adopted in case one of the parties is attacked or is threatened to be attacked."[9] The

[6] *Ibid.,* pp. 58–59.
[7] *Ibid.,* p. 58.
[8] *Ibid.,* p. 60.
[9] *Ibid.,* p. 59.

Foreign Office proposed to limit the pact to the exchange of "information on Communist activities and opinions regarding countermeasures to be adopted by each country" and to amend the agreement in such a way as to camouflage its aggressive nature.

It was for the same reason that the Foreign Office recommended that negotiations be conducted concurrently with Great Britain. It suggested that Great Britain be assured that her concessions in China would be respected and submitted to the government a draft treaty to be concluded with Great Britain for a period of five years, stipulating the establishment between the two powers "of frank relations with a view to the joint settlement of questions of importance to both countries."[10]

Premier Hirota Koki and Foreign Minister Arita Hachiro also sought to allay British and Soviet apprehensions in their statements during the discussion of this pact at the meeting of the Research Committee of the Privy Council on November 25, 1936.[11] Hirota assured the committee that the government "will refrain from taking any definite steps that might worsen relations with the Soviet Union" and "will attach most serious attention to settling diplomatic relations between the two countries in the best possible manner." He emphasized that the government "will invariably maintain and strengthen friendly relations between Japan and Great Britain and the United States of America and, especially, sincere relations with Great Britain."[12]

---

[10] *Ibid.*

[11] According to the procedure that existed at that time in Japan, important international agreements, laws and other documents drafted by the government were discussed preliminarily in the so-called Research Committee of the Privy Council and were subject to consideration at the meetings of the Privy Council to be presented later to the Emperor for ratification or approval.

[12] Soviet Archives, 436b, file 47, p. 27.

At the meeting of the Privy Council Arita stated that "the government did everything possible to avoid irritating the Soviet Union excessively." "In those articles of the Treaty which refer to the Comintern," he said, "we avoided such wording as might identify the Soviet Union with the Comintern and besides we have kept secret the annex to the Treaty and the appended official notes."[13]

Meanwhile the draft of the German-Japanese pact, put in final form by Mushakoji and Ribbentrop, had been initialled on October 23, 1936. The negotiations had been conducted in secret and the Japanese government had hoped to keep the matter quiet until it had concluded a new fisheries convention with the Soviet Union, but word leaked to the American and European press. When the chief of the Second Oriental Desk of the People's Commissariat for Foreign Affairs asked Chargé d'Affaires Sako Shuichi how credible were the rumors about a German-Japanese Agreement, Sako responded that "the Ministry for Foreign Affairs had instructed him to deny these rumors officially as utterly at variance with reality."[14] Foreign Minister Arita went even further in a talk with the Soviet Ambassador Konstantin Yurenev on November 16. He not only denied the conclusion of any agreement aimed against the U.S.S.R., but declared that Japan was striving to establish friendly relations with the latter and that the negotiations in progress with a third power could not reflect on Soviet-Japanese relations either directly or indirectly.[15]

The Soviet government was not fooled, however. A TASS dispatch of November 18 revealed Russian

---

[13] *Ibid.*, file 57, p. 30.
[14] *Pravda*, November 18, 1936.
[15] *Ibid.*

knowledge of the initialling of the Anti-Comintern Pact. "Though this agreement yet to be published refers to combating Communism," TASS wrote, "it is in fact a cover for a secret German-Japanese agreement on agreed actions on the part of Germany and Japan in case one of the countries is at war with a third state."[16]

The following day Yurenev called on Arita and told him that the Soviet government regarded the explanations concerning the character of the German-Japanese agreement which he had given on November 16 as unsatisfactory. He said that the Soviet government found it difficult to conceive that the German government might need the services of the Japanese police or that the Japanese government might need the services of the German police to combat Communism in their respective countries. The ambassador expressed the view that the agreement on combating Communism was only a cover for another agreement to be kept secret and directed against a third power, and warned that such an agreement might afflict a heavy blow to Soviet-Japanese relations.[17]

In the course of the discussion of the Anti-Comintern Pact at the meeting of the Privy Council on November 25, a number of questions were put to the government about the position of the Soviet Union concerning the pact. While assuring the Privy Council that the U.S.S.R. would not resort to any sanctions "even if the military preparations of Japan are inadequate," Arita admitted that the pact had an anti-Soviet orientation: "Soviet Russia must realize that she has to face Germany and Japan. . . ."[18]

[16] *Ibid.*
[17] *Ibid.*
[18] Soviet Archives, 436b, file 13, p. 167.

The final text of the pact, which was signed that day, incorporated the Japanese amendment that the obligations of the parties were limited to the exchange of information on the activities of the Comintern and the conduct of a joint struggle against it. But the Nazi diplomats succeeded in naming the Soviet Union in the appended Secret Agreement as the main target of the pact.

The text of the Secret Agreement became known only in 1947 during the Tokyo War Crimes Trial.[19] Like other aggressive agreements it was couched in defensive phraseology to camouflage its true nature. The preamble as well as the main body of the Anti-Comintern Pact contained references to the menace that international Communism presented to the existence of the signatories of the pact. It was agreed, therefore, in case one of them "become the object of an unprovoked attack by the U.S.S.R., the other High Contracting State engages itself to enter upon no measures of a kind which would have the effect of relieving the position of the U.S.S.R." and "immediately consult on what measures to take for the safeguard of their common interests." (Article I). During the continuation of the agreement (5 years) the sides undertook that they "will not, without reciprocal concurrence, conclude any sort of political treaties with the U.S.S.R. which are not in keeping with the spirit of this agreement."[20]

The notes exchanged between Ribbentrop and Ambassador Mushakoji after the signing of the pact were also kept secret. The German note stated that Berlin did not consider the provisions of the political treaties exist-

[19] United States, Department of State, *Documents on German Foreign Policy 1918–1945,* hereafter cited as "DGFP", Series "D", vol. I (Washington, 1949) doc. No. 463, annex.
[20] *Ibid.*

ing between Germany and the U.S.S.R., such as the Rapallo treaty of 1922 and the Neutrality Treaty of 1926, as contradicting the spirit of the Anti-Comintern Pact and the obligations ensuing therefrom.[21]

The year 1936 had seen numerous border clashes as the Kwantung Army and Manchurian forces had tested the Soviet frontier. Japanese authorities had repeatedly seized Soviet ships, and did not fulfill their obligations in connection with the sale of the Chinese Eastern Railway by the U.S.S.R. to Manchukuo.[22] With the conclusion of the Anti-Comintern Pact the Japanese intensified their anti-Soviet activities. On November 26, the day after the signing of the pact, Japanese and Manchurian forces crossed the Soviet border near Lake Khanka. A real military engagement ensued and the Japanese were forced to withdraw from Soviet territory.[23]

To increase its strength the Japanese Army put forward a long-term program, known as the Six-Year Plan of Military Preparations for the period from 1937 to 1942. The Ministry of Finance trimmed the budget estimate and lengthened the period of the plan by one year, but even in its pruned version the program provided for 38 billion yen—an enormous amount of money for the time.

Not all Japanese shared the aggressive views of the ultranationalists. Some of the business monopolies realized the risks with which such policy was fraught; they feared in particular that it would damage relations with the Western powers with which they had close economic ties. A number of Japanese newspapers attacked

[21] Soviet Archives, 436b, file 13, p. 147.
[22] Union of Soviet Socialist Republics, Ministry of Foreign Affairs, *Vneshnyaya politika SSSR. Sbornik dokumentov*, vol. IV (Moscow, 1946), pp. 80–235.
[23] Soviet Archives, 436b, file 17, p. 147.

the pact so sharply that Marshal Hermann Göring lodged a protest with Oshima.[24]

The signing of the Anti-Comintern Pact, the disruption of the Soviet-Japanese fishery negotiations, high military expenditures, rising prices (over 20% in less than two years), and the failure of negotiations with China combined to evoke serious criticism of the Japanese government in the Diet and in the country at large. Progressives in Japan regarded the signing of the Anti-Comintern Pact as an open transition to fresh acts of aggression. So strong was popular dissatisfaction in fact that the Hirota government had to resign. General Hayashi Senjuro, who succeeded as premier, did not change course, though he maneuvered somewhat on questions of foreign policy. In order to allay the fear of many prominent Japanese that relations with the Western powers would be hurt, the new Foreign Minister Sato Naotake made a statement in the Diet in which he criticized the Anti-Comintern Pact.

The German ambassador in Tokyo, Herbert von Dirksen, sounded a note of anxiety in his dispatch of March 27, 1937, when he informed Berlin that according to the statement made by Sato, the latter regarded the German-Japanese pact as an inescapable evil and considered that it had been concluded for technical reasons as a police measure against the Comintern. Dirksen called on Foreign Minister Sato to express his regret over the "fierce attacks" against the pact "from the press and the Parliament," noting that they created the impression abroad "that the political circles of Japan disapprove not only of the pact itself but also of the entire pro-German policy . . ." and that Japan might wish to annul the pact. He referred especially to the debate in the Diet,

[24] *Ibid.,* p. 47.

where various orators, including the liberal statesman Ozaki Yukio, spoke openly against the pact. Giving his own interpretation of the reasons for concluding the pact, namely the activities of the Comintern, Dirksen took issue with Sato's statement that from the point of view of Russo-Japanese relations the signing of the pact was "a deplorable and regretful event." But Sato did not go back on his words. He stated that "the Japanese Government, despite the existence of the Comintern, will try to improve relations between the two peoples . . ." and "will use the first opportunity to restore the sincere and friendly relations which existed for 12 years [since 1925] between Japan and Russia."[25] Pointing out that the hostile comments in the Japanese press had already provoked a corresponding response in Germany, Dirksen demanded that Sato tell a German correspondent "a few words for Germany in order to dispell the doubts in Germany and at the same time to shatter the hopes of our enemies [i.e., the enemies of Germany and Japan]."[26]

Sato expressed regret at the false impression gained in Germany regarding the Japanese attitude toward the pact and promised to take into account Dirksen's advice "to express his views when an opportunity offers itself." Yet in explaining the Japanese position, Sato confirmed that the Anti-Comintern Pact had worsened Russo-Japanese relations and foiled the signing of a fisheries agreement. Noting that Japanese public opinion had been greatly disturbed by this, Sato said that "his task for the immediate future was to establish better relations with Great Britain" in order to assure Japanese access to the markets of the third powers.

Dirksen retorted that "Germany, on her part, was

[25] Soviet Archives, 436b, file 47, pp. 46–47.
[26] *Ibid.*

striving to establish friendly relations with Great Britain." He indicated that "Germany will likewise welcome the establishment of friendly relations between Japan and China," because Germany wished to establish good relations with China "since it had considerable interests there."

At the end of the conversation Sato referred again to the instability of the situation in Japan and to the weakness of Manchukuo, and declared that he considered the "further deterioration of relations between Japan and the Soviet Union undesirable."

The conclusion of the Anti-Comintern Pact thus had not removed the contradictions between Japanese and German imperialism. Germany feared that further Japanese inroads into China might undermine her own economic position in the Far East. She had misgivings also that too deep an involvement in China might weaken Japan as an ally in German plans for world domination.

Not long before the provocation of the Lukouchiao or Marco Polo Bridge Incident, Ernst von Weizsäcker, secretary of the German Ministry for Foreign Affairs, wrote to Ambassador Dirksen in Tokyo that "the Japanese were going in a wrong direction in their attempts to act against Communism in China on the basis of the Anti-Comintern Pact." Referring to the fact that "the pact did not provide for combating Communism on the territory of third powers," Weizsäcker regarded the Japanese actions as "contradicting the spirit of the pact," because they stood in the way of unifying China and thus actually helped in spreading Communism in China. In support of his contention, Weizsäcker reported that Marshal Chiang Kai-shek had told the German Ambassador Oskar Trautmann that "it is necessary to take into account the possibility of Russian intervention in a possible future war" and that he himself "up till now has not concluded any agreements with Russia, but the situation has now changed."[27]

In June 1937 the German Ministry for Foreign Affairs warned the Japanese government that it must not expect German approval of their actions. It expressed displeasure at Japanese radio broadcasts which tried to convince German listeners of the need to side with Japan in the China conflict.[28] The Germans feared that Japanese aggression would intensify the national liberation movement in China and undermine Germany's influence with Chiang, whom she supplied with armaments and advisers for his anti-Communist campaigns.

German support of Chiang Kai-shek aroused Japanese protests. The Germans agreed to discontinue the delivery of military supplies—arms shipments actually continued until June 1938[29]—but refused to recall their military advisers. "This is out of the question," Weizsäcker wrote Dirksen, arguing that the recall of the advisers would be tantamount to Germany "becoming an enemy of Nanking" and result in their displacement by Soviet military advisers. Germany's willingness to instruct her advisers to abstain from taking part in military operations did not satisfy Japan. As the adjutant of the war minister pointed out, it "threatened the policy of cooperation with the Japanese army because the already existing opposition of individual groups of Japanese officers may become widespread."[30]

Japan's invasion of China in July 1937 did not meet with German approval. When Ambassador Mushakoji complained to Weizsäcker on July 28 that "Japan has lost

[27] Soviet Archives, 436b, file 13, pp. 173–174.
[28] *Ibid.*
[29] *Ibid.*, pp. 175–176.
[30] DGFP, vol. I, doc. 576.

the benefit of German understanding of the anti-Communist achievements as exemplified by the Japanese actions against China," "consistently tried to prove that Japan was working against Communism in China in our [i.e., German and Japanese] interests," and proposed the formation of a secret German-Japanese committee to which he could "explain the anti-Communist tendencies which have forced Japan to undertake her present actions in China," Weizsäcker replied that Germany could not "justify or morally support Japanese actions that might lead to the achievement of opposite purposes . . . to the encouragement of Communism in China and to pushing China into Russian hands as a result of such actions."[31]

In response to a query by Mushakoji about German arms shipments to China, Weizsäcker said that "Japan had no justifiable reasons to demand the discontinuation of German arms deliveries to China." His assertion that the German instructors had been ordered "not to interfere with tanks in the Sino-Japanese conflict" did not soothe Mushakoji, who made several remarks which sounded partly like a complaint and partly like a threat to the effect that his mission in Berlin had failed.[32]

When Japanese protests failed to halt German arms shipments to China and German officers continued to advise Chiang Kai-shek,[33] Japan threatened to annul the Anti-Comintern Pact unless her representations were heeded.[34] On October 19, 1937, Hitler officially ordered a halt to all deliveries to China, but two days later

[31] Soviet Archives, 436b, file 13, p. 178.
[32] Ibid.
[33] DGFP, vol. I, doc. 577. The number of military advisers reached 30 in August 1937 and 23 in April 1938 (Ibid., doc. 576).
[34] DGFP, vol. I, doc. 500.

Göring secretly allowed the deliveries to continue.[35] Germany had an important economic stake in Nationalist China. She stood third in volume of capital investment— behind Japan and Great Britain but ahead of the United States—[36] and second in import trade—behind the United States but ahead of Japan and Great Britain. Her purchases included not only foodstuffs (vegetable oil, egg products, soya beans) and textile raw materials (wool, silk) but invaluable strategic materials (tin, tungsten concentrate, antimony).[37] As Ambassador Trautmann wrote to the Ministry for Foreign Affairs on October 30, 1937:

> I should like to point out that it is of no advantage to us here to be lumped with Italian policy on Far Eastern questions. The Italians play a quite negative role in China and are regarded as allies of Japan. They can afford to carry on such a policy, whereas we have to protect our important economic interests in China, which are second only to those of the Anglo-Saxon powers and Japan.[38]

Needless to say, German armaments manufacturers also were opposed to a halt in military shipments to China. Firstly, they did not want to lose a profitable customer; secondly, they needed the strategic materials.

Germany had long withheld recognition of the puppet state of Manchukuo, set up by the Japanese in 1932, partly in order not to alienate the Chinese government, partly to use recognition as a lever for concessions from Japan in China. As the German Foreign Minister Kon-

[35] DGFP, vol. I, doc. 5.
[36] *China Economist*, April 10, 1948.
[37] M.I. Sladkovsky, *Ocherki razvitiya vneshneekonomicheskikh otno-shenii Kitaya* (Moscow, 1953), pp. 208, 211.
[38] DGFP, vol. I, doc. 511.

stantin von Neurath frankly told the Italian ambassador
on November 20, 1937: "We are not prepared to make
the Japanese a gift without something in return."[39] What
Germany wanted from Japan was more favorable treatment in the occupied territories of China than extended
to third powers; Japan was willing to guarantee only
"particularly favorable treatment of Germany."[40]

On January 26, 1938, Ambassador Dirksen urged
Berlin to make certain concessions to Japanese demands
to stop arms deliveries and recall military advisers in
view of the failure of German efforts to mediate an end
to the Sino-Japanese conflict and Japan's all-out offensive against the Chiang Kai-shek regime.[41] Dirksen
argued that the presence of German advisers in China
hurt German prestige. On one hand, the Chinese accused
the Germans of transmitting their plans of operations to
the Japanese; on the other hand, the Japanese believed
that the advisers worked out plans of operations for the
Chinese and helped to implement them. "Besides,"
Dirksen wrote, "repeated defeats sustained by the
Chinese army would undermine the prestige of the
German Army." He advised that the shipment of war
material to China be discontinued and that recognition
be accorded to Manchukuo while Japan had not yet
resorted to serious measures to bring pressure to bear on
Germany. "In my view it is impossible to procrastinate
any longer in the matter of according recognition,"
wrote Dirksen.[42] Believing that the recognition of Manchukuo might open the possibility of developing wide
political-economic ties with Japan, Dirksen suggested

[39] *Ibid.,* doc. 524.
[40] *Ibid.,* doc. 605.
[41] The same view was held by the German military attaché in Tokyo,
General Ott.
[42] Soviet Archives, 436b, file 13, pp. 198–199.

that it "might be a friendly gesture with regard to Japan which, if an opportunity presented itself (the anniversary of the founding of the Empire), will be no doubt appreciated there."[43] Dirksen thought it to Germany's advantage "economically and politically to concentrate on North China" rather than on Shanghai, Hankow and Chungking and asserted that the establishment of close relations with Japanese military and civilian authorities would give Germany the possibility to exploit these areas without obstacles.[44]

Dirksen's line of reasoning, Japanese military successes in North China and then in Central China, plus Japanese assurances of economic compensation in China changed the position of the Nazi government. In February 1938 it accorded recognition to Manchukuo and in June recalled its military advisers from China.[45] As noted, arms deliveries came to a halt the same month.

In the course of numerous talks which Ribbentrop had with Mushakoji's successor, Togo Shigenori, at the beginning of 1938, he recognized the special position of Japan in China and agreed with the Japanese ambassador that Germany and Japan should cooperate more closely in China in the economic field in conformity with the spirit of the Anti-Comintern Pact. While promising "to do everything possible to promote cooperation with Japan in the field of economy and technology," Ribbentrop expressed the wish that the Japanese government would act on its own on the same lines and would adopt a gracious and considerate attitude toward German trade in China.[46]

[43] *Ibid.*, p. 199.
[44] *Ibid.*
[45] Ribbentrop told Ambassador Togo on June 29, 1938: "Our military advisers will leave Hankow, probably on July 5. It was not an easy thing to arrange for their departure." (Soviet Archives, 436b, file 14, p. 214.)
[46] Soviet Archives, 436b, file 14, p. 210.

Important as the economic relations with Germany were to Japan, it had not been her wish, when she had allied herself with Germany against the U.S.S.R., to worsen her relations with Great Britain and the United States. Foreign Minister Hirota had observed concerning German demands for a privileged position in China: "Though we must give the greatest preference to Germany and Italy with regard to their participation in the economic development of North China, we cannot go as far as to grant them a status equal or even less privileged than ours, if that will allow them to have such advantages as may threaten to eliminate completely the participation of Great Britain and the United States of America in the economic life of the country in the future."[47]

It was the hope of the Japanese leaders that their adoption of a strong line would weaken the opposition of the capitalist powers to their conquests in China. The fact that the British government in April 1938 transferred to Japan the Customs Service on Chinese territory occupied by Japanese troops[48] and that Foreign Secretary Lord Halifax and his deputies in the House of Lords and the House of Commons made statements about the desirability of a peaceful solution of issues with Japan, strengthened their expectation that it might be possible to reach an amicable agreement with Great Britain against the U.S.S.R. at the expense of China. Nor did

[47] *Ibid.*

[48] General Ugaki Kazushige, who became foreign minister in June 1938, favored a rapprochement with Great Britain and the United States. In June–September of that year Ugaki conducted unofficial talks with the British ambassador in Tokyo, Sir Robert Craigie, on the question of the peaceful settlement of differences between Japan and Great Britain in China. For information about these negotiations, see L.N. Kutakov "Iz istorii podgotovki 'dal'nevostochnogo Myunkhena' (Yapono-angliiskiye otnosheniya nakanune vtoroi mirovoi voiny)," in *Mezhimperialisticheskie protivorechiya na pervom etape obshchego krizisa kapitalizma* (Moscow, 1959).

Japan wish to worsen her relations with the United States so long as the latter supplied her with strategic raw materials. Hirota deemed it necessary, therefore, to allot to Great Britain and to the United States a certain share of participation in the development of the Chinese economy.

The Japanese leaders intended to use their German and Italian allies as sources for the capital. Japan would need to develop China's natural resources. "The participation of Germany and Italy in the economic development of Northern China may find expression mainly in investments in various important branches of industry by Germany," wrote Hirota. He envisaged German participation in the following way:

(a) investments into the China Development Company and its branches (on condition that this would not affect Japan's right to manage those enterprises);

(b) underwriting debt obligations;

(c) granting credits in the form of machinery and granting shares of stock;

(d) joint management of certain enterprises by Germany and Japan or by Japan, Germany and China.

Hirota doubted that the first two points would be acceptable to Germany. With regard to point "c," he wrote that Japan might "depend to a great extent on Germany for materials to construct railways and for other equipment for transport and also for the production of machinery for mining and metallurgical industry." As for point "d," Hirota believed that Japan might seek from Germany as compensation for German participation in the management of certain enterprises "patent rights for machinery for converting coal into liquid fuel and equipment for those enterprises which will be placed under the joint management of Japan and Germany or Japan, Germany and China."[49]

Since the military shared his views and since Ribbentrop had made special efforts to obtain privileges for Germany in China, Hirota instructed Ambassador Togo to propose at an opportune moment that "if Germany gives a promise to recognize the present position of Japan in China, Japan will see to it that Germany does not find herself with regard to economic activities in North China in a worse position than other countries."[50]

The German position in China was discussed between Togo and Ribbentrop in May and June 1938. On June 29 Togo handed Ribbentrop a memorandum to the effect that the Japanese government was unable to secure for Germany more favored treatment than granted other countries and refused to formalize a special position of Germany in a treaty. Noting that Ribbentrop had recognized "the special position of Japan in China" and, agreeing with him that Japan and Germany should cooperate in China ever more closely in the economic field in conformity with the spirit of the Anti-Comintern Pact, and acknowledging the German government's expressed willingness for economic and technical cooperation with Japan," the Japanese government promised to "regard Germany's economic activities in China with special favor" and to grant her the most favored treatment enjoyed by third powers in Manchukuo. Yet the memorandum contained the qualification that "this preeminent position of Germany does not preclude, of course, Japan's economic cooperation with third powers."

[49] Soviet Archives, 436b, file 34, pp. 34–36.
[50] *Ibid.*, p. 37.

While stating that "German interests will receive particularly sympathetic consideration and will be granted at least the most favored treatment accorded to other powers,"[51] the memorandum made qualifications concerning the exclusive rights of Japan and left open the door for cooperation with other powers. A cursory examination of the memorandum sufficed for Ribbentrop to say, "I am not satisfied with the formula."

Togo tried to convince Ribbentrop that "the Japanese government would do everything necessary to protect German interests." "In actual practice," he said, "we are ready to grant [Germany] preferential treatment compared with other countries and intend to indicate this readiness in reality, but we cannot formalize it as a treaty commitment." When Ribbentrop remarked that the draft did not go beyond the most-favored-nation treatment, which could not be considered satisfactory in view of the special position of Germay, Togo began to speak of the hopeless position of Chiang Kai-shek, hinting that soon the whole of China would be laid low by the Japanese Army.[52]

In subsequent negotiations between Togo and Emil Wiehl, chief of the Trade and Political Department of the German Ministry for Foreign Affairs, Togo rejected the request that a statement be added to the memorandum to the effect that its provisions applied only to those regions of China that were under Japanese control on the ground that "the Japanese government hoped to extend its influence to the whole of China."[53] He objected strongly to the insistent demands that Germany

[51] Soviet Archives, 436b, file 34, pp. 210–212, "Pro Memoria", June 29, 1938, handed to Ribbentrop by Togo on June 29, 1938.
[52] Soviet Archives, 436b, file 14, pp. 213–214.
[53] *Ibid.*, pp. 216–217. Wiehl's memorandum of his conversation with Togo in July 1938.

be granted better conditions than third powers, and told Wiehl that he had been instructed to sign the text of the Pro Memoria as an interim agreement.[54]

German demands for preferential treatment had their origin in numerous complaints received by the Foreign Ministry from representatives of German business interests in the Far East, reciting numerous cases of Japanese discrimination against foreign interests in China, including those of Germany. A vivid picture of the economic policy of Japan in occupied China was contained in the "Report on the Situation of German Economic Interests in the Regions of China under the Japanese Occupation," dated July 24, 1938, and prepared by economic experts of the German Ministry for Foreign Affairs in cooperation with German consular officials in China.[55] While some restrictions could be attributed to the military situation, the report concluded that the Japanese military authorities intended to place the Chinese economy under Japanese domination, "to use the economy exclusively in the interests of Japan and relegate to the background and to drive away all foreign interests." Noting that "Japan intends to exploit China only in her interests" while the question of the participation of other powers "is raised only where the Japanese resources are insufficient and in such a manner as to ensure Japanese supremacy [the numerical superiority of the Japanese in mixed enterprises], the analysis warned that German interests "would fare no better than other foreign interests."[56] "The goal of the Japanese economic policy," the report declared, "is to gain control over all major branches of industry in Northern and Central China."[57]

[54] Ibid., p. 219.
[55] Ibid., p. 224.
[56] Ibid., p. 225.
[57] Ibid., p. 227.

The Japanese authorities took over all public or semi-public enterprises of the central government and the local administration, such as railways, telephone, telegraph and radio stations, arsenals and workshops, mines and salt mines. The major part of private industrial enterprises was destroyed, the equipment suitable for use was dismantled, the rest was shipped as scrap metal to Japan. The spinning factories of Central China were distributed among the Japanese spinning enterprises. Noting that according to Article 2 of the Japanese law for the creation of the Northern and Central China Development Society, "the government was to exert its efforts to force the new government of China to grant special conditions to the Society, which was being set up, and to its branches," the report indicated that "the results of the Japanese policy will have a great effect on German commercial activities in China."[58]

Having participated in the construction of the Shantung and Tientsin-Pukow railways, German financial and railway interests were concerned about developments in this area. By mid-July 1938 the Japanese had placed 7,000 out of a total of 11,000 kilometers of Chinese railway under the control of the South Manchurian Railway Company and had ordered exclusively from Japan 250 engines and 10,000 cars as replacement for the rolling stock, with which the Chinese troops had retreated. "We have lost the old Chinese railways as our clients,"[59] the report complained and noted that the Japanese authorities had ignored the demand for interest payments on the railway loans and income, totaling for the Tientsin-Pukow railway alone over one and a half million marks.[60]

[58] *Ibid.*
[59] *Ibid.*, p. 228.
[60] *Ibid.*

The situation was no better with regard to power stations, in which the Siemens company held important interests. The first steps of the Japanese authorities made it clear that foreign operations would not be tolerated. "The German firms have been completely ousted by Japanese firms from those areas where they had been the biggest purveyors," the report stated. "It is to be expected that the same will happen in all other fields where there are Japanese monopolies," it added and warned that as the Japanese army occupied the whole of China, "it will be just as inaccessible for our trade as are Korea or Formosa."[61]

Although the report indicated a difference in attitude toward the German interests in Northern and Central China—"the Kwantung Army," it said, "evinces a certain desire to cooperate with Germany while displaying a conscious attitude of animosity towards the British"[62]— it stressed that Japanese military and official circles in Central China shied from friendship with Germany.[63] "They usually only speak of cooperation with Germany and do it, as is only possible, in private circles, i.e., in order to reproach us or to ask us for something."[64]

[61] *Ibid.*, p. 231.

[62] *Ibid.*, p. 226.

[63] In May 1938, for example, the German Consul General Fischer approached his Japanese counterpart at Shanghai, Consul General Sone, concerning several factories connected with German capital. Sone replied that since he had not received any instructions concerning a special attitude toward German interests, he could not differentiate between the representatives of various foreign states. Fischer concluded, therefore, that the Japanese military authorities "do not recognize that the German interests should be an object of a specially thorough protection when stifling foreign trade." The experts noted in this connection that Fischer was "persona grata" for the Japanese military; Oshima, on his part, characterized him as "a person, approved by the Japanese military authorities." (See Soviet Archives, 436b, file 14, pp. 226–227.)

[64] Soviet Archives, 436b, file 14, p. 226. Report of June 23, 1938, from the trade experts in Central China. This was probably due to the fact that the Kwantung Army contained many military-fascist elements who harbored especially strong, aggressive, anti-Soviet sentiments. They regarded Germany as their major ally in a war against the U.S.S.R.

Like the nationals of other states the Germans were prohibited from visiting territories where "order has been established, since these territories are visited by Japanese merchants, commercial agents and other civilians." They were severely hurt when the export of hides and furs was forbidden from the ports of Tientsin, Chefoo and Tsingtao as of June 30, 1938, for German firms controlled 50 per cent of the exports. But the protest of the German trade representative was without avail, and he voiced fear that an embargo on the export of cotton would be next.[65] The report concluded, therefore, that the economic interests of Germany in China were suffering in the areas occupied by the Japanese as never before in China.

Under pressure from big business, the Nazi government took steps to ensure German economic interests in China. On July 27, 1938, Wiehl told Ambassador Togo that Ribbentrop considered the Japanese formula providing Germany only a "particularly favorable" treatment as unsatisfactory and insisted on a promise of a "more favorable position for Germany."[66] Depicting the demand as natural in view of the special relations between the two countries and "the great sacrifices" that Germany was making "in supporting the Japanese action in North China," Wiehl complained that in the areas of China occupied by the Japanese troops "all foreign trade was being ruthlessly eliminated and that German trade was by no means receiving more favorable treatment." Wiehl handed the ambassador a note of grievances against the attitude of the Japanese military authorities. He stressed the exclusion of Germany from fields in which German firms had for many years held a

[65] *Ibid.,* p. 232.
[66] *Ibid.,* p. 219. Wiehl's memorandum of July 28, 1938, of his conversation with Togo on July 27, 1938.

dominant position, i.e., in railroad equipment and in hydro-electric power. Togo replied that he had always done his best to meet German demands, but pointed out that "the suspension of deliveries of [German] war material to China and, in particular, the withdrawal of the military advisers had taken place so recently that there had not been time yet for these gestures of friendship to have an effect everywhere on the attitude of the Japanese authorities throughout North China."[67] He left the impression that he was very much interested in signing an agreement and that he could probably grant certain concessions on which he had maintained silence before.

Eager to safeguard its vital economic interests in China, the Nazi government decided to bring pressure directly in Tokyo through Ambassador Ott, who during his service as military attaché had made important contacts among the army leaders. As the Japanese military gave some promise of support, the Germans became more insistent in their demands. On October 6 Wiehl proposed to Togo the signing of a German-Japanese agreement guaranteeing German privileges in China.[68] In the course of the initial conversations in the German Ministry for Foreign Affairs, Togo seemed favorably disposed toward the German claims, but after communicating with his superiors in Tokyo he announced that the Japanese government could not agree to them.[69]

Turning to their military sympathizers in Japan, the Germans attained the recall of Togo and his replacement as ambassador by General Oshima Hiroshi, the former military attaché in Berlin, who was known for his fascist sympathies and was on friendly terms with Heinrich Himmler and Göring.[70]

[67] Ibid., p. 222.
[68] Soviet Archives, 436b, file 70, p. 41.
[69] Ibid.
[70] Ibid., p. 37.

On December 21, 1938, Wiehl informed Oshima that Foreign Minister Ribbentrop proposed in his memorandum to the Japanese government on German-Japanese co-operation the conclusion of a written agreement granting to Germany greater privileges in China than to third powers, and requested his cooperation in obtaining acceptance of the proposal. Wiehl pointed out that "considering the German support for Japan [the withdrawal of the military advisers and the discontinuation of war material shipments], the Germans have gained the right to enjoy a privileged position, particularly compared with the Americans or the English who have demonstrated time and again their ambitious policy in the conflict by granting . . . credits to China."

Oshima remarked that during the initial stages of the conflict there had been constant reports from the front that the Chinese used German-made arms. He himself agreed with what Wiehl was saying and had always worked in this direction, but opinions were divided in Japan. The military and some Foreign Office officials were in favor of meeting the German demands; business circles were opposed. He told Wiehl that he had sent a telegram to Tokyo on about December 9 insisting that an agreement on granting Germany special privileges and removing obstacles to her enterprises in China be signed or an explanation be given to the German representatives in Tokyo why this could not be done. Oshima promised to inform his government of the conversation by telegram and also by letter through a courier.[71]

In March 1939 Ott confirmed that Oshima had again cabled Tokyo "in accordance with our interests." Ott for his part thought it possible to realize the most favored treatment of Germany without putting it in writing. He

[71] *Ibid.*, p. 41.

did not, however, consider the "real measures" suggested by Japan as adequate.[72] As it turned out, Germany failed to secure the advantages she sought. The agreement that was initialed in July was but a provisional agreement governing trade relations between Germany and Japan.

Serious contradictions divided Germany and Japan on the question of the former German possessions in the Pacific. The Japanese were alarmed by Nazi slogans demanding their return. When Deputy Minister for Colonies Hagiwara told representatives of the press on November 27, 1937, that demands for the return of the trust territories in the southern seas were "completely groundless"—"the trust territories of the South Pacific are an integral part of Japan—"[73] Berlin instructed Ambassador Dirksen to lodge a protest against Hagiwara's statement and to inform the foreign minister that "Germany intends to start international discussion on the subject of her colonial claims" and that "she could hardly expect a refusal of help in this matter from her friends."[74]

Soon afterwards the German embassy learned that the Japanese navy, which had close connections with large monopolies and was determined to retain control of the strategic islands, proposed to return them to Germany nominally in order to repurchase them immediately. Such a step by the navy rather than the government was a reflection of the peculiar conduct of Japanese foreign policy, when military leaders communicated with foreign countries and entered into negotiations with them independently of the Foreign Office. On January 15, 1938, Maeda, chief aide to the commander-in-chief of the combined fleets, told the German military attaché

[72] Soviet Archives, 436b, file 14, pp. 240–241.
[73] DGFP, vol. I, doc. No. 555.
[74] Ibid.

in Tokyo that "the year 1938 would perhaps be decisive for Germany as regards German colonial questions." Noting that Japan, because of her South Sea mandate, had an interest in the matter, Maeda stated that Japan was prepared to contribute to a "mutually satisfactory solution" of the problem. "The Japanese navy would, if necessary, even take the initiative in arranging for the necessary conversations." As a "conceivable solution," Maeda envisaged that "without regard to the Peace Treaty of Versailles and the League of Nations Japan should simply return the South Sea mandate to Germany and then buy it back from Germany."[75]

Dirksen wrote to Berlin: "The position of Japanese policy with respect to the South Sea mandate is perfectly clear. Japan will under no circumstances, even at the risk of losing Germany's friendship, relinquish the South Sea Islands."[76] He urged, therefore, speedy clarification of the matter for the sake of upholding the Anti-Comintern Pact.

Maeda's proposal aroused a lot of interest in Germany. Foreign Minister Neurath instructed Dirksen to ascertain whether Maeda had acted on his own or whether his ideas were shared by the Minister for Foreign Affairs or by the government. On the positive side, Maeda's plan would mean the recognition by one of the principal Allied powers in the First World War of the obligation to return former German colonies; on the negative side, German consent to the repurchase would weaken her demand for the actual return of her colonies and leave the impression that it was possible to reach a monetary settlement with Germany. He felt for that reason that Japan should publicly announce her readiness to

[75] *Ibid.*
[76] *Ibid.*

discuss the colonial question with Germany, but that any agreement regarding this question should be kept strictly secret.[77]

Admiral Nomura Kichisaburo, chief of the Information Division of the Japanese Admiralty, backed Maeda's statement and led Dirksen to believe that the foreign minister would make a corresponding proposal.[78] Attaching great importance to solving the colonial question, Neurath instructed Dirksen to maintain a noncommittal attitude in case Hirota did so.[79]

When Foreign Minister Hirota raised the colonial question during a discussion of German-Japanese relations in general in early February, Dirksen asserted that apart from Germany's economic need for the South Sea islands she had a moral right to them in view of her nonrecognition of the Treaty of Versailles. Although Hirota retorted that he wished to clarify the colonial problem which was facing both Germany and Japan in order to strengthen German-Japanese relations, he mentioned the "greatest strategic importance" which they held for Japan.[80]

In view of Japan's clear unwillingness to return the islands but her readiness to give financial compensation, Ambassador Togo was instructed to negotiate:

(a) a public statement by the Japanese government to the effect that it recognized the justice of the German colonial claim and, on its part, was prepared to discuss with Germany the future of the South Sea mandates;

(b) a secret agreement, for the publication of which

[77] *Ibid.*, doc. 560.
[78] *Ibid.*, doc. 561.
[79] *Ibid.*, doc. 563.
[80] *Ibid.*, doc. 575.

Germany reserves the exclusive right, to the effect that it is prepared to waive her claim for retrocession in return for financial compensation to be specified more exactly later.

The compilers of the memorandum did not consider it necessary to make the solution of this question dependent on the solution of other problems which were facing both Germany and Japan.[81]

On February 22, 1938, Togo informed Ribbentrop that his government would be glad to do everything in its power to help Germany in realizing her colonial demands and was ready to entertain proposals on how this could be done. He pointed out, however, that "the mandates in the hands of Japan are vital for her defense and for that reason she could not relinquish them forever." Ribbentrop expressed his appreciation for Japan's readiness to co-operate, but refrained from making any specific proposals.[82] He did not consider the moment opportune for solving this question.

In early May, Foreign Minister Hirota told Ott that Togo had been instructed to repeat the proposals made to Dirksen.[83] As neither side would budge from its position, however, no progress was made until 1940, when the question was settled in a secret agreement during the negotiation of the Tripartite Pact.

The Anti-Comintern Pact and its addenda did not contain any military obligations on the part of its signatories. In January 1938, when Germany was making preparations for the annexation of Austria, negotiations were begun for the conclusion of a military-political

[81] *Ibid.,* doc. 568.
[82] DGFP, vol. I, doc. 571.
[83] *Ibid.*

alliance which would allow Germany, Italy and Japan to undertake joint military ventures against the U.S.S.R. and bourgeois-democratic states of the West in an attempt to redivide the world.

As the British Foreign Secretary Lord Halifax wrote to Ambassador Craigie, the alliance with Japan and Italy made it possible for Germany to threaten Great Britain with war simultaneously in the North, in the Mediterranean, and in the Far East. Italy, he believed, hoped "to partially divert the forces of the U.S.A. and Great Britain to the Far East while Italy would strive to achieve her aims in the Mediterranean Sea and in the Middle East." He noted that "the alliance could deter the U.S.A. and Great Britain from giving support to France and her resistance against the Italian claims and would compel France the sooner to yield to Italian demands."[84]

Bypassing the Japanese ambassador, Ribbentrop told Military Attaché Oshima, whose fascist leanings were well known, of his desire to establish closer cooperation between their countries. Oshima reported the conversation to the General Staff, which welcomed the idea of closer relations between Japan and Germany, noting that "the major factor to be kept in mind in developing such cooperation was an agreement on joint actions against Soviet Russia."[85]

At the beginning of June Oshima proposed to Ribbentrop a pact which would provide for consultation between Japan and Germany in the event of conflict between either of them and the Soviet Union.[86] Ribben-

[84] DGFP, vol. VIII, doc. 589.
[85] Soviet Archives, 436b, file 13, p. 236. Protocol of Interrogation of Oshima.
[86] *Ibid.*, file 13, pp. 236–237 and file 17, pp. 70–71.

trop replied several days later that Germany would not favor an agreement that provided only for consultation; instead he proposed the conclusion of a treaty of mutual assistance, aimed not only against the U.S.S.R., but also against Great Britain, France and the United States, the countries against which, Ribbentrop asserted, Germany and Japan would evidently have to war.[87] In talks that lasted throughout June, Ribbentrop succeeded in convincing Oshima of the need for a strong pact. Asking Oshima to find out the views of the Japanese army concerning such an agreement, Ribbentrop cautioned him to observe secrecy and not to communicate about this with Japan by telephone or radio, but only by special couriers.[88]

Secrecy was particularly necessary in view of Nazi efforts to conceal their aggressive designs by seeming to come to terms with the Western powers. Thus the Anglo-German Agreement of July 1 concerning the Austrian debt "created a favorable atmosphere in the field of foreign policy,"[89] as did the visit to London of Hitler's personal adjutant, Captain Fritz Wiedemann, in June 1938. Meetings between Halifax and Wiedemann were conducted in a friendly atmosphere, the British government welcoming enthusiastically the suggestion of a visit by Fieldmarshal Göring. Halifax told Wiedemann that "the most wonderful moment of his

---

[87] In his communication to the German ambassador in Tokyo, Ott described the project presented by Oshima in the following way: (1) consultations between the three powers in case one of them finds itself in a difficult political situation; (2) political and economic support in case one of the powers is threatened from outside; and (3) pledge of support in case one of the powers becomes an object of an unprovoked attack. (Soviet Archives, 436b, file 13, p. 263.)

[88] Soviet Archives, 436b, file 13, p. 237; file 17, pp. 70–72.

[89] Union of Soviet Socialist Republics, Ministry of Foreign Affairs. *Dokumenty i materialy kanuna vtorio mirovoi voiny*, vol. II, Dirksen's Archive (1938–1939) (Moscow, 1948), p. 178.

life will come when the Führer rides next to the King along the Mall[90] during an official visit to London."[91]

Had the English and French, who hoped to turn Hitler against the U.S.S.R., learned that the Germans were negotiating an alliance with Japan not merely against the U.S.S.R. but also against them, they might have blocked Hitler's seizure of Czechoslovakia. The need for secrecy may have given added stimulus for Ribbentrop's dealings with the Japanese military, because the Foreign Office contained many Anglophiles who might have leaked word of the nature of the negotiations.

At Ribbentrop's request Oshima sent Major General Kasahara Yukio, a member of his mission, to Tokyo with the German proposal. The General Staff conveyed the proposal to Foreign Minister General Ugaki Kazushige, who submitted it to the Five Ministers' Conference, at which he, Premier Konoe, Finance Minister Ikeda Seihin, War Minister Itagaki Seishiro and Navy Minister Yonai discussed the most crucial questions.[92]

It so happened that Soviet-Japanese relations were very tense at the moment in view of Japanese inroads into Soviet territory in the Lake Khasan region. With the army and the war minister favoring the escalation of hostilities against the U.S.S.R.[93] and the foreign minister and the finance minister who was closely connected

[90] The Mall is a street leading up to Buckingham Palace.
[91] *Dokumenenty i materialy kanuna vtoroi mirovoi voiny*, vol. II, p. 179.
[92] Soviet Archives, 436b, file 13, p. 239.
[93] Baron Harada, the private secretary of Prince Saionji Kinmochi, wrote in his diary on July 21, 1938, about a visit paid to the Emperor by the War Minister General Itagaki to obtain permission to use large military forces in the Lake Khasan region. Asked by the emperor whether the ministers responsible for this question agreed, Itagaki replied: "The minister of foreign affairs and the navy minister have expressed their agreement." In reality Ugaki and Yonai opposed the employment of large military forces, lest Japan be drawn into war with the U.S.S.R. The deception was discovered only later. (Soviet Archives, 436b, file 69, p. 23. From the diaries of Saionji and Harada, entry for July 21, 1938.)

with large business interests advocating better relations with Great Britain, France and the United States, the Five Ministers' Conference decided to strengthen the Anti-Comintern Pact, and Oshima was instructed to strive for a military alliance against the Soviet Union. In subsequent correspondence with Berlin, the Japanese government insisted that the preamble of a future agree· ment indicate clearly that it was "an extension of the Anti-Comintern Pact."[94] As Prince Konoe noted in his memoirs: "This was a plan to turn the Tripartite Anti-Comintern Pact, in force at the time, into a military alliance directed against the U.S.S.R."[95]

During the Munich Conference Hitler had broached the subject of a new pact to Benito Mussolini and the latter had agreed in principle to participate.[96] Mussolini reiterated this to Oshima, who visited Rome in December 1938, shortly after becoming ambassador to Berlin. Soon afterwards, Shiratori Toshio, who was an active advocate of a German-Japanese rapprochement, was appointed ambassador to Rome.

On January 7, 1939, Shiratori told Foreign Minister Count Galeazzo Ciano that Prime Minister Hiranuma favored such a pact, but that the new Foreign Minister Arita Hachiro was lukewarm to the idea. But he assured him that this might merely delay, not thwart the conclusion of the pact. Ciano noted in his diary that Shiratori "was very favorable to the idea of concluding the alliance, considering it to be the weapon with the aid of which Great Britain might be forced to yield those many things she owed us all."[97]

A week earlier, on January 1, Mussolini had told

[94] Soviet Archives, 436b, file 13, p. 239.
[95] *Ibid.,* p. 77.
[96] *Ibid.,* file 57.
[97] *Ibid.,* file 65, pp. 70–71.

Ciano that he had decided to accept Ribbentrop's proposal to turn the Anti-Comintern Pact into a military alliance. He had added that he wished it concluded by the end of January, since he expected a visit from Prime Minister Neville Chamberlain and Lord Halifax, and wished to demonstrate the might and solidarity of the Axis Powers, on the one hand, and to show, on the other hand, that not much could be expected from the visit of the British statesmen.[98] Ciano had written to Ribbentrop of Mussolini's willingness to sign the Tripartite Pact and on January 3, had informed thereof also the German Ambassador in Rome, Hans Georg von Mackensen, warning him that the matter was extremely secret.[99]

After that Ribbentrop, Oshima and Ciano worked out a draft agreement, providing for the following obligations on the part of the signatories:

1. In case one of the contracting parties is put into a difficult position by a nonsignatory power, "the contracting parties shall immediately begin discussions on measures to be undertaken jointly."
2. Political and economic support in case "one of the powers is threatened without cause, with a view to removing the threat."
3. "In case one of the contracting parties becomes the object of an unprovoked attack from a nonsignatory power or powers, the other contracting parties undertake to render assistance and support." In such an event they were to "begin immediate consultations and discuss measures necessary to implement the obligations."

The treaty was to run for 10 years.[100]

[98] *Ibid.*, p. 73.
[99] *Ibid.*, pp. 76–79. Mackensen's Memorandum of January 3, 1939.
[100] *Ibid.*, file 47, pp. 61–62.

The protocol on the signing of the treaty extended the German and Italian obligations of assistance to Manchukuo. Of special importance was a secret supplementary protocol, which provided for the priority of the treaty over other obligations and agreements which "contradict the provisions of this treaty" and placed the following obligations on the signatories:

(a) "to investigate at the earliest date after the treaty takes effect the possibilities of conflicts that might exist and in what way and to what extent the contracting powers will render each other assistance, support or help depending on the geographical conditions";

(b) "in case of a war which will be conducted by all contracting parties jointly, they pledge not to conclude a separate armistice or treaty."[101]

In view of serious resistance in Japan against the assumption of commitments for the joint waging of war against any third power, it was agreed that at the time of the signing of the agreement the Japanese ambassador would make a declaration to the effect that "Japan is able to implement the obligation and in conformity with Article III of the treaty assumes [the obligation] to render assistance and support by military force at present and in the immediate future only to a limited extent."[102]

As Oshima dispatched the drafts to Tokyo by special courier, he and Ribbentrop were certain that all that remained to be done were the technical formalities of finalizing the agreement.[103] Mackensen told Ciano that

[101] *Ibid.*, pp. 62–63. The draft treaty transmitted by Weizsäcker to Ott.
[102] *Ibid.*, file 13, p. 264.
[103] According to American data, reported to the British Foreign Office, a conference of six Japanese diplomats held in Paris in January 1939

in Ribbentrop's opinion the technical matters would require about three weeks. Mackensen recorded in his diary that Ciano looked at a calendar and said that the most convenient day for signing the pact would be the 28th or the 30th of January.[104]

But in February a mission arrived from Tokyo to spell out Japan's cautious position toward the pact. Ito Nobufumi, former ambassador to Poland who headed the mission, and the representatives of the Army and Navy General Staffs, Lieutenant Colonel Tatsumi and Captain Abe, made it clear that Japanese assistance must not be unconditional or automatic, and dashed hopes for the speedy signing of the treaty.[105]

Japan's vacillation encouraged Mussolini to drag his feet on the conclusion of the Tripartite Pact, for he feared that it might arouse the enmity of the United States, from which Italy obtained large loans, raw materials and fuel. Nor did Mussolini want to break with Great Britain, which in her attempt to use Italy against the U.S.S.R. and at the same time separate her from Germany was meeting Italian demands in the Mediterranean Sea and in the Near East. Mussolini felt "it might be a good idea to conclude a bilateral union without Japan, leaving the latter face to face with the Anglo-

---

unanimously recommended to the Japanese government that it sign the treaty of alliance in the form proposed by Germany and Italy. (DBFP, vol. VIII, doc. No. 488, footnote 2.)

[104] Soviet Archives, 436b, file 65. p. 79. Mackensen's memorandum of January 7, 1939.

[105] Despite the secret character of the Ito mission the *News Chronicle* of Great Britain reported about it on February 10. It wrote that there were differences of opinion among the proponents of the Tripartite Pact concerning its character and objectives and that Germany and Italy were insisting that the pact should be directed not only against the U.S.S.R. but also against Great Britain, France and the United States. Although the Japanese ambassador protested officially that the report was untrue, the British Foreign Office confirmed its veracity. (DBFP vol. VIII, doc. No. 488, Ronald to Craigie.)

French forces alone. In that case the pact would be neither anti-British nor anti-American."[106] In March 1939 Mussolini had expressed the fear to Ciano that Italy's union with Japan would "throw America into the arms of the Western democracies once and for all." When Ciano reported at the end of April that "the Japanese were insisting on their reservations with regard to the Tripartite Pact" and that "the signing has been postponed indefinitely," Mussolini replied that he was "very glad."[107]

While Mussolini was opposed to an alliance with Japan, he pushed for the speedy conclusion of a pact with Germany to strengthen him vis-à-vis the powers whose interests were threatened by expansion in the Mediterranean. In talks between Göring, Mussolini and Ciano the following month, Mussolini remarked that "total war was unavoidable." Göring agreed, but believed that Germany and Italy "must wait a little until their armament situation becomes more favorable compared with the democratic countries." It was agreed that "Germany and Italy will not allow themselves to be provoked into any conflict but will wait for the moment they will regard propitious for themselves." The two powers took it upon themselves to increase their armaments and to coordinate their efforts to attain self-sufficiency in the raw materials and foodstuffs necessary for waging a war. They decided to conduct joint air and naval operations. During the Ciano-Ribbentrop talks on May 6–7, agreement was reached to conclude a bilateral treaty of alliance.[108]

The unexpected delay of Japan in joining the Rome-

[106] Soviet Archives, 436b, file 65, p. 80.
[107] *Ibid.*
[108] *Ibid.*, pp. 80–81. From the Ciano diary, entries for April 25, May 6 and 7, 1939; *ibid.*, file 13, pp. 272–274.

Berlin Axis had been caused by strong differences of opinion among Japan's leaders concerning the direction and means of Japanese expansion. Some objected that an alliance with Germany and Italy would draw Japan into war with Great Britain, the United States and France. Others countered that the anti-Soviet nature of the pact would quiet Western opposition and assure Japanese success in defeating China. They felt that the threat of a two-front war would force the Soviet Union to make various concessions to Japan and conceived of a joint attack on the Soviet Union after China had been defeated. The army, impressed by German successes in Europe, favored a comprehensive alliance with Germany; the navy opposed it, lest a collision with the United States and Great Britain halt oil deliveries from the United States and the Dutch East Indies.

The foreign policy controversy had contributed to the fall of the Konoe government in January. But the Hiranuma cabinet was no less divided. Baron Hiranuma Kiichiro, an ultranationalist, and War Minister Itagaki, whose ministry had been involved in the early negotiations, advocated an unlimited alliance with Germany and Italy. Navy Minister Yonai and Foreign Minister Arita opposed the agreement, reiterating that Japan would not be able to conduct war successfully without the raw materials controlled by the United States and Great Britain. So acute was the struggle concerning the proposed agreement that the government devoted 75 meetings to this question in 1938. In the first stage opponents of a full alliance with Germany got the upper hand with the support of Navy Minister Yonai and his deputy, Admiral Yamamoto. They were supported by Saionji and the Court circles.

When Ito during his mission to Berlin had informed

Oshima and Shiratori that the Tripartite Pact must concentrate on the U.S.S.R., they had refused to convey this to the governments of Germany and Italy and had cabled to the Foreign Office that the text must be accepted without qualifications, threatening to resign and provoke a government crisis if this were not done.[109] The new foreign minister resolutely objected to the interference of the army in diplomatic questions. Arita told Harada that the Foreign Office had been completely unaware of Oshima's telegram to the General Staff about the strengthening of the Anti-Comintern Pact.[110]

The opposition of Arita and Yonai to a full rapprochement with Germany was rooted in the hope that Japan might be able to solve the China question with the aid of the Western powers. Such a hope was not groundless. On November 24, 1938, a United Press dispatch from Washington had reported about the intense activity of the British and American governments to compel China to reach a "peaceful settlement" with Japan. On December 5, 1938, the newspaper *Shanghai Shen-pao* had asserted that "if Japan could achieve a rapprochement with the democratic countries, Great Britain could reconcile herself to certain losses in the Yangtze River area for the sake of agreement with Japan."[111] On February 9, 1939, the Reuter Agency conveyed from Chungking the rumors that "an international Far Eastern conference will take up the question of the settlement of the Sino-Japanese conflict."

The conclusion of a military alliance against the Western powers would have disrupted plans for the solution of the China problem in the manner of Munich. Diplo-

---

[109] *Ibid.*, file 13, p. 248; *ibid.*, pp. 79–80, 248.

[110] *Ibid.*, file 69, p. 31.

[111] Chen Bo-da, *Chan Kai-shi—vrag Kitaiskogo naroda* (Moscow, 1952), p. 127.

matically astute circles in Japan hoped, therefore, to obtain Western support against China by taking a strongly anti-Soviet stance. The Japanese Emperor agreed with Arita's position and it was decided to recall Oshima and Shiratori if they would not implement the decisions of the Japanese government.[112] (Although the ambassadors had reported to Tokyo that they would not convey its proposals for a modification of the pact to the German and Italian governments and had demanded that they be signed without change, they had actually informed Ribbentrop and Ciano of the wishes of their government.)[113]

But Western appeasement of German and Japanese expansion strengthened the hand of the ultranationalists. When the United States protested half-heartedly against Japanese claims of sovereignty over the greater part of the Yellow Sea where the strategic Nanwei (Spratley) Islands were located and merely demanded an explanation of actions in connection with the bombardment of American property in China and discrimination against American business in the field of trade,[114] it gave encouragement to Japanese aggression and thus support to arguments for a military alliance with Germany. Consequently the Japanese government worked out a compromise text of the proposed Tripartite Pact, in which the desire to limit assistance to war against the U.S.S.R. was less explicit. Stating that political and economic factors did not allow Japan to act openly against the Western powers, it proposed that after the signing of the treaty, the British, French and American ambas-

[112] Soviet Archives, 436b, file 13, p. 32. From the diaries of Saionji and Harada.

[113] *Ibid.,* p. 265.

[114] United States, Department of State, *Foreign Relations of the United States* [hereafter cited as FRUS], 1939 (Washington, 1955), p. 15.

sadors be handed a declaration to the effect that the agreement was an extension of the Anti-Comintern Pact and not directed against their countries.[115]

Keeping Ribbentrop and Ciano informed of their correspondence with the Japanese Foreign Office, Oshima and Shiratori reported that the Japanese modification was not acceptable. Without instructions from Tokyo, but counting on the support of Hiranuma and Itagaki, Oshima and Shiratori assured Ribbentrop, who wanted a final decision, one way or another, before Hitler's speech, scheduled for April 28, that Japan would back Germany and Italy in military hostilities against Great Britain and France.[116]

When Arita demanded that the statement by Oshima and Shiratori be disowned, Hiranuma and Itagaki did not go along. Armed with the protocol of the meeting of the Five Ministers' Conference, Arita appealed to the Emperor personally on April 8, contending that Oshima and Shiratori had exceeded their authority. On April 11, the Emperor summoned Itagaki and told him that he regarded the actions of the ambassadors and their statement that Japan intended to take part in a war as an infringement upon his supreme power, and expressed displeasure at Itagaki's support of the ambassadors and his opposition on this question to the other ministers.[117]

But the Emperor's dissatisfaction did not impress the army leaders. On April 24 Home Minister Kido, who was close to the Court, told Harada that the army intended to avoid limitation of the pact to action against the Comintern and the Soviet Union. Fearful of a mili-

---

[115] Soviet Archives, 436b, file 13, pp. 265–266.

[116] *Ibid.; ibid.,* file 69, p. 34. From the diary of Saionji and Harada, entries for April 1939.

[117] *Ibid.,* file 34, p. 38.

tary coup, such as had been attempted in 1936,[118] the Court circles did not want to quarrel with the army, and the question was put again on the agenda of the Five Ministers' Conference.

Since Germany continued to insist on the unconditional adherence of Japan to the bloc, Oshima and Shiratori urgently requested their recall. As the ministers of war and of finance came out in support of the ambassadors, while the ministers of foreign affairs and of the navy opposed them, Hiranuma suggested as a compromise that a memorandum be sent to Hitler and Mussolini to explain the Japanese position and offer new concessions to the demands of the European partners. It was agreed to transmit such a communication through the German and Italian ambassadors in Tokyo, with Arita introducing the qualification that "neither at present nor in the future" would Japan be able to render Germany and Italy "any practical military assistance."[119]

In his message to Hitler, Hiranuma noted not only the efficacy of the Anti-Comintern Pact, but assured him of the sincerity of Japanese intentions to go hand in hand with Germany. Hiranuma wrote that "Japan firmly and irrevocably has decided to be on the side of Germany and Italy even if one of them becomes an object of attack by one or several powers without participation of the U.S.S.R. and to render them political, economic and, to the extent of her possibilities, military assistance." At the same time Hiranuma pointed out, as Arita had insisted, that "under the circumstances that obtained for Japan the latter neither at present nor in the near future will be able to render them [Germany and Italy] any military assistance," but qualified the qualification:

---

[118] *Ibid.*, p. 117. From the diary of Kido. Entry for April 19, 1939.
[119] Soviet Archives, 436b, file 13, pp. 267–27; *Ibid.*, p. 269.

"It stands to reason, however, that Japan would be glad to render them such support if that should become possible in view of changed circumstances." Eager to obtain German and Italian agreement not to publish the treaty, Hiranuma stated that "in connection with the international situation, Japan would have to observe extreme caution with regard to an explanation it may have to give when announcing the treaty."[120]

On the basis of information received from someone who worked with Itagaki, a conversation between the vice minister of war and the Italian military attaché, and his own conversations with officers of the Japanese Army General Staff, Ott reported to Berlin that army circles felt that the compromise reached by the prime minister was "a big achievement considering the present conditions and the conflict at the Five Ministers' Conference." Analyzing the major points of Hiranuma's message, the military believed that the point about the impossibility of rendering "an effective assistance at present and in the near future" was nullified in part by the reference to "changed circumstances," which would make an effective assistance possible in the future.

At the beginning of May the Japanese vice minister of war told the Italian military attaché that the treaty "binds Japan determinately to the Axis Powers." While remarking that Germany and Italy should understand that "Japan is isolated in the Far East and finds herself in a worse position than the European bloc of the Axis whose members can assist each other directly," he stressed the general significance of the treaty from the viewpoint of strengthening the positions of the three powers: "In case of war, however, irrespective of the start and development of Japanese military operations,

[120] *Ibid.,* pp. 268–269. Appendix to Ott's telegram of May 4, 1939.

the very fact of the existence of the treaty will have an effective influence on the enemy."

Ott reported that the Japanese army regarded Hiranuma's proposal as "flexible" and as "leaving the door open for negotiations and giving them favorable prospects." He singled out Vice Minister of the Navy Admiral Yamamoto Isoroku as the chief opponent of the agreement and pointed out that "in the government there exists a complete abyss between the friends and the foes of the agreement." "In case the agreement is reached," Ott wrote, "the army expects the Cabinet to resign, which would be an undesirable development at the present moment for international and domestic reasons."[121]

In Berlin, meanwhile, the Japanese embassy and the military attaché continued their adherence to the army line in disregard of the position of the government. When Counselor Usami Uzuhiko communicated to Foreign Minister Arita a new draft which Vice Minister of Foreign Affairs Friedrich Gaus had "unofficially" shown him, reiterating the German demands which Japan had declined to accept provisionally,[122] Arita pointed out to Baron Harada with indignation that the draft "was prepared by the Japanese Army and communicated to the Minister for Foreign Affairs through the military attachés."[123]

Since the message to Hitler and Mussolini had been delivered through the German and Italian ambassadors in Tokyo, Oshima had ignored it. He had informed Arita that when Ribbentrop had asked him "if it should be possible to consider that Japan was in a state of war

[121] Ibid., pp. 270–272. Ott's telegram to Ribbentrop of May 6, 1939.
[122] Ibid., file 69, p. 60.
[123] Ibid.

in case one of the contracting parties starts a war against a third party, even if Japan does not render military assistance (Germany and Italy do not expect assistance from Japan when she could not render it)," he had replied in the affirmative.[124] Arita fumed that Oshima's response had been "arbitrary" and "without the slightest justification" and told Harada that "he no longer could assume responsibility for the foreign policy."[125]

As Arita and Court circles anticipated, Hiranuma and Itagaki supported Oshima's reply to Ribbentrop at the Five Ministers' Conference on May 9. Though Arita's demand for a disavowal of Oshima's statement was backed by Yonai and though Arita warned that he would have to report the matter to the Emperor, Hiranuma made it plain that Oshima's answer would not be changed and that he was willing for Japan to be considered as "a country prepared to take part in a war in case of hostilities between Great Britain and France on the one hand and Germany and Italy on the other."[126]

In informing Oshima of Germany's intention to formalize her relations with Italy in order to inflict a counter-blow to the "political actions undertaken for propaganda purposes by the Western powers," which had started negotiations with the U.S.S.R., and to show "the unshakable character of the Berlin-Rome Axis," Ribbentrop observed that "the German-Italian pact contains elements which to some extent bind these two countries closer together than the provisions of the draft tripartite treaty under discussion." He reiterated that "the German and Italian governments would very much like to see the Japanese government come speedily

[124] *Ibid.*, p. 53.
[125] *Ibid.*, p. 60.
[126] *Ibid.*, file 58, pp. 60–62.

to a final decision so that the Tripartite Pact might be secretly concluded simultaneously with the signing of the German-Italian treaty."[127]

The proposal to conclude a secret pact was designed to dispel the anxiety of Japanese leaders who feared that Great Britain and the United States would react adversely if Japan joined the Axis. Bypassing Arita, with whose opposition he was familiar, Ribbentrop instructed Ott to communicate this point of view to Itagaki either through the "trusted person" he knew in the war minister's entourage or to him directly, in order to obtain "a speedy and positive decision."

Asserting that "the entire former line of behavior of the Japanese government was gradually producing some skepticism in Rome and in Berlin," Ribbentrop argued that "the fear in Japan that America may join Great Britain and France in case of war can in no way be used as an argument against concluding the Tripartite Pact because this pact will be the best means to keep America from entering the war." Turning to the subject which concerned Japan most—her war with China—Ribbentrop contended that Japan's position in East Asia and especially in China "depends in the first place on the superiority of the Axis powers over the Western powers" and insisted that it was in her interests "to reinforce this superiority by her participation and to avoid creating the impression among the Western powers that they could count on Japanese neutrality in case of a conflict with Germany and Italy."[128]

Ribbentrop's proposal for a secret pact made a strong impression in Tokyo. Ott reported that War Minister

---

[127] *Ibid.*, file 13, pp. 275–277. Telegram of Ribbentrop to Ott, of May 15, 1939.

[128] *Ibid.*, pp. 277–279.

Itagaki had assured him that the foreign minister would notify Germany "not later than on Sunday, 21 May, about a new positive decision that will be adopted at a meeting of the Japanese Cabinet."[129]

At the Five Ministers' Conference on May 20 Arita renewed his plea for the disowning of Oshima's reply to Ribbentrop, but was thwarted again by the resolute position of Itagaki and Hiranuma.[130] Arita did succeed in amending the Gaus-Itagaki draft of the Triparite Pact to the effect that the Japanese government, while agreeing to an unlimited alliance with Germany and Italy, reserved the right to enter (or not to enter) a war that might break out in Europe.[131]

Considering the amended text unacceptable, Oshima and Shiratori failed to transmit it to the German and Italian government as instructed.[132] They were encouraged in their sabotage by Itagaki, who cabled Oshima "to stand to the last and not to obey Arita in order not to hurt the negotiations between the parties in Tokyo." To calm Ribbentrop who was vainly waiting for the "positive decision of the Japanese government," Itagaki sent General Machijiri to Ambassador Ott right after the Five Ministers' Conference on the 20th with a letter in which he said that the army was prepared to sign the pact secretly and simultaneously with the signing of the German-Italian treaty of alliance in order to impart to it the character of a tripartite alliance.[133]

On May 27 Oshima secretly informed Ribbentrop of the decision of the Five Ministers' Conference and the amended draft treaty; at the same time he telegraphed

[129] *Ibid.*, file 34, p. 41.
[130] *Ibid.*, file 58, p. 29.
[131] *Ibid.*, file 34, p. 41. Ribbentrop to Ott, May 28, 1939.
[132] *Ibid.*, file 58, pp. 28–29.
[133] *Ibid.*, p. 29.

Arita bluntly that he would not communicate his instructions to the German government. Unable to cope with Oshima without support from the premier,[134] Arita wanted to resign, but Navy Minister Yonai persuaded him to remain in office.

Analyzing the situation, the British Ambassador in Tokyo, Sir Robert Craigie, wrote to Lord Halifax on June 3 that "in case of a world war Japan will have her hands more or less free in the Far East and will be able to achieve without special difficulties her purposes in China and realize her plans aimed at widening her influence in China." "These arguments," Craigie observed, "are perfectly in accord with the wishes of a segment of the army, which has the strong support of reactionary elements and believes that the outbreak of a second European war will give Japan the opportunity to solve such problems as the international settlements, the ending of the conflict with China and the establishing of their control over that country. . . ." The opponents of the agreement, Craigie remarked, were financial and business circles, led by former Finance Minister Ikeda, which felt that while Italy and Germany might render significant economic assistance, it was impossible for Japan to exploit China without British and American assistance. They feared, furthermore, "close friendship with the Axis powers will bring Japan sooner or later to an armed conflict with the United States."[135]

The struggle between the proponents and the opponents of the alliance was reflected in the press. While the *Nichi-Nichi* and *Chugai* took a relatively objective stand, voicing the opinions of both sides, most news-

---

[134] On May 23, Arita told Harada that when he sent his deputy to the premier the latter said that question would be solved in accordance with the wishes of the army. (*Ibid.*, file 69, p. 63.)

[135] DBFP, vol. VIII, No. 154. Craigie to Halifax, June 3, 1939.

papers took clearly opposing positions. *Yomiuri* and especially *Kokumin* and *Hochi,* which were connected with army circles, ardently supported the idea of strengthening the Anti-Comintern Pact, equating it with the conclusion of a military alliance in accordance with the German proposals.

On June 5 Ott reported to Ribbentrop that the Japanese government had modified its position to the extent of agreeing to "take part in a war against France and Great Britain, but with a qualification that Japan wanted to reserve for herself the right to enter the war at a moment propitious for her."[136] But the Nazis were not satisfied. Ribbentrop had warned Oshima and Shiratori in April that "if the question of concluding the pact remains for too long at the conversation stage, Germany may find it necessary to extend the hand to Russia in some way."[137] On June 16 he informed Shiratori that Germany intended to conclude a non-aggression pact with Russia, because Japan did not accept the German proposal.[138]

With the onset of economic talks between Germany and the U.S.S.R., the press was full of reports of a pending Soviet-German rapprochment. Alarmed, Oshima sent Usami to the chief of the Political Department of the Ministry for Foreign Affairs, Ernst Woermann, to obtain an official explanation. When he referred to a report in the *News Chronicle* that Russia and Germany were negotiating a non-aggression pact and that prominent German statesmen were said to be in Moscow, Woermann replied that all the rumors about political negotiations were an invention; the negotiations concerned purely

[136] Soviet Archives, 436b, file 14, p. 308. Ott to Ribbentrop, June 5, 1939.
[137] *Ibid.,* file 13, p. 260.
[138] *Ibid.,* file 34, p. 52.

economic questions, Germany being interested in obtaining a number of important commodities from the U.S.S.R.[139] On the basis of Woermann's assurances, Oshima reported to his government that "Germany will in no case conclude a pact with Soviet Russia."[140]

While the Japanese government was inclined to believe that Ribbentrop's talk of concluding a non-aggression pact with the Soviet Union was mere bluff,[141] the possibility provoked anxiety among the military who had plunged into a large-scale conflict with the Soviet Union at the Khalka River (the Nomonhan Incident) in May and desired more sizable support from Germany in order to compel the U.S.S.R. and the Mongolian People's Republic to make concessions and to transfer to Japan a number of areas belonging to the Mongolian People's Republic, and they put pressure on the government for a speedy conclusion of a treaty of alliance with Germany, insisting that German and Italian demands be met. Itagaki demanded of Hiranuma on August 7 that the question be reopened. He said that the army felt that the changes in the situation called for the signing of an offensive and defensive alliance with Germany and Italy.

Hiranuma convened the Five Ministers' Conference the following day, but according to Ott the discussion did not go beyond the June 5 proposal. Although Itagaki considered threatening to resign and precipitating the fall of the government in order to bring it around to his views and although Arita confided to Harada when he told him about the Five Ministers' Conference that the only solution was "either to agree unconditionally to

[139] *Ibid.*, file 48, pp. 12–14. Woermann's memorandum, July 19, 1939.
[140] *Ibid.*, p. 15.
[141] *Ibid.*, file 34, p. 53.

conclude the pact or to drop Itagaki,"[142] a showdown was avoided, Itagaki hoping to attain a compromise whereby Japan would give to Germany certain oral commitments.[143]

At the Five Ministers' Conference on August 15, Ott reported, Arita "was instructed to clarify again the text of the Japanese proposals of June 5 without its significant amendment." When Arita's draft was distributed among the participants of the conference, Itagaki rejected it and vainly demanded to go beyond the June 5 proposal.[144]

Although Itagaki did not resign, the days of the Hiranuma government were numbered. It fell on August 30, brought down not by the deadlock that had developed between the minister of foreign affairs and the minister of war, however, but by the shattering news of the signing of a nonaggression pact between Germany and the Soviet Union. To the Japanese who had been thinking in terms of fighting together with Germany against the U.S.S.R., the German action came as a betrayal of the principles of the Anti-Comintern Pact and Hiranuma, who had regarded the extension of the pact into a military alliance against Soviet Russia as the primary task of his government, could not but step down.[145]

When it had become clear that the U.S.S.R., having failed to secure a mutual assistance pact with Great Britain and France, was agreeable to accept the German proposal for a nonaggression pact, Germany had decided to make her intentions known to Japan. Ribbentrop had informed Oshima by telephone on August 21

[142] *Ibid.,* file 70, p. 12.
[143] *Ibid.,* file 63, p. 24. Ott to Ribbentrop, August 11, 1939.
[144] *Ibid.,* pp. 24–25. A telegram from Ott to Ribbentrop, August 18, 1939.
[145] *Ibid.,* p. 34. The speech of the Soviet prosecutor at the trial of the main Japanese War Criminals.

of his trip to Moscow. Agitated, Oshima had asked for an audience, but Ribbentrop had replied that he did not have time to see him before his departure. Weizsäcker, who had received Oshima at midnight, had assured him that Germany's intention to maintain friendly relations with Japan was unchanged. The German agreement with the Soviet Union, he had contended, would put Germany in a position to contribute to the furtherance of peaceful relations between Japan and the U.S.S.R. The primary enemy of both Germany and Japan, he had argued, was Britain.[146]

On August 25 Ott had called on Arita and reiterated Germany's wish to preserve friendly relations with Japan in the future, hinting also at the possibility of German assistance in stabilizing Soviet-Japanese relations. Leaving the matter of improving Soviet-Japanese relations for discussion at a later time, Arita had handed Ott copies of the instructions that he had dispatched to Oshima:

1. To notify the German government that the Japanese government regards the conclusion of the nonaggression pact as an action that constitutes a final annulment of the present negotiations regarding the Tripartite Pact.
2. The Japanese government states that the conclusion by Germany of the nonaggression pact with Russia constitutes a serious breach of the secret agreement connected with the Anti-Comintern Pact between Japan and Germany. It, therefore, protests strongly to the German government.

Privately, Arita remarked that "Japan is forced to make the statements contained herein, but is ready to con-

[146] *Ibid.*

tinue friendly relations with Germany and is searching for suitable ways."[147]

Although Oshima had received the note of protest on August 26 and had notified Tokyo that he had duly communicated it, he had, on Weizsäcker's advice, held on to the document until September 18. When finally transmitting the protest he had said: "If it should conform to the wishes of the Germans, this paper could be lost among the German documents."[148]

Ribbentrop had not given up the idea of an alliance with Japan. Germany needed Japan to divert British and French forces away from Europe and draw American attention to the Far East. As he told Oshima: "The idea of close co-operation between Germany, Italy and Japan is far from dead." He reiterated that such an alliance, backed by an understanding between Japan and the Soviet Union, would be directed "wholly against Great Britain."[149]

In offering his services as a mediator between Japan and the U.S.S.R., Ribbentrop spoke of a Japanese drive south.[150] At the moment war with the U.S.S.R. was not Hitler's immediate objective and Japanese inroads into the U.S.S.R. had been successfully repelled by the Red Army.

Oshima retorted, "the army no doubt approves the idea of establishing good relations with Russia, and it is to be hoped, therefore, that these ideas will soon be embraced by Japanese foreign policy."[151] Reporting this conversation to Ott, Ribbentrop instructed him to dis-

---

[147] *Ibid.*, file 13, pp. 282–283. Ott's telegram of August 25, 1939.

[148] *Ibid.*, pp. 283–284. Weizsäcker's memorandum on his conversation with Oshima on September 18, 1939.

[149] *Ibid.*, p. 286. Ribbentrop to Ott, September 9, 1939.

[150] *Ibid.*, p. 285. A telegram from Ribbentrop to Ott, September 9, 1939.

[151] *Ibid.*, p. 287. A telegram from Ribbentrop to Ott, September 9, 1939.

cuss it "absolutely frankly" with Prince Kanin Kotohito, chief of the General Staff of the Japanese army. Hitler and Ribbentrop talked on the same lines with General Count Terauchi Seiki, former minister of war, when the latter visited Germany in August–September 1939.[152]

The intensification of German efforts to improve Soviet-German-Italian-Japanese relations and turn Japan against Great Britain had been prompted by the signing of an Anglo-Japanese agreement, the Arita-Craigie Agreement, in July 1939. Wooing Japan in a sort of "Far Eastern Munich," the British government had gone so far as to "fully recognize the actual situation in China where hostilities on a large scale are in progress and note that as long as that state of affairs continues to exist, the Japanese forces in China have special requirements for the purpose of safeguarding their own security and maintaining public order in regions under their control, and that they have to suppress or remove any such acts or causes as will obstruct them." Stating that it had "no intention of countenancing any act or measures prejudicial to the attainment of the above-mentioned objects by Japanese forces,"[153] Great Britain had virtually recognized Japanese expansion in China and opened up prospects for a broad Anglo-Japanese deal.

Great Britain was concerned by rumors of the strengthening of the Anti-Comintern Pact. On November 1, 1938, Ambassador Craigie told Premier Konoe that the pact was widely interpreted in Japan as directed against his country even more than against the Comintern. Konoe's reply that "whatever the impression of the public, the pact has only one purpose and one purpose only,

---

[152] *Ibid.*, pp. 292–294.
[153] E.M. Zhukov (ed.) *Mezhdunarodnye otnosheniya na Dal'nem Vostoke (1840–1949)* (Moscow, 1956), pp. 504–505.

and that was to counter the activities of the Comintern," did not allay Craigie's fears. Nor did Prince Chichibu's assurance on December 1 that "any strengthening of the Anti-Comintern Pact would be directed solely against Russia."[154] "If Japan were now to enter into an alliance with the totalitarian powers (even though it were still nominally directed only against Soviet Russia)," Craigie reported to London, "the process of ultimate reconciliation with Great Britain, would obviously be retarded, if not completely arrested." While he had forecast at the time of Hitler's seizure of Czechoslovakia that Japan would remain neutral at least in the opening stages, he now felt that in the event a German-Japanese alliance were concluded, "the possibility of neutrality would be converted into the certainty of belligerency."

The proposals advanced by Craigie on the basis of this rather objective analysis were surprising from the point of common sense, though wholly in tune with the outlook of the Munich appeasers. To counter Japanese policy, Craigie suggested to accept the Japanese proposal of "cooperation" in China, though this amounted to recognizing all Japanese seizures, justifying his proposal on the grounds of the "big policy." "If the problem is regarded primarily as one in the economic sphere— namely the defense of our rights and interests in China— it would perhaps be best to leave the matter where it is and to continue to fight for these interests as best we can along the present lines. . . . Big political issues are now taking shape, the first of which is the possibility referred to above of the early conclusion of a triple alliance."[155]

Craigie's suggestion ran counter to the entire experi-

[154] DBFP, vol. VIII, doc. No. 295. Craigie to Halifax, December 1, 1938.
[155] *Ibid.*, doc. No. 308. Craigie to Halifax, December 2, 1938.

ence of dealing with Japan, Germany and Italy, which regarded such concessions as an encouragement of their aggressive actions and used them to consolidate their position, and Lord Halifax, though he said that he read Craigie's dispatch with "pleasure and interest,"[156] could not bring himself to accept the recommendation. Halifax feared that any attempt to compromise with Japan in China would inevitably be construed as the abandonment of China's cause and "would alienate the sympathy of the United States, weakening our chances of collaboration not only in the Far East, but everywhere else." He wrote to Craigie that "our aim must be active Anglo-American cooperation wherever possible, and we must be careful to do nothing which might jeopardize the movement in the United States for collaboration with like-minded governments in Europe."[157]

The foreign secretary's fears that an Anglo-Japanese deal would adversely affect relations with the United States were not unfounded. As the British chargé d'affaires in Washington Mallet wrote, even "a suspicion that we were considering some arrangement with Japan behind America's back and inconsistent with our obligations under the Nine-Power Treaty[158] would, in my

[156] *Ibid.*, doc. No. 483. Halifax to Craigie.

[157] Somewhat later, at the end of February, Halifax wrote to Craigie: "Any compromise, moreover, which gave Japan what she wanted in North China and left us in possession of a substantial portion of our investments and trade in a weakened but independent remainder, would, apart from other considerations, be out of the question unless it received the improbable concurrence of the United States, with whom we have been trying for some time to pursue a parallel policy." (DBFP, vol. VIII, doc. No. 519, Halifax to Craigie, February 28, 1939.)

[158] The Nine Power Treaty was concluded on February 6, 1922, at the Washington Conference by the United States, Great Britain, France, Japan, Belgium, Italy, Holland, Portugal and China. It obligated the participants to respect the sovereignty and territorial and administrative integrity of China and to observe the "open door" principle. It did not, however, provide for any means of enforcing the obligations.

opinion, arouse such a storm of criticism as to cost us the sympathy of this country at least for several months."[159]

Yet Halifax did not reject Craigie's proposal outright. He wrote him that he "should not wish to see any opportunity missed of doing something which might help to restore friendly relations with Japan." He merely wanted to have it done discreetly and safely, without endangering relations with the United States.[160]

The British ambassador to China, Sir A. Clark Kerr, was of a different opinion. Doubting that a new Japanese-German-Italian agreement would substantially change matters, he cautioned that Japan, if her hands were free and it suited her, "may be counted upon to throw her weight on to the side of the Berlin-Rome Axis." He considered it, therefore, a mistake to compromise with Japan in order to dissuade her from entering into an alliance with Germany.[161]

Actually, Halifax did not believe that a treaty of alliance between Japan, Germany and Italy might be signed soon. He wrote Chargé d'Affaires Mallet in Washington that he disagreed with the *News Chronicle* story of January 17, 1939, that Japan was ready to sign the alliance, for he presumed that Japan was willing to enter into a combination against the Soviet Union only, lest Great Britain and the United States respond with an embargo on sales of commodities which she required for the production of munitions and the conduct of war. Halifax surmised that, "Japan was so deeply committed in China she feared she might be involved by allies in a new adventure. Japan figures on solving

---

[159] DBFP, vol. VII, doc. No. 479. Mallet to Halifax, February 9, 1939.
[160] *Ibid.*, doc. No. 433. Halifax to Craigie, January 18, 1939.
[161] DBFP, doc. No. 441. Kerr to Halifax, January 23, 1939.

the China problem if there were a general conflict in Europe."[162]

Conscious of Britain's economic leverage, Craigie suggested to Arita on February 4, 1939, that "Japan, Great Britain, the United States and China come together in friendly cooperation," with Japan playing the role of "senior partner" so far as the Far East was concerned. If Japan relinquished her "monopolistic and exclusionist practices" and gave a less uncompromising turn to her foreign policy, Craigie said, the policies of Great Britain and the United States might become more favorable to Japan. If, on the other hand, Japan now were to join an alliance directed largely against Great Britain, he warned, "the last hope of friendly settlement might vanish and the two countries [might be] left to face each other in sterile economic conflict."

Arita replied that the negotiations with Germany and Italy had not been concluded and denied that the Tripartite alliance was anti-British. Depicting the projected alliance as merely an extension of the Anti-Comintern Pact, he said that he had been sincerely disappointed in 1936, when Great Britain had declined his invitation to participate in the pact. He promised to make "certain proposals" after the session of the Diet ended, which would go a long way toward improving the position of British interests in China.[163]

Thus, rather than give a stern warning to Japan against concluding a treaty with Germany, Great Britain only hinted that she might respond with economic sanctions, then substituted proposals of cooperation on broad lines.

---

[162] *Ibid.,* doc. No. 467. Halifax to Mallet, British chargé d'affaires in the U.S.A., February 4, 1939.
[163] *Ibid.,* doc. No. 473. Craigie to Halifax, February 5, 1939.

Advocates of a policy of appeasement toward the German-Japanese aggressors were found also in the United States. The American ambassador in Tokyo, Joseph C. Grew, for example, urged his government to refrain from imposing or threatening to impose drastic economic sanctions against Japan, such as halting the sale of oil and raw materials required by the Japanese in their war with China, lest Japanese hostility to the United States be aroused.[164] Grew's argument, which echoed the views expressed by Japanese journalists and publicists since 1931,[165] fell upon receptive ears in Washington, where many did not want the German-Japanese negotiations discontinued, hoping that Japan would become involved in war with the Soviet Union.

Secretary of State Cordell Hull, who had seen Halifax's dispatch to Mallet[166] in addition to Grew's report of February 8, which reviewed the negotiations between Germany and Japan, instructed Grew to warn Japan against concluding the alliance with Germany, but in doing so to avoid phrases which might bind the United States too closely to the position of Great Britain.

Hull shared Grew's view that the Japanese government would think it over before taking any decisive steps. He thought it best for the United States to restrict herself to half-measures—to warnings and the broadening of a "moral embargo"[167]—to limit the scope

[164] W.L. Langer and S.E. Gleason, *Challenge to Isolation* (New York, 1953), p. 19.
[165] See, for example, Sasa Hiro, *Taikoku Nihon no shorai* (Tokyo, 1935).
[166] DBFP, vol. VIII, doc. No. 467. Halifax to Mallet, February 4, 1939.
[167] Langer and Gleason, pp. 104–105. On July 1, 1938, the State Department notified American aviation companies that the United States government disapproved of the sale of aircraft and parts to countries which resorted to "inhumane bombardments." It was merely a gesture, made to deceive the American public and world opinion, because in 1937 the United States exported to Japan aircraft to the total sum of less than three million dollars while the exports of aircraft in 1938, when the moral

of the German-Japanese bloc to the struggle against the U.S.S.R.

When Grew conveyed Hull's message as his own opinion, the Japanese interpreted it as approval of their plans by the United States. On February 22 the Privy Council agreed to the adherence of Hungary and the puppet government of Manchukuo to the Anti-Comintern Pact. Foreign Minister Arita told the Privy Council on this occasion that the Japanese government was taking steps to strengthen the Anti-Comintern Pact and implied that its application would be confined essentially to the struggle against the U.S.S.R.

Arita understood the motives behind the American actions,[168] and told Grew on May 18, before the latter's departure for the United States, that there would be no military or political obligations in a treaty with Germany.[169] "So far as we are aware," a British Foreign Office official, Ronald, wrote to Mallet, "Grew has not made any comparable efforts to dissuade the Japanese from involving themselves in a formal alliance," and suggested that Mallet "try and get the State Department to instruct him to do whatever he [Grew] can in this sense."[170]

Aware that the deterioration of the European situation, which hampered British activity in the Far East, could be used by unscrupulous American politicians for the gradual subjugation of the colonial possessions and spheres of influence of Great Britain in the Far East,

---

embargo was in effect, grew by 15 million dollars to a total of almost 17½ million dollars. The total import of Japan from the U.S.A., which was made up mainly of strategic war materials, amounted in the period of 1937–1939 to 760 million dollars.

[168] *Ibid.*

[169] Langer and Gleason, p. 104.

[170] DBFP, vol. VIII, doc. No. 488. Ronald to Mallet, February 16, 1939.

the British Foreign Office, adopting a stronger line than its ambassador in Tokyo, sought to paralyze the United States in this regard and to safeguard the position of British imperialism in the Far East by involving its American competitor in an intensified struggle with Japan.

While prodding the United States into a more active policy against Japan in the name of "solidarity of interests" and "parallel actions" as a means of making Japan more amenable in regard to the China question and her relations with Germany and Italy, Great Britain could not herself make a deal with Japan. But neither did she take any serious steps, so that the Japanese could continue their aggression in the Far East and even bring pressure to bear on Great Britain, as in the case of the Soviet-British-French negotiations in the spring of 1939.

On March 29, the day after the Soviet news agency TASS had reported the arrival of the British Minister for Overseas Trade Hudson in Moscow,[171] Arita summoned Craigie and launched an attack on Soviet policy. He repeated that the British government "had been mistaken in not joining the Anti-Comintern Pact and that they would make a further mistake in trusting to Soviet Russia for military assistance."[172] He threatened that "if Great Britain were now to invite the U.S.S.R. to take part in any combination of powers, dangerous repercussion on Anglo-Japanese relations was inevitable."

In reply to a query by Craigie about the status of negotiations for the strengthening of the Anti-Comintern Pact, Arita lied that "negotiation had not started yet" and asserted that "in any case [the] Japanese government remained fully opposed to accepting any com-

---

[171] *Izvestiya,* March 28, 1939.
[172] DBFP, vol. VIII, doc. No. 586.

mitment or entanglements in Europe." He said that "Japan was prepared to combat Communism by all means and in association with powers holding the same view." As a result of the conversation Craigie gained the impression which Arita in fact sought to create. "I was left with strong impression," Craigie reported to London, "that the Japanese government has now de-cided—or virtually decided—to convert [the] Anti-Comintern Pact into an alliance against the U.S.S.R."[173]

In an effort to prevent a Soviet-British rapproche-ment the Japanese made the question of the Tripartite Pact directly dependent on the results of the Anglo-Franco-Soviet talks. On April 27 the Japanese Ambas-sador in London Shigemitsu Mamoru warned Halifax that "the suggestion that Great Britain was contemplating a military arrangement with the Russians" would give a stimulus to the supporters of the Anti-Comintern Pact."[174] On May 8 Arita declared in a speech at a conference of prefectual governors that "Japan could not regard Anglo-Soviet cooperation lightly, even if it did not extend to the Far East." "Japan intended," he said, "by strengthening the Anti-Comintern Pact, to meet the in-

---

[173] *Ibid.*, Craigie to Halifax, March 30, 1939. In subsequent telegrams Craigie tried to prove that it was dangerous for Great Britain to enter into an alliance with the U.S.S.R. Reporting at the end of April that Germany was exercising "the strongest pressure" on Japan, Craigie indi-cated that she was exploiting "alleged intention to extend proposed Anglo-Soviet agreement to include the Far East" and "proposed extension of non-aggression system to include China." At the same time, in order to avoid irritating the Japanese, Craigie told Arita in one of their conversations that "both allegations are unfounded," but that he could not guarantee what would happen if Japan were to commit herself further in favor of Ger-many. Asking his government to make a statement on the same lines, Craigie wrote to Halifax: "I believe such a statement would be useful to the [Japanese] prime minister and foreign minister who are stated to be putting up a good fight on this question against the army." (DBFP, vol. IX, doc. No. 20, Craigie to Halifax, April 25, 1939.)

[174] DBFP, vol. IX, doc. Nos. 24, 25, Halifax to Craigie, April 27, 1939.

ternational tension from an independent standpoint."[175]

At the beginning of May Craigie reported on the basis of information received from the Polish ambassador in Tokyo that "Japan replied in the negative to the German demand to enter an alliance against Great Britain and France."

But the Japanese government [Craigie cautioned] are still being strongly pressed by the German government and had decided that the question of an alliance with Germany would have to be reconsidered in either of the following contingencies: a) extension to the Far East of proposed Anglo-Soviet arrangement for defense against aggression in Europe; b) an arrangement between U.S.S.R. and China (with the approval of Great Britain) under which the Soviet government would undertake, in the event of war in Europe, to take the place of Great Britain and France in providing assistance to the Chinese government. Japanese government was stated to regard contingency b) as far more probable than a).

The source of the information and the activities of Arita and Shigemitsu make it clear that Japan deliberately put as many obstacles as possible in the way of Soviet-British negotiations. Japan knew that in the wake of the renewed Franco-Polish and Anglo-Polish friendship important information fed to the Polish ambassador in Tokyo would unavoidably reach London or Paris.

In his letters to Halifax, Craigie did not conceal his negative attitude toward the Anglo-Soviet negotiations and echoed Japanese arguments that there was a direct relationship between the Anglo-Soviet negotiations and the question of concluding a German-Japanese alliance. Reporting all sorts of rumors and versions about the Anglo-Soviet negotiations, Craigie never mentioned that

[175] *Ibid.*, doc. No. 76, footnote 2.

a rapprochement between the Soviet Union, Great Britain, and France might have a significant effect on the situation in the Far East; he merely repeated what the Japanese, who dreaded such a combination, had put into his head.

2

Japan and Great Britain: The Policy of Accommodation

In the preceding chapter reference was made to attempts on the part of Japan and Great Britain to reach an understanding on the basis of the division of China and the organization of an anti-Soviet front. Since little has been written on this subject in the U.S.S.R. or abroad it may be of interest to examine the background of this policy.

In 1938 Japan was steadily increasing the scale of hostilities in China. The naive expectations of quick victory had vanished after the first months of operations, and a mounting number of Japanese leaders had come to realize that the subjugation of China would entail a prolonged war and exhaust Japan's resources.

Confident that Great Britain, France and the United States were committed to a policy of "noninterference," and interpreting British appeasement of Germany as a reflection of British policy in general, the Japanese

69

sought to achieve an amicable accommodation with the Western powers in order to attract their capital for developing the newly acquired territories and restoring the ravaged economy.

Such plans were made first and foremost with regard to Great Britain, because Great Britain had the largest economic interests in China and was, therefore, most interested in their preservation. According to the press, British investments in China in 1937 amounted to 1½ billion dollars while those of the United States to only 295 million dollars.[1] The fact that in the initial stages of the "China Incident" Great Britain had been reluctant to worsen relations with Japan and had pressed China to grant concessions, had encouraged the Japanese in the belief that it would be possible to conclude an Anglo-Japanese agreement regarding the joint exploitation of China.

The idea of joint Anglo-Japanese exploitation of China was supported by such prominent figures as Prince Saionji[2] and Marquis Matsudaira Yasumasa as well as by business interests closely linked with the court, such as the Sumitomo, whose head, Baron Sumitomo Kichizaemon, was Prince Saionji's brother! (Both had been born into the Tokudaiji court family and adopted by the Sumitomo and Saionji respectively.) The Sumitomo concern was the major Japanese producer of non-ferrous and light metals; it had the largest aluminum, chemical, and electro-chemical plants in Japan, on Taiwan, and in northeastern China.[3] The volume of output of these enterprises depended in large measure

---

[1] *China Economist,* May 10, 1948.

[2] Prince Saionji was the last surviving genro (elder statesman); his views carried great weight.

[3] M.I. Luk'yanova, *Yaponskiye monopolii vo vremya vtoroi mirovoi voiny* (Moscow, 1953), p. 232.

on the delivery of tin and other non-ferrous metals from the British colonies. A number of Sumitomo subsidiaries were closely connected with large American trusts, such as the Aluminum Company of America, International Western Electric, and the Libby-Owens-Ford Companies.[4]

Prime Minister Prince Konoe also had family ties with the Sumitomo. He was Sumitomo Kichizaemon's son-in-law. It is not surprising that Craigie speaks of Konoe in glowing terms in his memoirs, for the ties that existed between the Sumitomo concern and the Anglo-American interests influenced Konoe to favor collusion with Great Britain.[5] Similarly business circles dependent on British raw materials, credits and markets sought to avoid a deterioration of relations with Great Britain. Former foreign minister Viscount Ishii, after visiting England on a "goodwill mission," declared on April 11, 1938, that "Great Britain understands the position of Japan."[6]

The spread of Japanese expansion to Central and South China alarmed the British, but Kajima Morinosuke, a journalist close to the Japanese Foreign Office, voiced confidence that an agreement with Great Britain remained possible, recalling that Great Britain had been first to recognize Japan's special interests in Manchuria after the Russo-Japanese War.

Kajima believed that if Japan were to guarantee British interests in China, Great Britain would deny support to Chiang Kai-shek and would recognize the Japanese position in North and Central China. If Great Britain recognized Japan's special rights and position in China

[4] United States, Department of State, *Report of the Mission on Japanese Combines*, Part I (Washington, 1946), p. 136.
[5] *Kaizo*, February 1938.
[6] *Asahi*, April 11, 1938.

and Germany and Italy did so, other powers would inevitably follow suit. Hence, he asserted, the government considered it necessary to reach an agreement with Great Britain and to cooperate with her.[7]

The prolongation of the war in China exacerbated the internal contradictions in Japan, for it led to an intensification of the struggle for control over the militarized economy between the major "Old Concerns" (Mitsui, Mitsubishi, Sumitomo, and Yasuda) and the "New Concerns" (Kuhara, Ayukawa and others) which had come into existence on the eve of the First World War and had strengthened their positions in the period of inflation, caused by the military preparations.

The ultranationalist and military extremist advocates of the Imperial Way—such men as Generals Araki Sadao and Mazaki Jinzaburo—had strong ties with the New Concerns, as did the command of the Kwantung Army, which operated in Northeast China. Their rivals in the military establishment, adherents of the Control Faction—such men as Generals Tojo Hideki and Nagata Tetsuzan—were closer to the Old Concerns, the main financial oligarchy, and the big landowners and the court bureaucracy. When the coup d'état attempt of the Imperial Way faction in February 1936 failed, the Control Faction and the Old Concerns gained influence.

In May 1938 Premier Konoe reorganized his cabinet in an effort to make use of the appeasement policy of the Western powers to bring the war in China to an end. War Minister Sugiyama Gen and Foreign Minister Hirota Koki, who refused to negotiate with the Chiang Kai-shek regime, were dropped from the government. The post of foreign minister was offered to Ugaki

[7] Kajima Morinosuka, *Saikin Nihon no kokusai-teki chi-i* (Tokyo, 1938), pp. 8 and 140.

Kazunari, who represented the circles most closely connected with the Old Concerns. Ugaki accepted on condition that "negotiations with China will be started" and the refusal to deal with Chiang Kai-shek, proclaimed in January of that year after the failure to come to terms with the Kuomintang Government, would be annulled if necessary.[8]

Ugaki and the circles which he represented understood the danger of a prolonged war for Japan and realized that Japan alone could not exploit China economically. He frankly stated in May 1938 that China was accustomed to long war and that the occupation of her vast territory would require "an enormous toll of human life and forbiddingly high expenditures." He added that Japan would hardly have enough capital to exploit so enormous an area as China.[9] Ugaki's view was shared by the new Finance Minister Ikeda Seihin, who headed the Mitsui concern and in 1937 had been appointed governor of the Bank of Japan.[10]

General Araki was appointed minister of education, General Itagaki Seishiro, one of the leaders of the Kwantung Army who was close to the Araki group, became minister of war.

Great Britain and the United States interpreted the appointment of Itagaki as a sign of the increasing influence in Japan of those who opposed an immediate drive southward.[11] And indeed, Ugaki and Itagaki in-

[8] *Istoriya voiny na Tikhom okeane* (Moscow, 1957–1958), vol. II, pp. 176–77.
[9] *Pravda*, June 1, 1938.
[10] In the words of the American ambassador: "Both Ugaki and Ikeda realize that the solution of Japan's problem in China will be impossible unless good relations are maintained with Great Britain and the United States, and Ugaki therefore proposes to do everything possible to see that their respective interests are protected." (Joseph C. Grew, *Ten Years in Japan* [New York, 1943], p. 246.)
[11] Grew, p. 248.

sisted that primary attention be given to war preparations against the Soviet Union. Controversy ensued over the degree of a rapprochement to be sought with Nazi Germany. Itagaki demanded that Japan should enter into an unconditional military alliance which would provide for assistance in case of war against any country of the world. Konoe, Ugaki, Ikeda and Navy Minister Yonai Mitsumasa, on the other hand, wanted the pact to be directed only against the U.S.S.R.[12] Konoe wrote in his memoirs of "turning the anti-Comintern pact which existed at that time into a military alliance spearheaded against the U.S.S.R."[13] By limiting the military alliance with Germany against the Soviet Union, Konoe, Ugaki and Yonai believed Japan would be able to subjugate China without any serious obstacle from the United States, Great Britain, and France, whose Far Eastern policy was based in large measure on the expectation of a conflict between Japan and the U.S.S.R. As Germany, which strove for a redivision of the world, insisted on a comprehensive military alliance oriented not only against the U.S.S.R. but also against Great Britain, France and the United States,[14] the military fascist group in the high command of the army, represented by Itagaki, demanded acceptance of the German proposal and abandonment of attempts to cooperate with the Western powers, arguing that resolute pressure on the Western powers could bring about the discontinuation of all their assistance to China and thus in its turn lead to the speedy capitulation of the Kuomintang. It was this controversy that ultimately was to topple the Konoe government in January 1939.

[12] Soviet Archives, 436b, file 13, pp. 239 ff.
[13] Ibid., p. 77.
[14] Ibid., p. 263.

Meanwhile the big business concerns, whose interests Ugaki and Ikeda voiced in the government, supported Araki and Itagaki in their campaign against the U.S.S.R., regarding increased pressure on the U.S.S.R. as a means of preventing the Soviet state from fulfilling its Five-Year Plan. Consequently, Soviet-Japanese relations sharply deteriorated, and Moscow's proposal of April 4, 1938, for the peaceful resolution of outstanding issues was not accepted.[15] Counting on collusion with the United States and Great Britain, Ugaki saw no need to improve relations with the U.S.S.R.[16]

A frenzied anti-Soviet campaign was under way in Japan. Almost every day newspapers printed statements about a crisis in relations between Japan and the U.S.S.R. and carried fictitious reports of border violations by Soviet frontier guards.[17] Japanese authorities impeded the normal navigation of Soviet ships, did not fulfill their obligations concerning the guaranty of payments by Manchukuo for the Chinese Eastern Railway (sold by the U.S.S.R. in 1935), detained aircraft carrying mail, and in violation of the Treaty of Portsmouth established restricted zones in La Pérouse Strait.[18]

On May 14, 1938, the Soviet government protested in a special note against the systematic campaign of slander and war propaganda against the U.S.S.R. Pointing to the mass of inflammatory articles and reports in the Japanese press and to the numerous communiques, booklets and pamphlets issued by the Ministry of War and various military organizations, the note complained that "despite their responsible position," a number of the most promi-

---

[15] "Concerning Soviet-Japanese Relations," *Izvestiya,* April 28, 1938.
[16] Foreign Commissariat report of conversation between Foreign Commissar Litvinov and Ambassador Shigemitsu, *Izvestiya,* April 5, 1938.
[17] "Concerning Soviet-Japanese Relations," *Izvestiya,* May 10, 1938.
[18] *Izvestiya,* April 10 and 28, June 29, 1938, and other issues.

nent leaders of the Japanese army went so far as to justify publicly and even approve of such a war, as was the case particularly in the recent interview with General Araki, who was a member of the Japanese government.[19] Yet the protest went unheeded and the tension was to culminate in the incursion of Japanese troops into Soviet territory in the region of Lake Khasan.

The prospect of another Russo-Japanese war appealed to the British and they were not averse to an accommodation with Japan at the expense of China to free the hand of the Japanese military for a conflict with the U.S.S.R. Unofficial Anglo-Japanese negotiations started at the end of June, shortly after Foreign Minister Ugaki had proclaimed at a press conference his desire to restore Japan's "special relations of traditional friendship with Great Britain."[20] (He told the American Ambassador Grew that he also "wished to do his best for developing good relations with the United States,"[21] and hoped to end the war in China through British mediation.)[22]

The Anglo-Japanese negotiations were conducted by Ugaki and Craigie in secret. Speculation about the talks in the press was much decried by Craigie and Halifax.[23] The documents on British foreign policy published after the Second World War[24] do not shed light on the es-

[19] Statement by Foreign Commissariat, *Izvestiya*, May 16, 1938.
[20] Irving S. Friedman, *British Relations with China, 1931–1939* (New York, 1940).
[21] Grew, p. 247.
[22] On June 24 the Conference of Five Ministers (Premier Konoe, Foreign Minister Ugaki, War Minister Itagaki, Navy Minister Yonai and Finance Minister Ikeda) adopted a program proposed by Ugaki. It envisioned the conclusion of the conflict with China by the end of the war with the aid of foreign mediation. (*Istoriya voiny na Tikhom okeane*, vol. II, p. 178.)
[23] DBFP, Third Series, vol, VIII, 1938 (London, 1955); Sir Robert Craigie, *Behind the Japanese Mask* (New York, 1945), p. 152.
[24] The first volume of the third series of the British collection of docu-

sence of the negotiations in their initial and most important phase. Commencing in August 1938, they conceal the outrageous deeds of the Chamberlain government, such as the placing of Chinese customs under the control of the Japanese authorities and their puppets, the curtailment of arms delivery to China, and the beginning of the negotiations between Ugaki and Craigie to achieve an amicable agreement for the joint plunder and division of China. Material pertaining to the initial phase of the negotiations between Craigie and Ugaki is confined to footnote comments by the compilers.

On March 22, 1938, Konoe had stated in the Diet: "I cannot name the borders where our operations will end nor a time when we can stop, but I can assure you that we shall never abandon a single inch of the territory of those regions which have been occupied by our forces."[25] Foreign Minister Hirota had told foreign correspondents on May 9 that, "since the main purpose of the [China] 'incident' was to make it possible for the peoples of China and Japan to cooperate economically and socially it was 'a small matter' whether the territory was Chinese or Japanese."[26] Now, in early July, in view of the forthcoming Anglo-Japanese negotiations, Prime Minister Konoe declared that Japan did not want an inch of Chinese territory and that upon the conclusion of hostilities the Chinese people would be helped, not governed, by Japan. "Vested rights and interests of

---

ments relating to events in 1938–1939 begins with a document, dated March 9, 1938. The late starting point is strange and leaves one with the suspicion that it was chosen to conceal the Anglo-German negotiations which had taken place in 1937. (See comments by E.A. Adamov and L.N. Kutakov "Angliiskiye fal'sifikatory istorii: Dokumenty Britanskoi Vneshnei Politiki, 1919–1939, Third series", in *Izvestiya Akademii nauk SSSR. Seriya istorii i filosofii,* vol. VII [Moscow, 1950], No. 2.)

[25] *Amerasia,* vol. II, No. 3 (1938).

[26] FRUS, *Far East,* 1938.

third powers in China will be fully respected, just as Japan has made every possible effort to respect them since the first fighting," Konoe promised. "It is not Japan's purpose to encroach upon the sphere of any foreign nation."[27]

The British, in turn, gave evidence of their readiness to agree to the Japanese program of exploitation of China and cessation of war on conditions favorable for Japan, by informing Chiang Kai-shek on July 19 of their decision to refuse him a loan.[28]

As far as can be determined from the published British documents, Ugaki and Craigie had their first meeting on June 19. As the question of terminating the hostilities in China came up, Craigie directed Ugaki's attention to Chamberlain's statement in the House of Commons on May 11, 1938, that His Majesty's Government would be glad to offer its services of mediation either alone or in conjunction with other powers, provided both sides indicated their willingness to accept such mediation.[29]

Craigie broached the matter again in his talk with Ugaki on June 28, but Ugaki retorted that "it would be difficult for Japan to accept any form of foreign mediation while China was receiving assistance in men and materials from foreign powers."[30]

Declaring its unwillingness to accept mediation from Great Britain and thereby showing its disinterest in ending the war, the Japanese government instead sponsored a peace proposal by the so-called North Chinese government, set up by the Japanese in Peking.

[27] *New York Times*, July 7, 1938.
[28] DBFP, vol. VIII, doc. 7.
[29] *Ibid.*, doc. 11, footnote 7; Great Britain, House of Commons, *Parliamentary Debates*, Fifth Series, vol. 335, col. 1558.
[30] DBFP, vol. VIII, doc. 12, footnote 3.

This plan called for the division of China into five independent states: North China, Inner Mongolia, East China (Shanghai and other maritime regions), Central China (the upper and middle reaches of the Yangtze River) and South China. The power in the first three "states" was to belong to Japanese henchmen—to the North China government in Peking, to Prince Teh Wang and to the Nanking-Reformed-Government of China; South China was to be placed under the control of the local Kwangsi and Kwantung militarists. Only Central China was to remain in Chiang Kai-shek's hands.

The plan provided also for the distribution of spheres of influence: North China and Inner Mongolia were recognized as the sphere of influence of Japan, the lower Yangtze with Shanghai as the sphere of influence of Great Britain, South China as the sphere of influence of Great Britain and France, and Shantung as the sphere of influence of Germany.[31] Since the lower Yangtze River and Shanghai were in an area controlled by a pro-Japanese government, Great Britain's sphere of influence here was actually reduced to naught. Thus, English and French imperialism were to dominate South China, and the United States and Great Britain Central China.

Such an arrangement did not satisfy Great Britain, the United States and France, and the negative position of the United States regarding the mediation of the conflict between China and Japan in August 1938, to be described below, was largely determined by this circumstance.

While not disclosing the nature of the Japanese overtures, Chamberlain made it clear that London was de-

[31] *New York Times,* July 2, 1938.

termined to defend British economic interests in China. "It cannot be said," he declared, "that we are disinterested as a country in the position in the Far East, because for a hundred years our interests in China have been of great importance, and when the Japanese Government claim that they are protecting their interests in China, I am sure they must recognize that we too have our interests in China and that we cannot stand by and see them sacrificed in the process." Reiterating his proposal of mediation, Chamberlain declared: "In the meantime we are resolved to do our utmost to see that British interests shall not suffer in a conflict for which we have no responsibility and in which we have no direct concern."[32]

That day Craigie submitted to Ugaki a list of problems, whose solution he deemed prerequisite for improving relations between the two countries. Included were removal of obstacles in the way of British control in the northern district of Shanghai, freedom of navigation on the Yangtze River, removal of restrictions on the activities of British-owned or British-controlled companies, the inspection by British and Chinese representatives of railways not located in areas of military operations and, lastly, the removal of restrictions on the work of the Whangpoo River Conservancy.[33]

In communicating these five demands, Craigie said that the British government did not put forward any problems without regard to the military situation. He stressed that the list contained questions whose immediate solution would be of great importance and that the attitude that Japan would show toward them would be a reflection of the actual position of Japan vis-à-vis

[32] *Ibid.*, July 27, 1938.
[33] DBFP, vol. VIII, doc. 12, footnote 2.

Great Britain. Ugaki promised a speedy resolution of the questions, but regarded the matter of shipping on the Yangtze River as a difficult problem, asserting that Japan could not permit free passage of foreign ships or of Nationalists to Wuhan and Nanking.[34]

In the course of the talk the question of the possibility of British mediation was raised. Ugaki said that the Japanese government did not believe in the sincerity of Chiang Kai-shek's intentions and that peace negotiations would therefore be very difficult at the present time. If, however, Chiang Kai-shek would show sincerity in trying to make peace with Japan, the Japanese government would reconsider the possibility of British mediation.[35]

The change in Japan's position was dictated by the deterioration in Soviet-Japanese relations due to the provocations engineered by the Japanese military. As for the British, they offered to mediate an end of the war in China with considerable reservations. Viscount Halifax instructed Craigie that "if we could persuade the belligerents to make peace, we should remove what may be the greatest danger of all to British interests, a Sino-Japanese compact jointly to exclude all foreign interests and trade." Halifax believed that Great Britain should set peace terms for the belligerents.[36]

The British government took advantage of a request by the Chiang Kai-shek government for mediation to plan joint Western action. On August 4 the Chinese ambassador in London had told Halifax that "the Chinese Government . . . suggests that the Governments of Great Britain and the United States acting

[34] *Ibid.*
[35] *Ibid.*, doc. 11, footnote 7.
[36] *Ibid.*

jointly or on parallel lines, in conjunction with the French government, if possible, should express both to China and Japan their willingness to offer their good offices for bringing the conflict to an end." He had added that if the offer was rejected by Japan, Great Britain and the United States should "take up a firm position and declare plainly their intentions to claim scrupulous respect for their rights in China."[37]

The start of negotiations between the Chiang Kai-shek government and Japan may be dated back to a telegram of greetings sent in June 1938 by Chang Ch'ün, vice-president of the Executive Yüan, to Ugaki when the latter took office, for Chang was a close friend of Chiang and the dispatch of the telegram cannot be viewed as a casual gesture. The Kuomintang was represented in the unofficial negotiations by K'ung Hsiang-hsi, president of the Executive Yüan. The peace conditions advanced by the Japanese side were based on demands which had been put forward earlier; they coincided with the position of Ugaki.[38]

The information about the negotiations, found in the published British documents by implication in the form of footnotes, suggests that the Chiang Kai-shek government was willing to consider the following peace terms: 1) the reorganization of Manchukuo; 2) the maintenance of Japanese garrisons for a limited period in Tientsin, Peking, Tsingtao and Shanghai; and 3) the granting of special economic and commercial facilities for Japan in North China.[39]

[37] Halifax to Kerr, August 4, 1938, *Ibid.*, doc. 5. Apart from trying to use the British to mediate an end to the war with Japan, the Kuomintang took steps to approach Ugaki directly, regarding him as a representative of circles which favored a rapprochement with the Western powers and the termination of hostilities in China.

[38] *Istoriya voiny na Tikhom okeane*, vol. II, p. 178.

[39] Telegram by Greenway, dated October 8, 1938, DBFP, vol. VIII, doc. 171, and doc. 144, footnote 2.

On the other hand, Craigie reported on the basis of "reliable sources," the Japanese Five Ministers' Conference, shortly before General Ugaki's resignation, had dropped the demand for compensations and, recognizing that the policy of establishing a "puppet government" in North China had been unsuccessful, had favored the creation of a government which could speak for the whole of China and thus ignore Chiang Kai-shek. The only way the latter could come to a "reasonable settlement" with the Japanese, Craigie believed, was to break with the Communists.

Failing to obtain Japanese consent to American and British mediation, the Kuomintang had made the above-mentioned overtures to London, Washington and Paris. But as Ambassador Kerr, who was well informed about the intentions of the Nationalist regime, wrote to Halifax in asking for mediation, "the Chinese have never contemplated anything but a public demarche made simultaneously to themselves and the Japanese, simultaneous action being intended to cloak the fact that the initiative came from themselves."[40] Halifax considered the proposal as an expression of doubt on the part of the Chinese "about their ability to continue the struggle."[41]

Notifying Craigie of the Chinese proposal, Halifax pointed to the possibility of enlisting German support at some stage.[42] He suggested that Craigie consult the American ambassador and, if possible, the German ambassador. Instructing Craigie to tell Foreign Minister Ugaki about the Chinese move, Halifax asked that any

[40] DBFP, vol. VIII, doc. 22.

[41] Halifax to Craigie, August 10, 1938, DBFP, vol. VIII, doc. 11.

[42] On January 14, 1938, Henderson had reported that Germany was unwilling to act as official mediator between China and Japan, but that she would resent being excluded in the event Great Britain, the United States and France undertook such a task. (DBFP, vol. XIII, doc. 11, footnote 4.)

British offer be confined to "good offices" and that he demand without reference to the Chinese requests that Japan observe meticulously the rights of other powers in China.[43]

The desire to enlist German help in resolving the Sino-Japanese conflict was undoubtedly connected with the appeasement of Germany in Europe by British and French statesmen in July and August. It was at this time that Marquis Londonderry made his trip to Berlin, while Wiedemann paid a visit to London with a personal communication from Hitler to Chamberlain and that British and French negotiators worked out the principles for solving the "Sudeten problem" on which the Munich agreement was to be based. At the beginning of August British appeasement reached its height as London sent notes to the government of Czechoslovakia demanding that it undertake resolute measures to preserve peace in Europe. Since this was also when Soviet-Japanese relations were in a critical stage because of the Japanese attack on Soviet territory in the Lake Khasan region, Halifax's idea of enlisting Nazi Germany in a mediation effort imparted an anti-Soviet flavor to the proposal of "good offices," for the prospect of ending the conflict in China encouraged the Japanese imperialists to act more aggressively against the U.S.S.R.

But Ambassador Craigie questioned that Japan would accept mediation by two or three powers, since the Tripartite Intervention of 1895, which had deprived Japan of some of the spoils of the Sino-Japanese War, was still fresh in her mind. He believed that the Japanese government would prefer either British or American mediation. He recommended, therefore, not "a joint and public demarche but rather a private sounding, either

[43] *Ibid.*

by my United States colleague or myself—not both."[44]
Convinced that no "mediatory action can now save
Hankow," Craigie believed that the fall of Hankow
would offer a good opportunity for proposing mediation. To be successful, however, Craigie believed, the
British initiative must be preceded by an easing in tension in Anglo-Japanese relations. He envisioned British
implementation of the Anglo-Japanese Customs Agreement, signed on May 5, 1938, and suspension of any
export credits to China pending the course of the mediation discussions on one hand, and Japanese acceptance of
the five above-mentioned demands on the other hand.[45]

The French Foreign Minister Georges Bonnet expressed support for the British desire to end the Sino-
Japanese war. He said to the British Chargé d'Affaires
Campbell on August 10 that "the Chinese Government's
approach to His Majesty's Government with suggestions
for a peace move was most important and should be
followed up."[46] Yet Halifax wrote to Craigie on August
13 that he agreed with him that undue haste should not
be shown in offering good offices.

The United States met the Chinese proposal and the
British initiative with indifference, if not hostility. The
Americans did not wish to see the Sino-Japanese conflict
settled under the auspices of Great Britain and within
the framework of the Anglo-Japanese negotiations. The
American counselor in London told Halifax on August
15 that the United States government felt "reluctant to
accept the position of a post office in transmitting from
one side to another proposals, many of which may be
inconsistent with the terms of the treaties by which the

---

[44] Craigie to Halifax, August 12, 1938, DBFP, vol. VIII, doc. 12.
[45] *Ibid.*
[46] *Ibid.*, doc. 16, footnote 1.

United States government set such store."[47] Desiring to set the peace terms itself, Washington preferred not to bind itself to British actions.

With the defeat of the Japanese forces by the Red Army near Lake Khasan British efforts to mediate an end to the Sino-Japanese war abated. The Soviet victory scuttled Ugaki's plans to solve the China question and defeat the Soviet Union in collusion with the Western powers.[48]

Ugaki's willingness to consider a negotiated peace aroused the wrath of ultranationalists who demonstrated carrying banners with such slogans as "Down with the negotiations between Ugaki and Craigie!" and simply "Down with Ugaki!" The militarists and the reactionary organizations which supported them were opposed to any compromises; they wanted to capture the whole of China. Their aggressive attitude was hardened by Germany's proposal for the strengthening of the Anti-Comintern Pact, put forward in January 1938 and discussed by the Japanese government from the beginning of July 1938. The army's support of the German plan to create a military bloc against the United States, Great Britain, and France, as well as the U.S.S.R., could not but affect Ugaki's position. When Craigie had talked with Ugaki on July 27, he had been hopeful that the negotiations might bear fruit, "but ever since that date," he reported in September, "the atmosphere has changed and General Ugaki's attitude has become that of a courteous and imperturbably, but nevertheless thoroughly stubborn counsel for the defense."[49]

<hr/>

[47] Halifax to Kerr, August 15, 1938, DBFP, vol. VIII, doc. 21.
[48] *Istoriya voiny na Tikhom okeane,* vol. II, p. 182.
[49] Craigie to Halifax, September 15, 1938, *Ibid.,* doc. 99. "I hardly think that synchronization of the time of the Ambassador's [Ott's] return and the date from which the stiffening anti-British attitude became ob-

Craigie believed that the change in Ugaki's attitude was the result firstly of the decision of the Five Ministers' Conference on August 16 to continue military operations "for the annihilation of the Chiang Kai-shek regime" while carrying on the "construction of New China."[50] Secondly, strong pressure had been exerted by the military on the Cabinet to discontinue conversations altogether.[51]

When Craigie saw Ugaki on August 18, the latter remarked that British refusal of a Chinese loan was a positive factor for improving relations between Great Britain and Japan, but asserted with serious displeasure that British criticism of Japanese policy in Parliament and in the press had aroused strong feeling against Great Britain in Japan. He told Craigie that the Japanese authorities in China were trying to meet the British demands. One hundred and thirty-four foreign factories, among them 54 British ones, had been reopened and over 136,000 Chinese workers allowed to return to the Northern Settlement area of Shanghai.

Although Ugaki spoke at length about the necessity of resolving the question amicably and of his hopes of improving Anglo-Japanese relations, he evaded Craigie's question whether his response was tantamount to a rejection of the five demands put forward by Great Britain by stating merely that it would take some time to improve relations. Craigie understood that Anglo-Japanese relations had come to a serious impasse. Yet it was also

---

servable can be mere coincidence", Craigie wrote. "It is evident that he must have been called back to Germany for some important purpose, and with my knowledge of Herr von Ribbentrop I suspect that this purpose was inimical to ourselves."

[50] Craigie to Halifax, August 10, 1938, DBFP, vol. VIII, doc. 33.
[51] *Ibid.*, doc. 32.

apparent that Ugaki did not want to break with Great Britain completely, for twice during the conversation he asked "whether Anglo-Japanese cooperation in occupied districts was possible."[52]

When Halifax questioned Craigie what he thought of Ugaki's feeler, Craigie took the inquiry to mean that he should do everything to come to terms with the Japanese. He cabled back that under the circumstances it was essential for the British press, particularly the *Times*, to "display special discretion in commenting during the next fortnight on Far Eastern affairs and preferably make no further reference at all to my conversation with Minister for Foreign Affairs."[53]

Interpreting Ugaki's query concerning Anglo-Japanese cooperation in occupied districts as an attempt on the part of Ugaki, who had been attacked by the ultra-nationalists for his intention to give concessions to Great Britain, to produce evidence that Great Britain would not remain "irretrievably hostile and uncooperative" even if she secured the more important of her "desiderata," Craigie considered it possible to tell Ugaki that, provided British interests were respected, the British were "quite prepared to cooperate in the sense in which we understood the word."[54] But this was too much even for Halifax. He wrote to Craigie on August 24 that the latter's proposal to "cooperate" with Japan had most dangerous implications. Halifax saw the danger first and foremost in the fact that the British promises would not remain secret and that upon their disclosure the British would be "exposed to every sort of suspicion and inevitably be attacked in Parliament and in the press, not

[52] Craigie to Halifax, August 20, 1938, DBFP, vol. VIII, doc. 39.
[53] Craigie to Halifax, August 22, 1938, DBFP, vol. VIII, doc. 41.
[54] *Ibid.*

to mention the effect in the United States of America and in China."[55]

Halifax had no illusions about the position of the United States. He understood that the Americans would resent strongly being bypassed, feeling that their own position would be endangered by deals of such kind. Hence the British government, engaged as it was in anti-Soviet intrigues in Europe, not only exercised caution with regard to the United States, but tried to shift the entire burden of the struggle against Japanese imperialism in China onto the shoulders of the United States. For that reason Halifax rejected the suggestion of Ambassador Kerr that Britain, in compliance with the request of the Chiang Kai-shek government, secretly offer her good offices to Japan to end the Sino-Japanese conflict and, should Japan reject the offer, make this public; he also rebuffed the suggestion that Great Britain jointly with the United States inform the Nationalist government of their willingness to act as mediators between it and Japan and publish a statement to this effect, if Japan refused their good offices, and that Great Britain herself start negotiations with Japan if a common policy with the United States could not be developed.[56]

While the British government understood that open cooperation with Japan could undermine its policy of deflecting Japanese aggression northward in the hope of

[55] Halifax to Craigie, August 24, 1938, DBFP, VIII, doc. 45.
[56] Kerr to Halifax, August 24, 1938, DBFP, vol. VIII, doc. 46; Halifax to Craigie, August 10, 1938, *Ibid.*, doc. 11. The British talked of "good offices", but in fact, as Halifax's instructions stated plainly, were primarily concerned in preserving British interests. Kerr advanced his proposal in the belief that any sign of collaboration between Great Britain and Japan would naturally be hailed in China as a betrayal of British pledges to China. He questioned that any form of Anglo-Japanese cooperation in the occupied areas could be to the benefit, and not to the detriment, of China.

preserving Britain's positions in China, it did not lose hope of reaching an agreement with Japan. The British position in relation to the Chinese complaint in the League of Nations against the Japanese aggression provides sufficient ground for this conclusion. When the Chinese ambassador called on Halifax on September 1 and expressed the opinion that the Chinese question should be included in the agenda of the forthcoming session of the Council and the Assembly of the League of Nations, Halifax, asked for the opinion of the British government concerning this matter, replied that he "could not see any prospect for this action to be of any benefit to China," in fact, that it could be only detrimental to the League of Nations. He pointed out that there was no precedent in the history of the League to show that its members "could be prepared to undertake any positive actions in the Far East of the kind provided for by Article 17."

Having learned of the Chinese intentions and being unsure of the position of the British government, the Japanese decided to bring pressure on London to prevent a decision by the League of Nations condemning the Japanese aggression in China. Asserting that the Japanese foreign minister was working to better Anglo-Japanese relations, Ambassador Yoshida Shigeru warned Halifax on September 9 that his government "feared the reaction upon public opinion in Japan" if Great Britain took further action in the League of Nations "in the sense desired by the Chinese Government." Halifax took the hint. Although he claimed not to have had time to inform himself "what precise action the Chinese Government was proposing to take" and that he "did not suppose that it would be at all likely that either the League of Nations or His Majesty's Government would be able to depart from the attitude that they had hitherto taken up in regard to these matters," he declared that the British government "wished to do nothing to make relations more difficult" between the two countries.[57] And, truly, the British representatives in the League of Nations, with the support of their French colleagues, did what they could to dissuade the Chinese government from requesting the League of Nations to apply Article 17.[58]

When Counselor Okamoto asked the British Foreign Office on September 20 to explain its position regarding the application of Article 17, he was told officially that it seemed inevitable that the request would be rejected, in other words, that there was no cause for Japanese anxiety. "As regards the application of sanctions under Article 16," Halifax informed Craigie, "Mr. Okamoto was referred to the public discussions which had been proceeding at Geneva and especially to pronouncements on the subject of the Netherlands and the Scandinavian countries who assert the non-compulsory nature of Article 16."[59] Halifax stated that it was "not possible to say definitely what action the Council will in fact recommend, but it is very improbable that there will be any question of sanctions."

When the Chinese delegation requested the Council to invoke the third paragraph of Article 17, the British representatives, on instructions from Halifax, stated that the possibility of applying economic sanctions against Japan had already been considered by the League and that even the application of sanctions by a limited number of states did not appear possible for the same reasons

---

[57] Halifax to Craigie, September 9, 1938. DBFP, vol. VIII, doc. 88.
[58] Halifax to Craigie, September 21, 1938, DBFP, vol. VIII, doc. 106.
[59] *Ibid.*

as stated before. In the British view the Council could not go beyond previous resolutions on the subject.[60]

Great Britain did not meet the Chinese request of September 1938 for a loan at least through other countries, nor did she agree to receive a special mission. When the Chinese proposed to send "something less than a mission"—a minister or a well-known political personality—the British government declared that such action would be undesirable.[61]

As no reply was made by London to Ugaki's query about Anglo-Japanese cooperation in occupied China, the Japanese government decided to take the initiative in putting forward its conditions for cooperation with Great Britain. On September 1, *Gaiko Jiho,* a journal close to the Foreign Office, carried an article with the significant title, "The Irresolute Policy of Great Britain in the Far East." The article asserted that "the only real and safe way for Great Britain to guarantee her interests in China would be to abandon her support of the Chiang Kai-shek regime completely and to cooperate faithfully with Japan in the Far East." This might hasten the termination of the China Incident, further the talks between Ugaki and Craigie, and lead to Anglo-Japanese cooperation.[62]

Hinting openly that lack of an agreement might imperil British interests in the Yangtze region and in Shanghai, the article warned that the creation of a new pro-Japanese government with jurisdiction over Shanghai, Nanking, and other cities and the restoration of ties between North and Central China would "create the possibility of setting up new enterprises under the guidance

[60] *Ibid.,* doc. 112.
[61] *Ibid.,* docs. 110 and 112.
[62] *Gaiko Jiho,* September 1, 1938.

of the Nanking government," which would increase the dependence of Great Britain on Japan, and that the fall of Hankow would weaken Britain's position further, and called upon the British government to abandon its irresolution in the negotiations.[63]

There can be no doubt that the article had been inspired by the Foreign Office, because a week later, in a meeting with the British ambassador, Ugaki recited its arguments almost word for word when Craigie failed to give a definite reply to the question of Anglo-Japanese cooperation in occupied China. He reiterated that if Great Britain would abandon her support of Chiang Kai-shek, an Anglo-Japanese settlement on the basis of mutual concession and understanding would be greatly facilitated; if she did not do so, she could not hope for a "rapid solution" of her difficulties.[64] Ugaki told Craigie that a new and powerful government of Central China would soon be formed and that he hoped that the foreign governments, including the British government, would take due note of this new situation, when it arose.[65] Turning to the five demands of Great Britain, communicated to him in June, Ugaki said that the Japanese government made the opening of the northern district of Shanghai dependent on the degree of "cooperation" between the Municipal Council and the Japanese side, by which Ugaki meant an increase in Japanese police representation and the adoption of measures to combat anti-Japanese activities, which was tantamount to the establishment of Japanese control over the territory of the settlement. The British demands for free navigation on the Yangtze River, the restoration of control over the

---

[63] *Ibid.*
[64] Craigie to Halifax, September 9, 1938, DBFP, vol. VIII, doc. 85.
[65] *Ibid.,* doc. 84.

railways and the removal of restrictions on British plants were not met on the pretext that military operations were still in progress and that they "would lead to similar demands from other powers." To avoid the impression of outright rejection, however, Ugaki said that the north station in Shanghai could be inspected and that navigation on the Yangtze River would be allowed under special circumstances.[66]

Ugaki realized that the Japanese position could not satisfy Great Britain. "Ugaki's reply left us almost exactly where we were before," Craigie reported to London, and observed "I am beginning to believe General Ugaki has capitulated to military."[67]

The Foreign Office took advantage of Hitler's speech before the Nuremberg Congress of the Nazi party on September 12 to put pressure on the British. In a public statement which referred to Hitler's allegation that Czechoslovakia served as a base for the activities of the Comintern in Europe and that a similar role was played by China in Asia, the Foreign Office expressed Japan's readiness to join forces with Germany and Italy to fight against the "Red Menace" and expressed the hope that "such great powers as Great Britain and France will take a definite cognizance of it and act accordingly for the sake of world peace,"[68] i.e., would not interfere with German and Japanese plans.

Convinced that the Foreign Office statement was intended to inflame public opinion in Great Britain,[69] Craigie hesitated to ask Ugaki for an explanation, fearing "this might drive the Japanese government to clarify

---

[66] Craigie to Halifax, September 9, 1938, DBFP, vol. VIII, doc. 86.
[67] *Ibid.*; Craigie to Halifax, September 8, 1938, DBFP, vol. VIII, doc. 85.
[68] Craigie to Halifax, September 14, 1938, DBFP, vol. VIII, doc. 95.
[69] Craigie to Halifax, September 14, 1938, DBFP, vol. VIII, doc. 94.

statement in manner unfavorable" to Great Britain.[70] Hence his talk with Ugaki on September 14 was extremely cautious, with hints and promises concerning the future but without any definite pledges given. Both sides waited to see what course events in Europe would take. As Craigie reported, "in the present circumstances we cannot hope to do much more than mark time."[71]

British concessions to Germany and Italy triggered renewed Japanese pressure for British acceptance of Japanese control of China's public utilities and industrial enterprises[72] and the termination of British assistance to Chiang Kai-shek. Although British assistance to China was insignificant, Ugaki tried to secure a statement agreeing to its discontinuance in order to demonstrate to the military that his course was more successful than their brazen policy.

The Japanese vice-minister assured Craigie that there had been no change in Japanese policy and that the delay in solving the questions raised by Great Britain was "due not only to present wave of anti-British feeling but also to real difficulties inherent in the problems themselves." He strongly urged Craigie to continue his conversations with Ugaki, holding out results satisfactory to Great Britain. The vice-minister tried to soften the harsh impressions that may have been given by Ugaki's tough statement of September 14 in the wake of Hitler's speech and Prince Konoe's press interview the following day concerning the proposed strengthening of the Anti-Comintern Pact.[73] He "categorically"

---

[70] *Ibid.* A week later Halifax stated to Craigie that he did not think that any useful purpose would be served by his making any inquiry. (DBFP, vol. VIII, doc. 103.)

[71] Craigie to Halifax, September 14, 1938, DBFP, vol. VIII, doc. 96.

[72] Craigie to Halifax, September 15, 1938, DBFP, vol. VIII, doc. 99.

[73] Konoe said that there was a need for strengthening the Anti-Comintern Pact.

rejected the contention that the Foreign Office statement meant that Japan intended to ally herself with Germany and Italy if the Czechoslovakian crisis led to war and asserted, in regard to Konoe's declaration, that "the government had been turning over in their minds various ways of strengthening the Anti-Comintern Pact but always with a view to combating Communist activities and not with any wider political objective." When Craigie rejoined that "any such strengthening of the pact at this stage would be interpreted as bringing Japan into closer political association with the totalitarian powers, thus further complicating the solution of existing Anglo-Japanese difficulties," the vice-minister pointed out that membership in the Tripartite Pact had not prevented Italy from concluding the recent Anglo-Italian agreement,[74] and added maliciously that it was his understanding that His Majesty's government was trying to "reach an amicable settlement when possible with totalitarian powers."[75]

On September 22 Craigie had the last interview with Ugaki prior to the latter's resignation. Suggesting that Great Britain "assume towards the Japanese authorities in China an attitude similar to that which she had adopted vis-à-vis the Franco Government in Spain," Ugaki insisted again on the discontinuance of British assistance to Chiang Kai-shek. Craigie retorted that Great Britain did not really furnish Chiang any concrete assistance, but Ugaki cited the League of Nations' resolution of as-

[74] The vice-minister had in mind the Anglo-Italian agreement of April 16, 1938, in which Great Britan promised to work for League of Nations' recognition of Italian sovereignty over Ethiopia; it sanctioned the armed assistance of Italy to Francisco Franco in return for Italy's pledge to recall her volunteers after the civil war in Spain was over. Great Britain also recognized the equality of Italian rights in Saudi Arabia and Yemen.
[75] Craigie to Halifax, September 9, 1938, DBFP, vol. VIII, doc. 102.

sistance, statements made by British ministers in the House of Commons and articles critical of Japanese policy in newspapers published in the International Settlement in Shanghai in support of his contention that Great Britain was supporting Chiang. As for the five British demands, Ugaki said that he agreed to the restoration of a "normal" regime in the northern district of the Shanghai Settlement on condition that there would be cooperation with the Japanese authorities in the maintenance of order and that the Japanese demands regarding the policy of the Municipal Council would be met. He left the cardinal question of navigation on the Yangtze River unresolved. Agreeing to the complete restoration of the Council's authority in Hankow and Yangtzepoo, Ugaki demanded a full investigation of the silver reserves in the Federal Reserve Bank and their transfer to Japan.[76]

The major questions raised by both sides were not resolved. The British could not meet the Japanese demands because the concessions did not further the anti-Soviet plans of British imperialism and because Craigie had received reports from the Dutch and French ambassadors that the Japanese were about to drive into South China and capture Canton, where Britain's most important business interests were concentrated.[77]

Sir A. Clark Kerr insisted on the discontinuance of the concessions.

[76] Craigie to Halifax, September 22, 1938, DBFP, vol. VIII, doc. 108.
[77] Craigie to Halifax, September 15, 1938, DBFP, vol. VIII, doc. 98. On September 15 the Dutch ambassador informed Craigie that he had gained the impression from recent contacts with German circles that the German and Italian embassies were pressing the Japanese government to attack Canton and the southern provinces after the fall of Hankow. The Germans believed that the campaign in China could be brought to a rapid end only by cutting South China off completely from the Pacific supply routes. The information about the contemplated attack on Canton was confirmed by the French ambassador, who added that he had received news about the concentration of military ships for a new expedition.

I see no reason [Kerr wrote to Halifax] why we
should give away to the Japanese everything we have
secured during these past months. . . . As we
clearly cannot make any headway at present, I recommend that as far as possible these matters be temporar-
ily left in cold storage. If conditions in Europe deteriorate, the Japanese will sooner or later settle these
and other issues under threat of force. If conditions
improve we may be able to take a firmer line.[78]

Halifax agreed with Kerr.

Acceptance of the Japanese proposals for full cooperation [he wrote] would mean in practice that the
control of the municipal administration would pass
rapidly into Japanese hands. If that must come about, I
think it is better that they should take it illegally by
force majeure than that we should surrender the
position voluntarily. In the former case we should at
least have the moral support of the Americans and
other nations interested in maintaining the international status of the Settlement. In the latter, we should
be blamed by those nations for selling the past. Moreover, even if we agreed to Japanese demands, there
would still be no guarantee that they would continue
to respect our rights to interests in China in the event
of the international situation deteriorating.[79]

The failure of the strong policy versus the Soviet
Union, as evidenced by the defeat of the Japanese forces
near Lake Khasan, and the inability to secure a profitable
agreement with Great Britain were the major causes of
Ugaki's resignation. Ostensibly he resigned over a dispute whether the China Council was to be placed under
the Foreign Office or the War Ministry, but as Craigie
reported, "the real reason for Ugaki's resignation was
not the question of setting up a China organ but the un-

[78] Halifax to Craigie, September 26, 1938, DBFP, vol. VIII, doc. 111.
[79] Halifax to Craigie, September 30, 1938, DBFP, vol. VIII, doc. 118.

popularity in many quarters of the conversations in which General Ugaki and I were engaged."[80]

Premier Konoe, who assumed simultaneously the portfolio of foreign minister upon Ugaki's resignation, declared that there would be no change in Japanese foreign policy.[81] He reassured Ambassador Grew that the Japanese government would fully respect the Open Door rights and interests of the United States of America in China,[82] and made a statement to the effect that the Anglo-Japanese talks could be continued, if Great Britain so desired.[83]

Regarding Konoe's statement as affording "a favorable opportunity for trying to get a conversation for the improvement of Anglo-Japanese relations on to a higher level,"[84] Craigie requested an audience with Konoe. The meeting, which took place on October 12, constituted the resumption of Anglo-Japanese negotiations. Craigie raised two questions: the situation in Shanghai and navigation on the Yangtze River. Konoe echoed Ugaki's assertion that the delay in meeting the British demands concerning the former was due to the need for maintaining order, concerning the latter due to the necessities of the military situation. Reiterating that "the two countries should cooperate for future development of China and for establishment of a lasting peace," Konoe emphasized the difficulties which his government faced in trying to settle Anglo-Japanese relations. "There were in Japan," he said, "elements unfriendly to Great Britain who desired to see the British interests driven out

[80] Craigie to Halifax, October 7, 1938, DBFP, vol. VIII, doc. 130.
[81] *Ibid.*
[82] FRUS, *Far East,* vol. I (Washington, 1954), pp. 781–785. Grew brought it to the attention of Craigie. (Craigie to Halifax, October 4, 1938, DBFP, vol. VIII, doc. 125)
[83] Craigie to Halifax, October 3, 1938, DBFP, vol. VII, doc. 122.
[84] Halifax to Craigie, October 7, 1938, DBFP, vol. VIII, doc. 128.

of China, but the Japanese Government did not share these views and, on the contrary, wished to solve all these matters by friendly compromises."[85]

Konoe proposed the following agenda for their talks:

1. The settlement as far as practicable of outstanding differences.
2. The restoration of peace.
3. A general settlement between Japan and Great Britain of all outstanding proposals under consideration before the outbreak of the present incidents.[86]

Conscious that in the past wide publicity had complicated Anglo-Japanese negotiations and prevented their successful conclusion, Craigie and Konoe agreed to avoid publicity as much as possible.[87] Yet the Japanese press continued to agitate against making concessions to Great Britain and, as Britain's position in Europe deteriorated, called for British concessions in the Far East. The Japanese press applauded Britain's "realistic" policy in Europe, especially the Anglo-Italian agreement, non-interference in the Spanish question, and the Munich agreement. In an article entitled "The Guiding Principle of British Diplomacy," *Gaiko Jiho* extolled the "realistic" policy of Chamberlain, emphasizing that it was necessary for Great Britain to be at peace with Japan, because her position in Africa was threatened by Italy, which had subjugated Ethiopia, and her position in Europe by Germany, which had occupied Austria and the Rhine region. Pointing to Great Britain's need "to secure her interests in China," the magazine intimated clearly that Great Britain could

[85] Craigie to Halifax, October 12, 1938, DBFP, vol. VIII, doc. 140.
[86] *Ibid.*
[87] Craigie to Halifax, October 12, 1938, DBFP, vol. VIII, doc. 141.

gain what she wanted "by settling Anglo-Japanese relations." "Only in this way," it wrote, "can Great Britain secure her interests."[88]

As the Japanese drove into South China, where British imperialism had especially important interests, Chiang Kai-shek told the British chargé d'affaires, Mr. Greenway, on October 13 that "many people regarded the invasion of the south as a direct challenge to Great Britain" and requested from the British government "an authoritative statement for his private information" with regard to British policy in China.[89]

British attempts to come to an agreement with Japan were hindered also by the United States of America. As stated above, the United States had disrupted an Anglo-French attempt in August 1938 to negotiate an end to the Sino-Japanese war. The United States was opposed to Anglo-Japanese cooperation in occupied China and, as talks between Craigie and Konoe ensued after Ugaki's resignation, tried to prevent a rapprochement between Great Britain and Japan.

On October 10 Grew handed to the Japanese government a note protesting Japanese discrimination against American trade in China. The note, dated October 6, asserted that Japan, contrary to her numerous promises, had been violating the Open Door and was not respecting the interests of the foreign powers in occupied China or Manchuria; it cited numerous examples of Japanese restraints, such as the introduction of a new customs tariff and the closing of the Yangtze River to foreign shipping.

The note contained a thinly veiled threat of retaliation, the first such warning by the United States. Point-

[88] *Gaiko Jiho,* October 15, 1938.
[89] Greenway to Kerr, November 13, 1938, DBFP, vol. VIII, doc. 151.

ing out that while "the Government of the United States has not sought either in its own territory or in the territory of third countries to establish or influence the establishment of embargoes, import prohibitions, exchange controls, preferential restrictions, monopolies or special companies, designed to eliminate or having the effect of eliminating Japanese trade and enterprise," a great and growing disparity had developed "between the treatment accorded American nationals and their trade and enterprise by Japanese authorities in China and Japan and the treatment accorded Japanese nationals and their trade and enterprise by the Government of the United States in areas within its jurisdiction,"[90] it demanded that measures of discrimination against American trade and enterprise be discontinued.

The American démarche could not be ignored by the makers of British foreign policy who had become increasingly United States-oriented. Their complicity in German aggression by virtue of their appeasement policy had created for themselves increasing difficulties in Europe, with the result that Great Britain found it difficult to retain her position in the Far East. Turning her back on the collective security proposals advanced indefatigably by the Soviet Union, Great Britain sought to extricate herself from her predicament by drawing closer to the United States. The American démarche made it clear that an Anglo-Japanese rapprochement would arouse the displeasure of the United States. On the other hand, Great Britain could not afford a confrontation with Japan for the time being. "We are not in a position effectively to defend our interests in the Far East at the moment," wrote Halifax to Kerr, "and the situation is bound to continue until the

90 FRUS, *Japan 1931–1941*, vol. I, pp. 789–790.

position in Europe lightens or we are sufficiently re-armed to enable us to maintain a force of ships in Far Eastern waters sufficient to engage the Japanese navy."[91] Not until 1942 would there be such a fleet according to Admiralty plans; meanwhile one principal fleet would be kept at home and another in the Mediterranean.[92]

In view of the Chinese and American actions, Halifax indicated to Craigie on October 13 that Great Britain should not show a readiness to be more accommodating than the United States. "We ought to be prepared to go as far as they in the matter of inducements to negotiate a settlement of our respective demands," he cabled. He instructed Craigie to acquaint the American ambassador with the British proposals "for improving the atmosphere." They included:

1. to receive and investigate any complaints or suggestions by the Japanese, but to see to it that they "are not short of doing anything legally improper or detrimental to China's interests";
2. to renew the offer of good offices "as and when both sides desire them";
3. to offer help to Japan and China alike upon the end of hostilities in the economic reconstruction of China;
4. to continue negotiations for a general comprehensive settlement with Japan.[93]

A former Dutch envoy to Peking, who had visited Japan on business, had been given to understand by Japanese spokesmen that Japan would be willing to re-

[91] Halifax to Kerr, October 17, 1938, DBFP, vol. VIII, doc. 158.
[92] Letter from the Admiralty to the Foreign Office, dated February 29, 1939, DBFP, vol. VIII, Appendix.
[93] Halifax to Craigie, November 13, 1938, DBFP, vol. VIII, doc. 149. Grew told Craigie that the American government was thinking along the same lines. (*Ibid.*, doc. 207.)

ceive British loans for the rehabilitation of China—one
leading capitalist mentioned the sum of 200 million
pounds. The Japanese knew, of course, that the "confidential" information would be conveyed to the British
Foreign Office in view of the diplomatic ties of Great
Britain and Holland and the close interweaving of the
interests of the Dutch and English bourgeoisie. It was
their hope to lessen London's resistance to Japanese expansion in China by giving British capital a share in the
exploitation of subjugated China.

On October 19 Halifax inquired of Craigie by telegram "as to the sort of help, if any, which Japan expects
to receive from us and Americans after hostilities cease
and on what terms." Feeling that the proffer of economic aid might give Great Britain "one of the rare
cards in our hands," Halifax advised Craigie to make it
clear to the Japanese that "British investors in assessing
risks attaching to such a loan will . . . obviously take
into account Japanese behavior towards us between now
and cessation of hostilities."[94]

Another reply to the Japanese soundings may be
found in Chamberlain's speech in the House of Commons on November 1. Rebutting the contention of the
opposition leader Clement Attlee that a successful
Japanese offensive would mean the closure of the potentially greatest market in the world to other countries,
Chamberlain declared that "China cannot develop into
a real market without a large injection of capital" and
that it was "absolutely clear that Japan cannot furnish
such capital." Asserting that it would be "tantamount
to ignoring the facts" to assert that Japan would establish
a monopoly over the Chinese trade, Chamberlain argued
that "when the war is over and reconstruction of China

[94] Halifax to Craigie, October 19, 1938, DBFP, vol. VIII, doc. 162.

begins, the latter will not be able to effect reconstruction without a certain assistance from Great Britain."[95]

Needless to say, the cynicism of this utterly "business-like" statement by the premier, who promised Japan assistance in the exploitation and development of the seized parts of China, evoked criticism from the Kuomintang leaders, who were normally subservient to the American and British bourgeoisie, and the British government amended Chamberlain's exceedingly frank statement. On November 10, Halifax conveyed to Greenway the remarks made by the Parliamentary under-secretary in the course of a debate in the House of Commons on November 9, namely that in contemplating economic assistance Great Britain was not "looking at the end of the war to lend money to Japan in order to enable the latter to complete her domination of China."[96] The statement was not made, however, until it had become clear that the loan offer had not met with Japanese approval and had not helped advance the Anglo-Japanese negotiations which had been resumed between Craigie and Konoe on November 1.[97]

It is interesting to note that the British government concealed from Parliament and the public the attempt to resume negotiations with Japan after Ugaki's resignation.[98] The published diplomatic correspondence might lead one to believe that at the end of October 1938 the British were considering such action against Japan as the denouncement of the Anglo-Japanese trade treaty,

[95] Great Britain, Parliament, *Parliamentary Debates, House of Commons*, Fifth Series, vol. 340, col. 69, 82.
[96] Halifax to Greenway, November 10, 1938, DBFP, vol. VIII, doc. 225.
[97] See also *Ibid.*, doc. 193.
[98] Halifax to Craigie, November 5, 1938, DBFP, vol. VIII, doc. 209. On November 2 the parliamentary under-secretary for foreign affairs stated that the discussion of the question which has taken place that year had not been resumed with the new minister.

because the Japanese had seriously encroached on the positions of British imperialism, particularly with their expansion into South China, and because world public opinion was calling for the adoption of certain measures. But proposals for reprisals were received very unfavorably by the British ambassador in Tokyo. Arguing that there would be no advantage in the policy of reprisals, Craigie opposed the denunciation of the trade treaty on the ground that this could be tantamount to abandoning the status of the most favored nation. In his opinion, Great Britain need not run this risk, the more so as denunciation could take effect only after one year, while practical results could not be expected before the beginning of 1940.

Craigie did not consider it wise to condemn Japanese aggression for the sake of observing the League of Nations resolution. Somehow he believed it would mean the disruption of friendly relations with both belligerents, and proposed that Great Britain "put up with temporary losses which British interests have suffered in China" in order that she might play her "proper part during these negotiations and afterwards."[99] His arguments fell on willing ears because cooperation with Japan was a traditional policy of Great Britain. By not alienating either Japan or China she hoped to be in a position of mediating peace between them when both had reached the stage of exhaustion, and British interests could be secured during the peace talks.[100]

[99] Craigie to Halifax, October 23, 1938, DBFP, vol. VIII, doc. 175.
[100] In the course of subsequent correspondence discussion was begun in response to Halifax's proposal concerning the use of "petty administrative vexations" toward Japan (though Craigie reacted even to this proposal with many reservations) and also concerning economic pressure in order to restrict the scope of the treaty of commerce. In Craigie's opinion the following measures would have harmed Japan more than Great Britain: increasing the export duty on certain materials obtained by Japan from

The Japanese refusal to meet the British demands and indications that the Kuomintang regime might make peace with Japan[101] compelled Great Britain once again to focus on the question of ending hostilities in China, particularly as the Japanese occupation of South China was inimical to British interests. The matter was given impetus by the query of the German Ambassador Ott in the course of a private conversation with the British Military Attaché Piggott, with whom he was on friendly terms, what he thought of the idea of Germany using all her influence on Japan to propose reasonable peace terms as soon as Hankow had fallen and Great Britain exerting all her influence on Chiang Kai-shek to accept them.

Seizing upon the idea, which Piggott did not regard as entirely a private one of the ambassador,[102] Craigie advised London that in his view an Anglo-German proposal of good offices (not of mediation, as proposed by Ott), might have the greatest chance of success. Recalling that the United States had disrupted the British attempt at mediation some two months before, Craigie proposed to act without the United States and to inform Germany through the military attaché that Great Britain was favorably inclined toward Ott's suggestion.

Meanwhile a Japanese financier, Viscount Kano Hisao of the Yokohama Specie Bank, approached Wardlaw-Milne, a member of the British Parliament, and tried to convince him that now was a favorable

---

the crown colonies (for example, iron ore from Malaya), purchasing within the British empire various commodities presently received from Japan, and a further reduction in the colonial quotas for Japanese textiles. (Craigie to Halifax, November 4, 1938, DBFP, vol. VIII, doc. 208.)

[101] Chiang Kai-shek's request for mediation and the secret talks between Ugaki and K'ung Hsiang-hsi are evidence of the Kuomintang's readiness to make peace with Japan.

[102] Craigie to Halifax, October 25, 1938, DBFP, vol. VIII, doc. 176.

moment for the British government to offer its services in ending the hostilities in China, that the Japanese military as well as civilians would welcome "any approach for mediation." Kano alleged that Japan would agree to peace on the following basis:

(a) Complete Japanese withdrawal from China.
(b) No concessions, but complete equality of opportunities with other powers.
(c) A Sino-Japanese agreement for the cessation of official Chinese participation in anti-Japanese activities, particularly the trade boycott.

The British government, Kano said, should join the agreement, without, however, taking upon itself the responsibility for its observance. He contended that if Craigie approached Konoe with the offer to mediate on the basis of the above terms, the result would be "astonishing."[103]

Halifax, whom Wardlaw-Milne informed of Kano's views on October 25, was skeptical, but believing that the Kano proposal might serve as a pretext for reopening negotiations, he authorized Craigie to seek an informal interview with the prime minister and talk to him on the lines suggested by Kano but without mentioning the latter and renew previous assurances of the British government's readiness "to exert their good offices in a mediatory capacity either as a channel of communication between the two parties or in any other way which may seem useful or desirable."[104] At the same time Halifax agreed with Craigie's suggestion to react favorably to Ott's feeler concerning collaboration with Germany in ending the war, writing that "it is not unlikely that

---

[103] Halifax to Craigie, October 26, 1938, DBFP, vol. VIII, doc. 178.
[104] *Ibid.*

it has been prompted by the German Government or the Japanese Government or both."[105]

On October 29, Arita Hachiro was appointed foreign minister, but Craigie chose to deal with Premier Konoe, convinced that the latter was opposed to the war in China.[106] When he saw Konoe on November 1, he took it upon himself to modify the suggestions put forward by Kano, for he did not think that points "a" and "b" would be acceptable to the Japanese as phrased.[107] The former was changed to read "Complete but gradual withdrawal from China," the latter "Complete equality of opportunity between all powers."

Konoe welcomed the British offer of good offices but declined to give an immediate reply, saying that this was an "important" and "delicate" matter and must await the general policy statement that was being drafted in time for the Emperor's birthday on November 3. Konoe and Craigie agreed that the British offer should be regarded as strictly confidential,[108] but this did not prevent Craigie from informing the French and American ambassadors about the talks.[109]

The Japanese policy statement on November 3rd declared that the Kuomintang government had ceased to exist except as a local regime and that Japan would not lay down arms until it had been crushed. It contended that Japan sought the establishment of a New Order which would ensure permanent stability in East Asia.[110] The statement and Konoe's speech indicated clearly that the government had shifted from Ugaki's policy to a

[105] *Ibid.*

[106] Craigie to Halifax, October 20, 1938, DBFP, vol. VIII, doc. 167.

[107] On November 7 the Foreign Office approved the position taken by Craigie.

[108] Craigie to Halifax, November 2, 1938, DBFP, vol. VIII, doc. 193.

[109] *Ibid.*

[110] DBFP, vol. VIII, doc. 195, footnote 3.

new course, though this did not exclude, as will be seen, further fluctuations in Japanese policy and a fierce struggle over the direction of Japanese expansion. Stating frankly that Japan had decided to effect substantial changes in the Far East and to weave a new fabric of peace, Konoe declared that Japan would cooperate with the Western powers, notably Great Britain and the United States, only if they "understand the real intentions of Japan and devise a policy in accordance with the new situation."[111]

In spite of the uncompromising tenor of these statements, the British did not lose hope of receiving a favorable reply to their proposal for mediation and thought it possible to improve Anglo-Japanese relations. Ugaki's resignation had precipitated a struggle between the advocates of further expansion southward, inimical to British and American interests, and a close rapprochement with Germany and Italy on the one hand, and the proponents of the Ugaki line of reaching a mutual understanding with Great Britain and the United States on the other. The former worked for the appointment of Matsuoka Yosuke as foreign minister. Matsuoka had been president of the South Manchurian Railway Company and had close connections not only with business companies operating in Manchuria but also with military circles, particularly officers of the Kwangtung Army, who supported his candidacy. Yet Matsuoka was passed over in favor of Araki, who was backed by the real masters of the country, the big monopolies.[112]

Arita's appointment left Craigie optimistic, though he realized that Arita was a considerably weaker personality than Ugaki and that "the real power remains

[111] FRUS, *Japan 1931–1941,* vol. I, p. 480.
[112] Craigie to Halifax, November 3, 1938, DBFP, vol. VIII, doc. 200.

in the Five Ministers' Conference and the position of
the key members of that body is in no way affected by
these latest additions to the Cabinet."[113] The well-known
magazine *Chuo Koron* characterized Arita as friendly
to Great Britain and as a believer in methods of con-
ciliation.[114] When he had served as vice-minister for
foreign affairs some years earlier, he had found himself
in direct opposition to Shiratori Toshio, the director of
the Information Bureau, over the issue of withdrawal
from the League of Nations. He had been foreign minister at the time of the conclusion of the Anti-
Comintern Pact, but, as Craigie reported, the negotiations had been conducted by Oshima, and Arita had
actually had little say about the pact. Craigie concluded
consequently, "there seems to be good reason to believe
that Mr. Arita is not personally antagonistic to Great
Britain and may be counted upon to give sympathetic
consideration to our point of view."[115]

Craigie recommended that Great Britain "play for
time in the expectation that both sides [Japan and China]
will eventually become sufficiently exhausted" to permit
British help in bringing about "a reasonable settlement
of this tragic conflict."[116] In order to ensure British
influence in the peace negotiations or "in the post-
settlement period of reconstruction," Craigie considered
it necessary to establish "a yet more intimate relationship between Japan and the totalitarian powers."[117] He
anticipated that the Japanese peace terms would be
"more moderate than the objective circumstances might
be held to warrant," believing that the "educated opin-

[113] *Ibid.*
[114] *Ibid.*
[115] Craigie to Halifax, November 4, 1938, DBFP, vol. VIII, doc. 207.
[116] *Ibid.*
[117] *Ibid.*

ion" in Japan understood the limitations of Japan's economic position.[118] He was convinced that given the establishment of a well-disposed central government in China, the Japanese forces would gradually withdraw from the greater part of the areas they had occupied.[119] Thus, Craigie argued, Great Britain should protest against infringements on British rights on the part of the Japanese while withholding credits from the Chinese and hope that "continued resistance by General Chiang Kai-shek, despite the fall of Hankow and Canton, might induce a more reasonable frame of mind among the Japanese to agree to a compromise solution of the China problem."

The astonishing short-sightedness of many British diplomats who failed to understand the growing contradictions between the imperialist powers and the aggravation of the struggle for the redivision of the world and believed erroneously that all these contradictions could be solved by the establishment of a bloc of powers against the U.S.S.R. was shared by the British government. British diplomats provided the government with information that agreed with the latter's ideas about the state of international relations and the character of the policy of foreign states. It was not surprising, therefore, that the point of view of Craigie, who was openly formulating British policy in the Far East, was fully shared by the British government. His program of action was followed with only minor exceptions up to the conclusion of the Arita-Craigie agreement in July 1939, which constituted a further step towards collusion with Japanese imperialism and an extension to the Far East of the Munich appeasement.

[118] *Ibid.*
[119] *Ibid.*

Craigie's recommendation that "a fair and reasonable settlement of this most deplorable conflict"[120] be achieved jointly by Great Britain, France, Germany and Italy was well received in the Foreign Office, which was aware that there had been little or nothing in the way of Anglo-German cooperation anywhere since Munich and felt that the Far East might offer "a not too unpromising field" for Anglo-German cooperation.[121] While believing that "the early restoration of peace in the Far East may . . . be regarded as a matter in which Great Britain and Germany have a common interest,"[122] officials in London realized that an Anglo-German rapprochement in the Far East would not be welcomed by the United States. They hoped, however, that "the United States Government might be brought to regard Anglo-German cooperation as calculated to help in some measure the general world appeasement."[123]

American approval of the Munich agreement, which the British expected to form the basis for broad Anglo-German cooperation, stimulated British plans for the solution of many problems both in Europe and in the Far East. The British intended to make Anglo-German cooperation a cardinal point in their world strategy and wished to build an anti-Soviet front under the guise of a peaceful settlement. In this they hoped for American support,[124] despite the threat to American interests inherent in an Anglo-German rapprochement. And indeed, American diplomats, notably Ambassador Grew, favored a policy of appeasing Japan.[125] Thus the British

[120] *Ibid.*
[121] Howe to Craigie, November 25, 1938, DBFP, vol. VIII, doc. 288.
[122] *Ibid.*
[123] *Ibid.*
[124] *Ibid.*
[125] In his talk with Craigie on November 25, Grew opposed a joint démarche against Japan. Warning that "joint Anglo-Franco-American

government initially paid little heed to the new course of Japanese foreign policy, and Craigie merely sent a note of protest against interference with the freedom of navigation on the Yangtze River.[126] There was little that Great Britain and the United States did beyond filing protests against Japanese violation of the Open Door in China.[127] Great Britain was to grant China some financial aid for stabilizing her currency in the hope of prolonging Chinese resistance, while the United States was to impose only a "moral embargo" on the sale of aircraft material to Japan— weak measures to combat Japan's New Order in Asia.[128]

Western appeasement emboldened the Japanese imperialists. The prominent newspaper *Tokyo Nichi-Nichi* wrote that Arita was ready to resume negotiations with Craigie provided Great Britain recognized the new situation in Eastern Asia.[129] On November 7 Vice-Minister for Foreign Affairs Sawada Renzo handed Craigie a note in reply to his letter of October 31, in which he reiterated the explanations given by Ugaki and Konoe concerning the temporary obstruction of the interests of third countries in occupied areas, namely that the war in China required the mobilization of all natural

---

measures of the type contemplated would involve a serious risk of war," he declared: "In any case it should not be envisaged unless the three countries were prepared to face war in the last resort." In reporting Grew's words to London, Craigie could not conceal his pleasure. "The fact that he considers that even tripartite counteraction may lead to war," Craigie commented, "affords striking confirmation of my own view that action by Great Britain alone would involve us in most serious risks." (Craigie to Foreign Office, November 25, 1938, DBFP, vol. VIII, doc. 285.)

[126] Similar notes were sent by the French and American governments. (DBFP, vol. VIII, docs. 210–214.)

[127] Halifax to Craigie, November 10, 1938, DBFP, vol. VIII, doc. 288.

[128] Lindsay to Halifax, October 10, 1938, DBFP, vol. VIII, doc. 229.

[129] *Trans-Pacific,* November 3, 1938.

resources and that under the circumstances "one cannot expect much from Japan." Although agreeing to consider isolated cases, the Japanese government did not promise to pay greater attention to British interests, as Ugaki had always done. Stressing that in the immediate vicinity of the front line and in the occupied areas "in the existing situation . . . the activities of third countries will at times be unavoidably restricted,"[130] the note left no doubt that Japan was going to treat South China as her own possession. It requested the British government to devise "immediate and appropriate measures" in the areas of future hostilities—Kiangsi, Hupeh, Hunan and Kwangsi—specifically to discontinue flights of civil aeroplanes; it warned that journeys by British nationals in those areas would be undertaken at their personal risk. It asked that British nationals withdraw from these areas to other places for their own safety and demanded that British rights and interests in these regions be reported to the Japanese authorities. The note warned that the Japanese authorities would not assume responsibility for the protection of Chinese property transferred to third powers.[131]

In his talk with Craigie on November 17 Arita was even more outspoken in indicating that a change in Japanese policy had taken place. When Craigie pointed to the specific assurances given by Arita's predecessors in regard to the British rights and interests and the principle of equal opportunity and complained that they had not been honored, Arita replied that "it was necessary to recognize that a complete change had come over the situation in China and that assurances given earlier

[130] Craigie to Halifax, November 11, 1938, enclosure I, DBFP, vol. VIII, doc. 235.
[131] Craigie to Halifax, November 9, 1938, DBFP, vol. VIII, doc. 222.

might not be wholly applicable to new situations which had developed."[132]

In support of Japan's policy of creating the Greater East Asia Co-Prosperity Sphere, Arita stated that the "economic appeasement" of which the world stood in such need should find expression not only in the economic groups already in existence, such as the British empire, the United States (which he linked with Latin America) and Russia, but also in the grouping of smaller countries in economic blocs. "For East Asia," Arita said, "a natural grouping was Japan, China and Manchukuo." He stressed that he also felt it unfair that the principle of "the Open Door and equality of opportunity" be applied to China only. He left the impression, as Craigie reported, that the Japanese plans had crystallized and that "Japan was evidently trying to establish economic domination in China."[133]

On November 18 the Japanese government rejected the American protest of October 6. In its reply the Japanese government did not confine itself to denying that there had been any discrimination against American trade and enterprise on the part of the Japanese authorities in China, but went so far as to challenge the demand of the United States for the observance of "the Open Door principle" in China.[134] In a talk with Counselor Dumont the following day, Arita stated plainly that the principle of the Open Door as understood in the United States and other countries was incompatible with the New Order Japan was going to create in East Asia.[135]

The British offer of mediation received short shrift.

[132] Craigie to Halifax, November 17, 1939, DBFP, vol. VIII, doc. 249.
[133] Craigie to Halifax, December 2, 1938, DBFP, vol. VIII, doc. 308.
[134] FRUS, 1938, p. 800.
[135] Ibid., p. 804.

Even before an official reply was made, the Japanese ambassador designate to Rome, Shiratori, who was known for his connections with the army and had great influence in the Foreign Office,[136] mentioned to the financial adviser of the British embassy that the three points proposed by Craigie to Konoe as a basis for peace negotiation were unacceptable, particularly points "b" and "c," and showed a complete lack of understanding of the Japanese attitude. He declared bluntly that "Japan was now in a position to impose what terms she wished on China and she would brook no interference." While asserting that third power interests would be respected, Shiratori said that "Great Britain must resign herself to lose the dominant position she had hitherto held in China."[137]

On November 24 Arita officially declined Craigie's proposal of November 1, telling him that "the moment was not considered opportune for any mediation between Japanese Government and Chiang Kai-shek." Yet Craigie did not lose hope. He still considered that the door had not been closed to a British initiative,[138] a view shared by the British Foreign Office.

The Domei News Agency reported from London that the prime minister and foreign secretary were hopeful of reaching an understanding with Japan and wrote of the "indefatigable work" of Ambassador Shigemitsu who was said to have had numerous interviews with British officials and British leaders, among them Sir H. Wilson and Sir F. Leith-Roth.[139]

The United States was less optimistic. Acting Secre-

---

[136] After Ugaki's resignation, Shiratori was considered as a possible candidate for the post of foreign minister. (DBFP, vol. VIII, doc. 200.)
[137] Craigie to Halifax, November 17, 1938, DBFP, vol. VIII, doc. 251.
[138] Craigie to Halifax, November 25, 1938, DBFP, vol. VIII, doc. 284.
[139] Craigie to Halifax, November 27, 1938, DBFP, vol. VIII, doc. 262.

tary of State Sumner Welles told the British Ambassador Lindsay on November 28 that the State Department interpreted the Japanese reply as indicating that "the Japanese had every intention of excluding the United States, Great Britain, and France from those possibilities of commerce in China which should be secured by the observance of the Open Door principle." Welles remarked to the British ambassador that "the time seemed to be drawing near when the American and British Governments might have to devise together economic measures to protect the legitimate interests in China."[140] In another talk with Lindsay several days later on December 1, Welles again stressed the need for concerted economic action in the defense of British and American interests.[141]

Ambassador Grew held a different view. Although he discussed with Craigie the possibility of granting to China an Anglo-Franco-American stabilization loan, the denunciation by Great Britain, France, and the United States of commercial treaties with China, and the opening of the Indo-China border,[142] he saw no way of recommending joint action, because, in his words, "the public opinion of the United States concentrated its attention on the contradictions with Germany" and did not pay attention to Japan. Grew feared that even joint Anglo-Franco-American action could mean "a risk of war."[143]

Grew did not deem it possible to alter Japanese policy by means of economic pressure or sanctions, a view which he reiterated in a letter, dated December 7. "Representations are not likely to lead to any substantial

---

[140] Lindsay to Halifax, December 1, 1938, DBFP, vol. VIII, doc. 298.
[141] *Ibid.*
[142] Craigie to Halifax, November 25, 1938, DBFP, vol. VIII, doc. 28.
[143] Craigie to Halifax, December 4, 1938, DBFP, vol. VIII, doc. 311.

moderation of the Japanese policy in China, and he cannot conscientiously recommend his Government's recourse to economic sanctions," Craigie reported.[144] By arguing that opposition to the Japanese entailed the risk of war without chance of altering Japanese policy, Grew joined Craigie in justifying British and American appeasement, and hence encouragement, of Japanese aggression.

Craigie used Grew's views and rumors about the German-Japanese negotiations for the strengthening of the Anti-Comintern Pact by a military alliance as pretexts for considering cooperation with Japan. The scheme of cooperation, proposed by Craigie, provided the basis for the notorious Arita-Craigie agreement that was to be concluded the following year. On one hand, Craigie believed that cooperation with Japan would be prejudicial to British interests and that it would be best, therefore, to leave matters where they stood. On the other hand, he felt that cooperation with Japan would not be reprehensible if judged in terms of the "big policy" and "the task of delaying the conclusion of a tripartite alliance." In Craigie's view, "to win back ultimate Chinese independence" would be possible only "through cooperation both with China and Japan by establishing that assured market and that source of raw material which represents Japan's primary needs in the economic field."[145] Recognizing that such an approach to the question "would mean recognition of the actual fact of Japan's military and economic predominance in China today," the British ambassador proposed none other than the amicable division of China, covered up with talk about Chinese "independence" and the wish

[144] Craigie to Halifax, December 12, 1938, DBFP, vol. VIII, doc. 332.
[145] Craigie to Halifax, December 2, 1938, DBFP, vol. VIII, doc. 308.

to prevent Japan from entering into a tripartite military alliance.[146]

It soon became clear, however, that the division of China would not satisfy Japan. On December 4 Arita spoke to Craigie about the possibility of creating a new central government for China and inquired whether he thought the British government would recognize it.[147] This showed that the Japanese had designs on all of China.

In a statement on December 22, Konoe propounded Japan's plans for a New Order in East Asia, which contained the following conditions for peace: (1) Chinese recognition of Manchukuo; (2) Chinese accession to the Anti-Comintern Pact; (3) the retention of Japanese troops in certain places in China and the conversion of Inner Mongolia into a special Anti-Comintern area as a guarantee of China's adherence to the Anti-Comintern Pact; (4) the granting to Japanese nationals of the right to exploit the natural resources of China; (5) Japanese readiness to abolish extraterritoriality and to liquidate foreign concessions for the sake of the complete "independence" of China.[148]

At last even Craigie became alarmed. "One cannot overestimate the seriousness of recent statements for our relations with the Japanese Government," he wrote to Halifax and recommended that economic sanctions be applied against Japan to defend the British position in

[146] Ibid.

[147] Craigie to Halifax, December 4, 1938, DBFP, vol. VIII, doc. 308. The Japanese sought to make use of the Chinese militarist Wu Péi–fu, who had left the political arena after the victory of Kuomintang, and negotiated with him for several months. But Wu insisted on the withdrawal of Japanese troops and advisers from China and the creation of a Chinese army of which he would be the commander-in-chief. Wu's demands were unacceptable to the Japanese, who meanwhile had begun negotiating with Wang Ching-wei, who was more cooperative.

[148] Kiyosawa Kiyoshi, Nihon gaiko-shi (Tokyo, 1943), p. 563.

China. "The present moment," he wrote, "is the most favorable for such action." With the Japanese army deeply committed in vast areas of China, the Japanese economy was beginning to show signs of strain.[149] An embargo on Japanese exports, Craigie believed, would therefore "rapidly prove disastrous to Japan's economy."[150] "The simplest and most effective first step," Craigie thought, "would appear to be for Great Britain, the United States, and France to refuse the purchase of any further gold from Japan," assuming arrangements could be made to prevent Japanese gold from reaching those countries through third parties.[151]

Yet the British government did not implement even these modest sanctions, lest chances for an understanding with Japan be destroyed. Although Japanese expansion could have been blocked by English collaboration with the U.S.S.R., the British did not want an Anglo-Soviet rapprochement. Instead, they tried to preserve their position in China by exploiting Soviet-Japanese contradictions, Craigie having reported that "Japan's failure to reach the usual *modus vivendi* with the U.S.S.R.[152] can at any moment develop into a first-class crisis."[153]

Meanwhile Tokyo, conscious of Japan's vulnerability to resolute economic sanctions and desirous of the continuance of British and American appeasement, tried to appear reasonable by making minor concessions to Great Britain and the United States. The statements and actions of Ugaki, Konoe and Arita, described

[149] Craigie to Haifax, January 1, 1939, DBFP, vol. VIII, doc. 384.
[150] For details see Craigie to Halifax, January 1, 1939, DBFP, vol. VIII, doc. 382.
[151] *Ibid.*
[152] This refers to the Soviet Union's unwillingness, under the circumstances, to conclude a new fisheries convention.
[153] DBFP, vol. VIII, doc. 304.

above, including their attempt to shift the blame for Japanese expansion on the alleged disobedience of the military, leave no doubt that the various foreign ministers followed a single, consciously adopted policy. Internal contradictions existed with different groups contending for control, but there was little disagreement among them about Japan's ultimate objectives in China.

A report made by Morishima Goro, adviser of the Japanese embassy in Shanghai, in the spring of 1939 at a meeting of the Diplomatic Association of Japan in Tokyo is illuminating. Morishima stated that Japanese policy in China was determined to a large extent by the positions of the U.S.S.R., Great Britain, the United States and France; the positions of Germany and Italy were of secondary importance. Since the U.S.S.R. could be expected to cooperate with Chungking to the end, Morishima noted, it would be "extremely difficult" to draw her to Japan's side. As for France, she followed in British and American footsteps. Hence it was on the relations with Great Britain and the United States that Japanese policy makers must focus, Morishima pointed out. Since Hirota, Ugaki and Konoe had officially stated that they would respect the Open Door and the "equal-opportunity" principles and Arita had reiterated that Japan "respects the acquired rights and interests of Great Britain and the U.S.A.," Morishima believed that if Japan wanted to conduct negotiations with London and Washington on the basis of her "new target," she must simultaneously "resolve outstanding problems in Shanghai." While Japan's ambitions in the north might arouse little British and American opposition, Morishima calculated, her policies in Central China must be moderated if differences with Great Britain and the United States were to be solved. Morishima expressed the view that the most important British demand, that of granting freedom of navigation on the Yangtze, could be met only after Japan's dominant position on the river had been secured by an increase in the number of Japanese ships, the installation of facilities necessary for Japanese trade, and the removal from circulation of Kuomintang currency in Central and South China. Even so, Morishima did not consider it possible to open navigation along the entire Yangtze River.

While the interests of the Western powers were identical, Morishima felt that Japan could and should prevent action on their part. This was facilitated, he thought, by the fact that "there were no signs of a joint struggle of these countries against Japan," because the United States and France believed that "if the question with Great Britain were solved, they would have the same possibilities." Morishima, therefore, regarded the negotiations between Arita and Craigie as a correct step, which could give Japan an opportunity "to make use of the conditions that obtained to solve controversial questions and at the same time to accumulate and strengthen the real forces of Japan."

Morishima spoke out in favor of conducting peace negotiations with Chiang Kai-shek. The need to end the war in China had been discussed increasingly in Japan and Great Britain. On March 28 Craigie wrote of a "secret conference" that had been held in Tokyo at the beginning of the year to consider possible means of securing an early peace. He reported that Generals Kito, Doihara and Hata had worked on this question and that the idea of concluding peace was supported by "the leading members of both the moderate and the more advanced groups." The Japanese plan, according to Craigie, envisaged the withdrawal of Japanese troops in Central and South China, north of the Yellow River or Lunghai Railway, as a conciliatory gesture. Great Britain, France and the Unied States would then be invited to mediate on the following basis: China would make economic concessions to Japan in North China and would recognize Manchukuo; Japanese troops would be withdrawn from China, except for garrisons in the North regarding which there could be a reversion to the status quo.[154]

At a small dinner party given by Marquis Tokugawa, General Koiso Kuniaki, recently appointed minister for colonies, in the presence of Yada, former minister to Switzerland and the British Military Attaché General Piggott, proposed that a meeting be arranged between Chiang Kai-shek and the Japanese premier or foreign minister on neutral territory. Although Koiso claimed to be expressing his personal opinion, Craigie thought it likely that "Arita knew of the intended party" and that the proposal indicated "the possibility of a change in Japan's policy of ostracizing Chiang Kai-shek."[155]

Japanese peace feelers were made also directly to Chungking. The Chinese Ambassador Kuo T'ai-ch'i mentioned to Halifax on April 18 without going into any details that some peace proposals had been made by the Japanese side to T. V. Soong during his visit to Hong Kong.[156]

On July 15 Arita handed Craigie a draft agreement, whereby the British government was to recognize the

---

[154] The representatives of the more extreme group wanted to hold the plan in abeyance for four months to see whether "real progress" could be achieved during that time by military means; if no such progress was made by the following August, they would go along with the plan. (Craigie to Halifax, March 28, 1939, DBFP, vol. VIII, doc. 585.)

[155] Craigie to Halifax, June 14, 1939, DBFP, vol. IX, doc. 201.

[156] Halifax to Kerr, April 18, 1939, DBFP, vol. IX, doc. 11.

actual situation in China and refrain from any acts or measures which might interfere with the Japanese military forces in implementing their special tasks.[157] Although British business circles which had interests in China resolutely objected to the adoption of the Japanese proposals, realizing that this might result in further acts of discrimination against the British firms and their complete ouster from China in the future, the Foreign Office and the War Office deemed it necessary to accept Arita's proposal, lest the Japanese without the limitations of an agreement intensify their offensive against the British, particularly if the failure of Anglo-Soviet negotiations left the latter defenseless in the Far East.[158]

In accordance with the instructions of Halifax, who could not see any way out but to accept Arita's proposals,[159] Craigie on July 24 signed the Arita-Craigie agreement, whereby Great Britain recognized the Japanese seizures in China. The agreement declared that "the Japanese forces in China have special requirements for the purpose of safeguarding their own security and maintaining public order in the regions under their control, and they have taken the necessary steps in order to suppress or remove any such acts or causes as will obstruct them or benefit their enemy."[160] Great Britain officially recognized the legitimacy of Japanese aggression in China and obligated herself not to aid China in her struggle against Japan, for the British government stated that it had "no intention of countenancing any act or measures prejudicial of the above-mentioned objects by Japanese forces" and promised to make it plain

[157] Craigie to Halifax, July 15, 1939, DBFP, vol. IX, doc. 325.
[158] Craigie to Halifax, July 17, 1939, DBFP, vol. IX, doc. 332.
[159] Halifax to Craigie, July 22, 1939, DBFP, vol. IX, doc. 359.
[160] Craigie to Halifax, July 23, 1939, DBFP, vol. IX, doc. 365.

to British officials and nationals in China that they should refrain from such action.[161]

In an interview with foreign correspondents that day Craigie confirmed that Great Britain recognized by the agreement Japanese seizure of vast territory in China. He stated plainly that the sphere of the agreement extended to "all areas seized by the Japanese army in North, Central and South China.[162]

The Arita-Craigie agreement, which constituted a Far Eastern version of the Munich concessions, was a logical consequence of the entire previous policy of British imperialism in the Far East. The events recited above show that the Arita-Craigie agreement had not been forced on the British government by the aggravated situation in Europe in the summer of 1939 as asserted by bourgeois historians,[163] but was a manifestation of the time-honored strategy of directing German and Japanese aggression against Russia. It must be kept in mind that the secret Anglo-Japanese negotiation dated back to June 1938, when Chamberlain and Halifax had tried most energetically to appease Germany and had striven to extend the principles of European policy to the Far East in an attempt to come to terms with Japan.

The Arita-Craigie agreement was anti-Soviet in character. Signed at a time when the Kwantung Army had plunged across the border of the Mongolian People's Republic and collided with Soviet forces, it represented an attempt by the British to encourage the Japanese drive against the U.S.S.R. and thereby prevent further Japanese expansion southward.

---

[161] *Ibid.*

[162] Soviet Archives, 146, file 5, p. 136.

[163] See, for example, the preface by Professor E. L. Woodward, editor of the *Documents on British Foreign Policy,* in volume VIII.

The agreement was a great success for Japanese diplomacy, which regarded it as a base for further inroads on Britain's position in China. The British were mistaken in their calculation that Japan's policy could be moderated by appeasement. Already in August 1939 the Japanese government demanded that Chinese silver kept in the banks in the British settlement in Tientsin be transferred to it, and Japanese troops disembarked near Hongkong at the Kowloon Peninsula, bringing to a halt the work of the Anglo-Japanese round-table conference that had been convened in July for solving specific questions arising out of the Arita-Craigie agreement. Nor were British expectations of an intensification of Soviet-Japanese hostilities justified. The devastating defeat sustained by the Japanese forces at the Khalka River strengthened the influence of those in Japan who believed that their country's primary objective should be the seizure of the Western colonies in Southeast Asia and in the South Pacific. Needless to say, such a policy set Japan on a collision course with Great Britain and the United States. Thus the attempts to solve the economic contradictions between the capitalist powers "politically" had failed, and the main contenders for the markets and resources of the Far East were to clash in war.

3

Japan and the Soviet Union: The Policy of Ambivalence

Following the establishment of diplomatic relations between the U.S.S.R. and Japan in 1925, the Soviet government strove to develop economic and cultural ties with the latter in the hope that the desire of Japanese business companies for concessions in the Russian Far East might be used to stabilize the international situation and counteract the aggressive designs of the Japanese militarists. In 1926 and again in 1927 and in 1931 the Soviet government proposed the conclusion of a nonaggression treaty with Japan. The Soviet ambassador to Tokyo, Aleksandr Troyanovsky, and senior aides of the People's Commissariat for Foreign Affairs vainly pointed out that such a pact would contribute to the stabilization of the international situation in the Far East. Japan declined the Soviet proposal under the pretext that since both Japan and the U.S.S.R. had signed the Briand-Kellogg Peace Pact it would be redundant to conclude a special nonaggression pact.

The Soviet government, which had concluded such pacts with its neighbors, countered on January 4, 1933, that "in its view there were no issues between the U.S.S.R. and Japan which could not be solved or which it would not agree to solve peacefully." It stated that "its proposals were not made on the spur of the moment, but were the result of its policy of peace and they will remain in force for the future." But although the general public spoke out in favor of concluding such a pact, in the course of the wide discussion that ensued in the Japanese press, the military, the Foreign Office and reactionary leaders objected to a détente with the U.S.S.R.

The Japanese imperialists never lost sight of the possibility of war against the U.S.S.R. They turned Northeast China and North Korea into military bridgeheads and strengthened the Kwantung Army, building ever more military installations, barracks, and air fields, and setting up special units for bacteriological warfare, and joined Nazi Germany in the Anti-Comintern Pact directed against the Soviet Union.

A Soviet proposal on April 4, 1938, to settle all outstanding issues by peaceful means did not meet with Japanese acceptance.[1] Thinking in terms of an accommodation with Great Britain and the United States, Foreign Minister Ugaki showed no desire to improve relations with the U.S.S.R. As he began his above-mentioned negotiations with Ambassador Craigie in June 1938, making various concessions to Great Britain, Japan intensified her pressure on the Soviet Union.

A frenzied anti-Soviet campaign was under way in Japan. Almost daily newspapers printed reports about the "crisis" in Soviet-Japanese relations, fabricating

[1] *Izvestiya,* April 28, 1938.

stories of Russian border violations, so that the Soviet Union had found it necessary already in May to protest against the systematic campaign of slander and war propaganda against her, frequently with the participation of public officials and organizations. The Japanese government did not live up to its guaranty of the payments by Manchukuo for the Chinese Eastern Railway, sold by the Soviet Union in 1935 to remove a major source of friction between herself and Japan. It impeded Soviet shipping, establishing, in violation of Article IX of the Treaty of Portsmouth, restricted zones in La Pérouse Strait. La Pérouse Strait was of great importance both for navigation near the Pacific shores of the Soviet Union and for communication with the ports on the shores of the Okhotsk Sea, Sakhalin and Kamchatka; it also provided the best passage from the Japan Sea into neighboring waters. Frequent, dense fogs, strong currents, and an abundance of underwater reefs made navigation in the straits extremely difficult under normal conditions; prohibition by Japan under the military secrets of October 7, 1937, of Soviet entry into restricted zones near the southern tip of Sakhalin and northern Hokkaido greatly added to the hazards and resulted in heavy damages and catastrophes. When the Soviet ship *Refrigerator No. 1* was damaged on May 31, 1938, the Japanese authorities did not provide help; instead they seized the ship and arrested its crew and started judicial proceedings against them for violating the restricted zone.[2]

Article IX of the Treaty of Portsmouth forbade the construction of military fortifications on Sakhalin and adjacent islands, and Japan had undertaken not to obstruct the free navigation of La Pérouse Strait. On June

[2] DBFP, vol. VIII, docs. 11–12.

28 the Soviet government, therefore, lodged a protest in Tokyo, stating that it expected the Japanese government to take the necessary measures "to restore in La Pérouse Strait and its shores the regime established by the Portsmouth Peace Treaty."[3]

At the beginning of July 1938 the Japanese border troops west of Lake Khasan were reinforced by regular troops, which were assembled on the eastern bank of the Tumen River, a little further to the west. Between the river and the lake lay a hilly region which afforded a good view of the surrounding area, including important railway lines and roads which led to the Soviet maritime region and the city of Vladivostok. The Japanese desired acquisition of these strategic heights in order to deny to Mongolian and Soviet forces observation of their lines of communication. As far back as 1933, the Kwantung Army had made a detailed topographic survey of the region with "military hostilities against Soviet Russia" in mind.[4]

On July 13, 1938, the Japanese press claimed that some 40 Red Army soldiers had invaded the area west of Lake Khasan on July 11 and had occupied territory belonging to Manchukuo.[5] When Chargé d'Affaires Nishi Haruhiko visited the People's Commissariat for Foreign Affairs on July 15 and demanded that the Soviet frontier guards be removed from this region, the Soviets produced maps which had been appended to the Hunchun Agreement of 1886 between China and Russia, showing clearly that the entire Lake Khasan was located in Soviet territory, and that, therefore, no vio-

[3] *Izvestiya,* July 2, 1938.
[4] M. Yu. Raginsky and S. Ya. Rozenblit, *Mezhdunarodnyi protsess glavnykh prestupnikov* (Moscow, 1950), p. 258.
[5] *Asahi Shimbun,* July 13, 1938.

lation of the border by the Soviet side had taken place.[6] Meanwhile a group of Japanese ultranationalists who had been distributing inflammatory leaflets burst into the grounds of the Soviet embassy in Tokyo on July 19, without hindrance from the Japanese police on duty at the gate.[7]

Ambassador Shigemitsu, who had been away in Western Europe, hastened back to Moscow and on July 20 demanded the withdrawal of Soviet troops from Zaozernaya Hill (Changkufeng), insisting that that area belonged to Manchukuo and that the Manchurian population conducted religious rites on the hill. Accusing the Soviet side of having violated the status quo, he declared that "an immediate withdrawal of the Soviet troops" was necessary "to bring calm."[8]

Foreign Commissar Maksim Litvinov reminded Shigemitsu that Nishi had been shown the Hunchun agreement and maps, which proved that the territory in question was Russian. He rejected flimsy arguments to the contrary and insisted that Soviet troops had every right to be on the hill west of Lake Khasan and that no interference by another state could be tolerated. Litvinov stressed that the Soviet Union maintained armies for the defense of her borders, not to dispatch them abroad. It was alive to its responsibilities of protecting the inviolability of the frontier.[9]

Shigemitsu replied that his government would hardly be satisfied with Litvinov's answer and threatened that if the Soviet Union did not withdraw her forces, "Japan

[6] *Pravda,* July 18, 1938.
[7] *Izvestiya,* July 22, 1938.
[8] Shigemitsu Mamoru, *Japan and Her Destiny* (New York, 1958), p. 158; *Izvestiya,* July 22, 1938.
[9] *Ibid.*

will have to come to the conclusion that it is necessary to resort to force." Litvinov reiterated that the Japanese demands for the withdrawal of Soviet troops were not supported by documentary evidence and thus were unacceptable; as for the threat of using force, Litvinov remarked, intimidation might work elsewhere, but not in Moscow.[10]

Unable to attain their ends by diplomacy, the Japanese turned to direct military pressure. When the Minister of War General Itagaki Seishiro requested imperial sanction for the use of armed force, the Emperor asked whether the respective ministers concurred. Itagaki falsely asserted that the foreign minister and the navy minister had expressed their agreement, but his deception soon came to light. Because of the unfinished war in China, Prince Konoe and the court circles feared hostilities with the Soviet Union, and the Lord Keeper of the Privy Seal Kido Koichi told Baron Harada on July 21 that Konoe would resign as premier should the army succeed in its advocacy of war with the U.S.S.R.[11] The following day the Five Ministers' Conference decided "to proceed with preparations in such a way as to safeguard against any contingency, to bring the armed forces into action in accordance with the Emperor's edict after agreement is reached between the representatives of the respective organs."[12]

On the strength of this decision, the army dispatched to the Zaozernaya Hill region a division of 10,000 men plus a heavy artillery unit from Korea plus about two thousand troops from Manchuria. The forces were headed by Colonel Naga Isamu, a member of the nation-

<hr />

[10] *Ibid.*
[11] Soviet Archives, 436b, file 69, p. 335.
[12] *Istoriya voiny na Tikhom okeane*, vol. II, 180–181.

alistic Cherry Society, who had been active in the seizure of Northeast China in 1931.[13]

On July 26 the Foreign Office issued a statement by the Chief of the Information Bureau accusing the Soviet authorities of infringing on the rights of Japanese concessionaires on northern Sakhalin. It hinted threateningly that Japan might have to defend her interests by armed force.

On July 29 two Japanese-Manchurian detachments crossed the Soviet frontier and tried to capture Bezymyannaya Hill, located north of Lake Khasan, two kilometers from Zaozernaya Hill, but the Soviet frontier guards drove them back from Soviet territory. The next day, the Soviet chargé d'affaires in Tokyo lodged a resolute protest with the Japanese government and demanded the punishment of those responsible for the incident. He warned that the Soviet government held it fully responsible for the consequences that the actions of its organs in Northeast China might entail.

On July 31 Japanese troops moved into Soviet territory under the cover of an artillery barrage and after heavy fighting captured the Zaozernaya Hill and Bezymyannaya Hill. A Soviet counterattack on August 2 and 3 failed to dislodge them, because there were insufficient Soviet troops in the area.[14]

The Soviet Union lodged another resolute protest in which she warned the Japanese government of the dire consequences of Japanese violation of Soviet territory. At the same time she began to concentrate the necessary forces near Lake Khasan to drive out the intruders.

On August 4 Shigemitsu called on Litvinov to tell him

[13] Shigemitsu, p. 159.
[14] *Istoriya Velikoi Otechestvennoi voiny Sovetskogo Soyuza 1941–1945*, vol. I (Moscow: Voyenizdat, 1961), pp. 232–34.

that the Japanese government was prepared to solve the Lake Khasan conflict by peaceful means as a local incident. He proposed that hostilities be halted by both sides. Litvinov retorted that any peaceful intentions on the part of the Japanese government were belied by the actions of the military. Had they not crossed the Soviet frontier, there would not have been an incident. If the Japanese would stop their invasion and shelling of Soviet territory and withdraw all their troops from it, the Red Army would have no need to continue its retaliatory action, and the Soviet government would be ready to start diplomatic discussion of proposals which the Japanese government might wish to advance.

When Litvinov declared that the inviolability of the Soviet border must be ensured in accordance with the Hunchun Agreement and the map appended thereto, Shigemitsu questioned the validity of the map, asserting that the Japanese had not seen the map before. "It would not be reasonable, therefore," he argued, "to resolve the incident on the basis of such map." He did express his government's willingness to discuss the treaty and the map, noting that the question of the demarcation of the Russo-Japanese frontier by a joint commission had been considered earlier.

The Soviet Union rejected the Japanese attempt to negotiate a change in her frontiers by disregarding time-honored international agreements and to halt hostilities while Japanese troops remained on her soil. "Borders between states are subject exclusively to international agreements, and maps are not regulated on the basis of subjective opinion or the desires of governments and military circles or unofficial data," Litvinov declared. Pointing out that Japanese opposition to the documents delineating the frontier was based entirely on their desire for a change, he stated that the occupation of Manchuria by Japan did not give her the right to demand an alteration in the frontiers. The Soviet government had no intention of revising her borders and would not consider the replacement of the Hunchun treaty by some other agreement.[15] Litvinov stated emphatically that the hostilities could be terminated only if the status quo prior to July 29 were restored, the shelling of Soviet territory stopped, and all Japanese troops withdrawn. He warned resolutely that the Soviet people would not tolerate the presence of foreign troops on an inch of Russian soil and would not stop at any sacrifice to free this territory. The Soviet government thus reserved the right to take any action so long as the attacks on Soviet territory continued and a single Japanese soldier remained on Russian land.

On August 7 Shigemitsu called Litvinov again to reiterate his proposal for the termination of hostilities, with the troops of both sides remaining where they were at the time the ceasefire would take effect, and the formation of a Soviet-Manchukuoan commission which with Japanese participation would redemarcate the frontier.

Litvinov pointed out that since the local situation was subject to change and both sides would strive to occupy the most advantageous positions by the time the agreement would take effect, the proposal encouraged the continuation of the hostilities. "In any case," he repeated, "no agreement is possible so long as Soviet territory is occupied by a Japanese military unit of any size." Litvinov added that while the Japanese government was proposing to end the fighting in one area, a Japanese unit had invaded the Soviet Union in another region, at Grodekovo. He warned that "from this moment

[15] *Izvestiya,* August 5, 1938.

on the Soviet government will not allow to go unpunished the periodical killing or wounding of its frontier guards or any temporary occupation of Soviet territory by Japanese troops, and it is fully determined to resort in such cases in the future to the strictest measures, including the use of artillery and aircraft." He called on the Japanese government to "force the Kwantung and Korean armies to respect the existing border."[16]

Meanwhile, Soviet troops, in a fierce offensive on August 6–9, completely freed the Soviet territory from the invaders.[17] On August 10 Shigemitsu accepted a Soviet proposal to terminate hostilities the following day, with troops remaining in the positions occupied on August 10. A joint commission was to be set up for the redemarcation of the disputed area. The Soviet side insisted that the commission should take as the basis of its work the treaties and maps signed by the plenipotentiary representatives of Russia and China; the Japanese proposed that account be taken of other materials, which they promised to present later.

The hostilities were ended on August 11. An attempt by the Japanese to violate the provisions of the armistice by advancing 100 meters was frustrated when Litvinov categorically demanded their withdrawal.

The Japanese did not succeed in concealing their defeat. The Soviet government gave wide publicity through TASS dispatches to the clashes near Lake Khasan, the casualties incurred by both sides, and the negotiations with Shigemitsu. When an American correspondent asked at a press conference, called by the Japanese Foreign Office, whether it was true that the

[16] *Izvestiya,* August 8, 1938.
[17] For further detail, see *Istoriya Velikoi Otechestvennoi voiny,* vol. I, pp. 234–36; Marshal G. K. Zhukov, *Vospominaniya i razmyshleniya* (Moscow, 1969), pp. 152–78.

Soviet flag waved atop Changkufeng hill, the most that the Japanese spokesman could state was, "not at the very top but a little to the side. . . ."

Japanese propaganda sought to conceal the responsibility of the Japanese military for the Lake Khasan incident by contending that the Soviet Union had begun hostilities with a view to disrupting the Japanese offensive in the Hankow area, but the International Military Tribunal for the Far East, which tried the main Japanese war criminals after the Second World War, recognized that Japan had been the aggressor in the events near Lake Khasan. As the indictment stated, the attack of the Japanese troops near Lake Khasan had been deliberately planned by the General Staff and Minister of War Itagaki and had been sanctioned by at least five ministers who had participated in the meeting on July 22, 1938.

> The purpose of this attack could have been either to test the strength of the Soviet Union in this area or to seize a strategically important area on the hill range overlooking the communications leading to Vladivostok and the Maritime Area. The attack, which had been planned and was implemented with the use of considerable forces, could not be viewed as merely a clash between patrols of frontier guards. The Tribunal considers it also established that these hostilities were started by the Japanese. Though the military forces engaged in the conflict were not of considerable strength, the above-mentioned purpose of the attack and the results which could have been obtained in case of its success were sufficient in the Tribunal's view to consider these hostilities a war. The Tribunal considers that the operations of the Japanese forces were of an openly aggressive nature.[18]

[18] Raginski and Rozenblit, pp. 259–60.

Despite the exhaustive indictment and the facts of the case, official Japanese publications such as a short history of a century of Japanese diplomacy, issued by the Foreign Office in 1948, and diplomatic memoirs, such as those of Togo Shigenori, Shigemitsu and Sato Naotake, assert that the events had been incidental, not a deliberately planned aggressive action on the part of Japan.

> Neither the Japanese Government nor the General Staff planned an aggressive war for an object of such strategic insignificance [Shigemitsu writes in his memoirs]. Moreover all the classes in Japan followed with the greatest anxiety the development of the incident. One could add that the Army at the time of the event dispatched a great number of troops to take part in the Wuhan campaign and desired only peace and tranquility in all other places.[19]

In an earlier book, Shigemitsu had also contended that Japan had not planned to attack the Soviet Union, but had admitted that "one could not deny that the officers of the army stationed in Korea showed indiscretion and worsened the situation."[20]

The defeat near Lake Khasan demonstrated the futility of seeking to cow the U.S.S.R. by military pressure. It undermined the whole basis of the diplomacy of Ugaki of seeking to obtain from the Western powers a free hand in China by posing as the champion of anti-Communism. Ugaki's attempt to come to terms with Chiang Kai-shek added to the dissatisfaction of the military, who desired full control over China and common action with Nazi Germany against the Western powers

---

[19] Shigemitsu, p. 160.
[20] Shigemitsu Mamoru, *Showa no doran* (Tokyo, 1952), p. 151.

as well as the U.S.S.R., and on September 27 Ugaki was forced to resign.

In November 1938 the Japanese government proposed the negotiation of a new Soviet-Japanese fishery convention, based on a draft considered but not signed in 1936. In doing so, it referred to the Treaty of Portsmouth, in which Japanese fishing in Russian waters had been stipulated, and accused the Soviet government of violating its provisions.

Foreign Commissar Litvinov reminded Ambassador Togo on November 27 that Japan had aborted the signature of a new fisheries convention in 1936 by her conclusion of the Anti-Comintern Pact and told him that it was known in Moscow that Japan was now conducting negotiations with Germany concerning a military alliance directed against the Soviet Union.[21]

On November 28 Litvinov handed to Togo the Soviet reply to the Japanese proposal for the conclusion of a new fisheries convention. Rejecting Japanese claims of Soviet violation of the Treaty of Portsmouth, he stressed that the treaty did not put any obligations on the U.S.S.R. as to the number of fishing lots leased to Japanese nationals or the terms of lease; they must be determined by an amicable agreement between the two sides. He took the opportunity to point out that Japan had violated the Treaty of Portsmouth by occupying Northeast China and maintaining there a huge army, and by fortifying La Pérouse Strait and hindering the passage of Soviet ships through it. "It cannot be tolerated," Litvinov declared, "that the Japanese government, while violating its own obligations toward the U.S.S.R., should insist that the latter not only fulfill her obligations but meet Japanese demands beyond the

[21] Soviet Archives, fund 146, file 031/I, p. 35.

limits of these obligations."[22] He added that the Soviet government would not begin negotiations concerning a new fisheries convention until the Japanese government had met its obligation to guarantee the payments for the Chinese Eastern Railway.[23]

The Soviet government did agree to conclude a provisional fisheries agreement for one year. Notifying Japan that auctions had been scheduled for February 1939, it informed it of its intention to withdraw 40 fishing grounds from Japanese exploitation for strategic reasons.

The Japanese took advantage of the fishing and crabbing lots and of the right of Japanese fishermen to pull up at the Soviet shores during the fishing season in order to process the catch at the canning factories to engage in sabotage and espionage against the U.S.S.R. The twenty thousand-odd workers whom the Japanese brought to these lots every fishing season were mainly young people of conscription age, organized in military fashion. The administrators of the fisheries were officers. In 1937–38 12 groups were found spying. The solid structure erected by the Japanese at their fishing bases and canning factories were suitable for military purposes. Japanese warships, which visited the area of the leased lots and surveyed the shores, violated Soviet territorial waters. Thirty-two such cases were registered in 1937 and 26 in 1938.[24]

When Togo replied to Litvinov's criticism of Japanese policy in December that the northeastern provinces of

[22] *Izvestiya,* December 8, 1938.
[23] Manchukuo had failed to make the final installment payment of about 6 million yen, due on March 23, 1938, raising unfounded claims of over 5 million yen against the U.S.S.R. Although Japanese guaranty of the payments had been a condition of the sale, Japan had declined to intervene.
[24] Soviet Archives, 0146, file 26, p. 85.

China had become independent, and that Japanese troops were stationed there in accordance with agreements concluded between Japan and Manchukuo, Litvinov remarked that the promulgation of Manchukuo's "independence" had been the result of the movement of Japanese troops into northeastern China and that their presence there in large numbers was contrary to the Treaty of Portsmouth. He reiterated the Soviet position that since Japan had no right to construct military installations on the shores of La Pérouse Strait, there should be no restricted zones in that region.[25]

The Japanese government declared that it would be willing to consider the matter of payments for the Chinese Eastern Railway, only if the Soviet Union signed the draft fisheries convention, formulated in 1936, by December 10, 1938, but Litvinov rejected the condition which bordered on an ultimatum.

On December 13 discussions were begun concerning the provisional agreement. Togo sought to do away with the auction system, and objected to the withdrawal of the above-mentioned 40 fishing grounds from Japanese exploitation.

Meanwhile the Japanese press accused the Soviet Union of deliberate delay in the signing of the fisheries convention and threatened the U.S.S.R. with unrestricted fishing in Soviet waters. On December 22 Vice-Admiral Kanazawa declared that the Japanese Navy was following the negotiations between Togo and Litvinov very closely and was ready to defend the fishing rights of Japan. He warned that if the Soviet government did not agree to sign the agreement by December 24, it would be impossible to conclude the pact before the expiration of the current provisional agreement

[25] *Izvestiya,* December 10, 1938.

and Japan would have to resort to "free fishing."[26] Tension mounted as the Lower House of the Diet passed a resolution on February 14, 1939, calling on the government to take measures to protect Japanese interests, but the Soviet government resolutely rejected Japanese pressure and warned that any attempt at unrestricted fishing would be regarded as an attack on the U.S.S.R. and would be met as such.[27]

The firm stand of the Soviet government left the Japanese no choice but to sign an extension of the provisional fisheries agreement for one year on Russian terms. The Soviet victory had broad implications. As the government noted at the third session of the Supreme Soviet of the U.S.S.R. on May 31:

This agreement with Japan on the fisheries question has great political significance, the more so since the Japanese reactionary circles did everything in their power to stress the political aspects of this matter, resorting even to threats of various kinds. But the Japanese reactionaries had another chance to convince themselves that threats against the Soviet Union never succeed, and the rights of the Soviet State are strongly safeguarded.[28]

Soviet-Japanese relations were marred also by disputes over the Japanese oil and coal concessions in Northern Sakhalin, which had been granted in accordance with contracts signed between the U.S.S.R. and Japan on December 14, 1925, for a 45-year period. Japanese failure to exploit many of these concessions and constant violations of the concession contracts gave rise

[26] Soviet Archives, 416, file 031/1 p. 49.
[27] *Ibid.*, pp. 49–50.
[28] Union of Soviet Socialist Republics, Verkhovnyi Sovet, *Tret'ya sessiya Verkhovnogo Soveta SSSR 25–31 maya 1939 g. Stenograficheskii otchet* (Moscow; 1939), pp. 474–75.

to frictions and disputes, which were used by the Japanese military along with the fisheries question to aggravate Soviet-Japanese relations. Threatening speeches were made in the Diet. On February 14, 1939, Minister of Commerce and Industry Hatta Yoshiaki stated that the appropriate authorities were discussing measures for the preservation of Japan's important rights.[29] On March 16 Finance Minister Ishiwatari Sotaro remarked at a meeting of the Budget Commission of the Lower House that "in the future measures will be taken to end the unlawful pressure on the part of the U.S.S.R."[30] On April 27 the Japanese government formally protested that Soviet authorities were allegedly exercising pressure on the oil company in North Sakhalin, putting obstacles in the way of normal operations.[31]

On June 16 Ambassador Togo communicated to the People's Commissariat for Foreign Affairs a note in which he demanded that permission be granted immediately to Japanese concessionaires to bring Japanese workers to the U.S.S.R. as well as to hire Soviet workers, and that the existing collective agreements be repealed. The note ended with an ultimatum:

> In view of the aggravated local situation, the Japanese side demands that the Soviet governments give as soon as possible, but not later than June 18, an explicit answer to all the questions. Otherwise the Japanese government will have to resort to corresponding measures to protect its interests deriving from the treaty.[32]

[29] Asahi, February 15, 1939.
[30] Asahi, March 17, 1939.
[31] Union of Soviet Socialist Republics, Ministry of Foreign Affairs, *Vneshnyaya politika SSSR. Sbornk dokumentov*, vol. IV (Moscow, 1946), p. 432.
[32] Soviet Archives, 146, file 4, pp. 25–27.

Angered by the arrogant tone of the Japanese document, the Foreign Commissariat replied curtly that "in view of the fact that the document of June 16 contains threats and has the character of an ultimatum, the People's Commissariat for Foreign Affairs does not deem it possible to accept the document and returns it without giving it consideration.[33]

A week later, on June 24, the Soviet government gave a detailed answer to the Japanese memorandum of April 27. Denying that the authorities in North Sakhalin had imposed unlawful restrictions, it asserted that the Foreign Commissariat had ample evidence of direct violations by the Japanese concessionaires of the concession contracts and of Soviet laws. It pointed out that the coal and oil concessions had made no lease payments to the Soviet government since December 14, 1925, for the property transferred to them for their use, and that the concession company systematically violated safety regulations. Listing all the violations by the Japanese of the concession contracts, the Soviet government alleged that "the Japanese concessionaires systematically violate the concession contracts in an effort to secure for themselves in the U.S.S.R. conditions of economic activity, analogous to those which are being imposed in Manchuria, occupied by Japan."[34]

The German seizure of the remaining part of Czechoslovakia in March 1939, the Italian annexation of Albania the following month, and German demands on Poland prompted the ultranationalists in Japan to renew their clamor for the intensification of hostilities in China and aggression against the Soviet Union and the Mongolian People's Republic, confident that the Soviet

---

[33] *Ibid.*, file 2, p. 33.
[34] *Vneshnyaya politika SSSR*, vol. IV, pp. 437–38.

government was too preoccupied with European affairs to take a strong stand in the Far East.

The Japanese military calculated that the conquest of the Mongolian People's Republic, which did not have a large army, would bring Japanese forces close to the Soviet border below Chita and put them within easy striking distance of the Trans-Siberian Railway, the Soviet Union's most vital artery of communication; at the same time it would enhance Japanese prestige and expedite the conclusion of a military alliance with Germany and Italy. They thought it might also disrupt the Anglo-Franco-Soviet mutual assistance talks and halt Soviet aid to China. They were not worried by the possibility that the U.S.S.R. might actively side with the Mongolian People's Republic, confident that the Japanese army could successfully cope with the Soviet forces in the Trans-Baikal region.[35]

On March 28 General Itagaki Seishiro, chief of staff of the Kwantung army who shortly was to become minister of war, told Foreign Minister Arita:

If Outer Mongolia [the Mongolian People's Republic] is incorporated with Japan and Manchukuo, the security of the Soviet Far East will sustain a very heavy blow. In case of necessity, it would be possible to do away with the influence of the U.S.S.R. in the Far East almost without a struggle. For that reason, the Army intends to extend Japanese and Manchurian influence to Outer Mongolia with all the means at its disposal.[36]

As a pretext for military hostilities the Japanese militarists advanced the theory of the "disputability" of the

[35] At his trial in Khabarovsk in 1949, Ataman Semenov, one of the former White Russian leaders, testified concerning Japanese plans to invade the Trans-Baikal region and wrest the territory east of Lake Baikal from the Soviet Union with the aid of emigrés in Inner Mongolia.

[36] Soviet Archives, 436b, file 16, p. 121.

Mongolian frontier, even though it was fully in conformity with official Chinese maps and had never been questioned before by anyone, including the Japanese-Manchurian side. All the maps, printed by authoritative publishing houses throughout the world, including Japanese maps issued before 1935, showed the border between Manchukuo and the Mongolian People's Republic as running east of the Khalka (Khalkhin-gol) River. In 1935 the Kwantung army brought out new maps of Manchukuo, moving the frontier between the Mongolian People's Republic and Manchukuo 20 kilometers to the west so that it ran along the Khalka River. Maps showing the old border, particularly those prepared by the Research Bureau of the South Manchurian Railway, were removed from distribution.[37]

In preparation for their attack the Japanese made a detailed survey of the area and constructed a railway line to the border. By 1939 units up to platoon strength began to cross into the Mongolian People's Republic; there were over 30 violations of the frontier in the spring.

On May 11, 300 Japanese soldiers penetrated 15 kilometers into Mongolian territory in the Lake Buir Nor region. On May 14 they advanced to the Khalka River, driving back the frontier units of the Mongolian People's Republic.

In conformity with the Protocol of Mutual Assistance, units of the 57th Special Corps of the Red army were stationed in the Mongolian People's Republic. Some of these were rushed to the scene of the Japanese invasion.[38]

Japanese propaganda alleged that the Mongolian side

[37] Tsuji Masanobu, *Nomonhan* (Tokyo, 1947).
[38] *Istoriya Velikoi Otechestvennoi voiny,* vol, I, pp. 236–38.

had violated the border, but when Premier Hiranuma Kiichiro, informed of developments, demanded that the conflict be arrested, the military demurred.[39] The history of Japanese diplomacy, complied by the Foreign Office, contends that "initially Japan did not plan to widen the conflict, but hostilities between the U.S.S.R. and Japan gradually widened;"[40] it does not explain who was responsible for the broadening of hostilities and why the Japanese government continued to send fresh troops to the region. Numerous memoirs, published in Japan before the Pacific War, also depicted the Japanese invasion as an ordinary "frontier clash," caused by the dispute over the location of the boundary line between the Mongolian People's Republic and Manchukuo.[41]

On May 19, 1939, the People's Commissar for Foreign Affairs lodged a protest with Ambassador Togo.

Recently, on May 11 and 12 as well as subsequently, the border of the Mongolian People's Republic was violated several times by Japanese-Manchurian units, which attacked Mongolian units in the region of Nomonhan, Burt-Obo, and also in the area Dongur-Obo. There are killed and wounded among the troops of the Mongolian People's Republic. Japanese-Manchurian aircraft participated also in this thrust into the Mongolian People's Republic. I must warn that there is a limit to patience, and I ask the Ambassador to convey to the Japanese government that there must be no repetition of such acts. It will be better that way in the interests of the Japanese government itself. . . . It is an indisputable fact that the Japanese-Manchurian units violated the border of the Mongolian People's Republic and opened military hostilities, that this attack on the territory of the Mon-

[39] Raginsky and Rozenblitt, p. 262.
[40] Japan, Foreign Office, *Nihon gaiko hyakunen shoshi* (Tokyo, 1958), p. 157.
[41] Shigemitsu, *Japan and Her Destiny*, pp. 172–73.

golian People's Republic was committed by Japanese-Manchurian troops and aircraft. We will not tolerate this. One cannot tax the patience of the Mongolian government and believe that this will pass unpunished. My statement is in complete conformity with the provisions of the Pact of Mutual Assistance concluded between the U.S.S.R. and the Mongolian People's Republic.[42]

The Japanese ignored the warning of the Soviet government. Having assembled a force of about 2,500 men with artillery, armored cars and 40 aircraft, they launched an offensive on May 28, and were beaten and driven back to the border.

On May 31 the Soviet government repeated its warning. Speaking at the third session of the Supreme Soviet of the U.S.S.R., the head of the government, Vyacheslav Molotov, declared that the Soviet Union, in compliance with the Treaty of Mutual Assistance, would defend the borders of the Mongolian People's Republic as resolutely as if they were her own.

It is time to understand that the Japanese allegations that the government of the Mongolian People's Republic is guilty of aggression against Japan are ridiculous and absurd. It is time to understand likewise that there is a limit to patience. It would be better, therefore, to discontinue in time the continuously repeating provocative violations of the border of the U.S.S.R. and the Mongolian People's Republic by Japanese-Manchurian military units.[43]

The Japanese militarists did not heed the warning and sent fresh units to the Khalka region. By the beginning of June they had gathered two divisions and two regiments of the seventh division, and two tank regiments—

---

[42] Soviet Archives, 146, file 15, p. 151.
[43] *Tret'ya sessiya Verkhovnogo Soveta,* p. 475.

a total of 38,000 officers and men with 145 tanks and armored cars, 310 guns and 225 planes. They attacked again and were beaten again, though their forces outnumbered the Soviet-Mongolian troops three to one.

As the military conflict between the Soviet Union and Japan took on the form of an undeclared war, the United States tried to exploit the situation. Ambassador Grew had a number of talks with Foreign Minister Arita and Premier Hiranuma in mid-May. At one of them, on May 18, Hiranuma declared that it would be possible to achieve the closest cooperation between the United States and Japan on the basis of seeking means for solving the contradictions in Europe.[44] When Grew left Japan at the end of May, Hiranuma proposed to Counselor Dooman that an international conference be convened to discuss problems of international policy, including the Far Eastern situation. The conference was to be composed of delegates from the United States and Japan, as well as of Great Britain, France, Germany and Italy, and was to decide the destiny of China in Munich-fashion.[45]

When Secretary of State Hull conferred with Ambassador Horiuchi Kensuke in Washington in June and July 1939, he warned Japan that she must respect American rights in China. Yet he seemed to sympathize with the Japanese position vis-à-vis the Mongolian People's Republic and the U.S.S.R., and on July 20 stated that the United States and other powers were against strengthening the Soviet Union.[46]

Emboldened by the American stance and the conclu-

---

[44] United States Congress, Joint Committee on the Pearl Harbor Attack, *Hearings before the Joint Committee on the Investigation of the Pearl Harbor Attack* (Washington, 1946), part 20, p. 4158.

[45] Soviet Archives, 436b, file 59, p. 128.

[46] *Hearings,* part 20, pp. 4188–4189.

sion of the Arita-Craigie agreement, discussed above, the Japanese military began preparations for a new offensive, concentrating in the Khalka region the 7th and the 23rd divisions, a brigade of Manchurian soldiers, three artillery regiments and three cavalry regiments, combined in the 6th army—a total of 75,000 officers and men, supported by over 300 planes, 500 guns, and 182 tanks.[47]

Meanwhile the Soviet command, determined to annihilate the invaders and restore the borders of the Mongolian People's Republic, moved enough forces into the disputed area to gain a numerical superiority over the enemy in personnel and equipment. The Red army assembled 1½ times more men, 4 times more tanks, 2 times more guns and 1.6 times more planes than the Japanese and Manchurians.

On August 20 the Soviet-Mongolian troops went to the attack and by August 31 routed the Japanese army. The Japanese suffered between 52,000 and 55,000 casualties, including 25,000 dead; the Soviet-Mongolian troops lost less than 10,000 men, including those killed and wounded.[48]

The Kwantung Army was eager to assemble more troops and strike back at the Soviet forces, but this time the government, shaken by Germany's conclusion of a nonaggression pact with the U.S.S.R., intervened, halted further operations by an imperial edict, and dismissed the commander-in-chief of the Kwangtung Army and his chief of staff.[49]

On September 9 Ambassador Togo visited the People's Commissariat for Foreign Affairs and proposed the

[47] *Istoriya Velikoi Otechestvennoi voiny,* vol. I, p. 240.
[48] *Ibid.,* p. 244.
[49] Shigemitsu, *Japan and Her Destiny,* p. 173.

conclusion of an armistice, the creation of two commissions to demarcate the borders between the Soviet Union and Manchukuo and between the Mongolian People's Republic and Manchukuo respectively, and of another commission to settle future conflicts between the U.S.S.R. and Manchukuo. He raised the question of making the Khalka region into a demilitarized zone and expressed the desire of his government to conclude a treaty of commerce with the Soviet Union to increase the economic relations between the two countries.[50]

The foreign commissar replied the following day that the Soviet government deemed the establishment of the two border redemarcation commissions reasonable and that it accepted also the proposal for the creation of a commission to settle conflicts. The Soviet and Mongolian governments rejected, however, the idea of the demilitarization of the Khalka region; they wanted the restoration of the *status quo ante bellum*—the reestablishment of the old borders between the Mongolian People's Republic and Manchukuo and the withdrawal of troops from this border. The Soviet government agreed to the negotiation of a treaty of commerce with a view to improving relations between the U.S.S.R. and Japan.[51]

The Japanese government did not go along with the restoration of the former border line in the Khalka area and the mutual withdrawal of Soviet-Mongolian and Japanese-Manchurian troops from the frontier. It proposed on September 14 that the Japanese-Manchurian and Soviet-Mongolian troops remain in the positions occupied as of September 15, 1939. To speed a settlement, the Soviet government consented, and a communiqué,

[50] Soviet Archives, 0146, file 1219, p. 52.
[51] *Ibid.*

issued the same day, announced the termination of hostilities. But though it was agreed to set up a commission, composed of two representatives from the Soviet-Mongolian side and two from the Japanese-Manchurian side, to determine the border line between the Mongolian People's Republic and Manchukuo in the disputed region and that the commission commence its work immediately upon formation,[52] the Japanese balked at implementing the agreement and new negotiations had to be begun in autumn.

The defeat sustained by the Japanese in the Khalka region was of great significance for the further development of Soviet-Japanese relations, for it deflected Japanese expansion southward.[53] An official publication of the Japanese Foreign Office admits that the Japanese government decided on the basis of the lessons learned from this failure to change the direction of Japan's advance to the South. The southward direction was encouraged by Germany, which did not contemplate war with the Soviet Union at this stage and wanted Japan to divert the forces of Great Britain, France and the United States from Europe. Ribbentrop, therefore, offered to mediate an improvement in relations between Japan and the U.S.S.R.[54] Assured by Ribbentrop that "the idea of close cooperation between Germany, Italy and Japan is not at all dead,"[55] Ambassador Oshima remarked that the Japanese army accepted the idea of establishing good relations with the Soviet Union, and expressed the hope that the idea would soon be reflected in Japanese foreign policy.[56] At the same time German diplomacy sought

[52] *Vneshnyaya politika SSSR*, vol. IV, pp. 461–62.
[53] *Nihon gaiko hyakunen shoshi*, p. 157.
[54] Soviet Archives, 436b, file 13, p. 287.
[55] *Ibid.*, p. 286.
[56] *Ibid.*, pp. 292–94.

to worsen Japanese relations with Great Britain by undermining the Arita-Craigie agreement.

The defeat near the Khalka River proved to be a turning point in the attitude of Japan toward the Soviet Union. Political groups oriented toward Germany and Italy and, of course, business circles involved in dealings with the U.S.S.R., such as oil concessionaires, spoke out in favor of improving relations between the two powers. The malicious anti-Soviet tirades of old were replaced by more balanced and quieter accounts in the press. Newspapers began to give special attention to Soviet-Japanese problems. The influential paper *Yamato*, for example, repeatedly stressed the need to settle relations with the Soviet Union before coming to terms with the United States and Great Britain. *Asahi* called upon the Soviet Union to join in the establishment of "peace in the Far East" and *Nichi-Nichi* advocated the conclusion of a nonaggression pact between the Soviet Union and Japan.[57] The move to stabilize relations with the Soviet Union was prompted in part by the need to have a safe rear when striking southward. It was designed also to acerbate the contradictions between the U.S.S.R. and the capitalist powers and between the United States and Great Britain.

On October 4 Ambassador Togo communicated to the Foreign Commissariat concrete proposals for a trade agreement, providing for the barter of certain goods at a 1 to 1 ratio, all transactions to be done on the basis of a clearing system. The Japanese offered to conclude an agreement, embodying most-favored-nation treatment in trade and navigation.

The meetings of the new Soviet Ambassador Konstantin Smetanin with the new Japanese Foreign Minister

[57] *Soviet Archives*, 0146, file 1219, p. 53.

Nomura Kichisaburo received wide coverage in Japan. Contrary to diplomatic practice, the first talks of the ambassador with the foreign minister were not confined to formalities. During their first meeting on November 15, prior to the presentation of Smetanin's credentials, Nomura transmitted a draft agreement on the functions of the agreed-upon frontier commissions and a draft fisheries convention, since the provisional one was about to expire.[58] Since Nomura expressed the desire of his government to conclude a long-term fisheries convention on the basis of the 1936 draft, "to assist actively in the settling of the question of payments concerning the Chinese Eastern Railway," and to speed up the negotiation of a treaty of commerce,[59] the Nomura-Smetanin talks were hailed by the Japanese press as the beginning of "a new era" in Soviet-Japanese relations.

Meanwhile, on November 13, Ambassador Togo communicated to the Foreign Commissariat a list of outstanding issues—the fisheries convention, a treaty of commerce, and the establishment of commissions for the settlement of conflicts. Appended to the list were draft proposals for the establishment of the various commissions.

On November 19 agreement was reached on the composition, functions and place of work of the joint commission on redemarcation of the border between the Mongolian People's Republic and Manchukuo in the Khalka area. The commission was to start its work in the city of Chita and conduct the second half of its meetings in Harbin.

[58] A similar draft was transmitted directly to the Foreign Commissariat in Moscow on December 1.
[59] Soviet Archives, 0146, file 1087, p. 151.

On the same day the Soviet government informed Nomura of its willingness to start negotiations concerning a treaty of commerce with Japan along the lines suggested by the Japanese government. It expressed the hope that the conclusion of such a treaty would be accompanied by the removal of misunderstandings between Japanese firms and Soviet organizations in connection with the implementation of Soviet orders. The Matsuo Dockyard Company, which had agreed in September 1936 to build three ships for the Soviet Union and had received an advance in the amount of over 1½ million yen, had neither fulfilled the order nor refunded the money. Officials in the ministries of trade, finance and foreign affairs had declined to become involved, and when the Soviet trade mission had taken the matter to court in Tokyo in December 1938, the case had been postponed repeatedly.

But the fisheries convention draft, submitted by the Japanese, was based on the draft of 1936, rejected by the Soviet government. Furthermore, as in 1938, Moscow did not deem it possible to conclude any new fisheries convention so long as the final installment for the Chinese Eastern Railway had not been paid. On December 15 the Foreign Commissariat informed Togo:

> The Soviet government, while deeming it impossible to conclude the fisheries convention on the basis of the Sato-Kozlovsky draft, rejected already in 1936, 1937, and 1938, is prepared, nevertheless, to start negotiations concerning the conclusion of a fisheries convention for a long term. What is necessary for this, is for the Japanese government to discharge at least in a preliminary fashion its obligations as a guarantor of the payments for the Chinese Eastern Railway.[60]

[60] *Ibid.*, p. 54.

Angered by the firm position of the Soviet government, the Japanese made another attempt to exert pressure on the Soviet Union. Newspapers were filled with all kinds of accusations and threats. On December 11 all newspapers carried a lengthy statement of the semi-official Domei Tsushin news agency, declaring that "fishing rights on the Kamtchatka peninsula, gained by blood and sweat in the course of the Russo-Japanese War, cannot be ceded to the U.S.S.R., and if the latter will continue to adhere to its arrogant and ambitious policy, this may force Japan to take resolute steps to perpetuate her fishing concessions." The same day, the newspaper *Kokumin,* an organ of the Foreign Office, printed lengthy commentaries in an anti-Soviet spirit.[61] War Minister Hata Shunroku told an *Asahi* correspondent on December 13 that the Japanese failures were the result of insufficient vigilance towards "the workings of the red devil."

The Japanese press criticized especially the Soviet linking of the last installment for the Chinese Eastern Railway with the conclusion of a long-term fisheries convention. It printed lengthy computations to show that the last installment was allegedly more than offset by the debts of the Soviet government to the administration of the Chinese Eastern Railway.

In the meantime, on December 7, the joint commission on the redemarcation of the border between the People's Mongolian Republic and Manchukuo had commenced its deliberations. But although a number of meetings were held in Chita through December 25 and in Harbin from January 7 to January 30, 1940, no agreement could be reached, because the Japanese would not recognize the authority of the above-mentioned documents, and the

[61] *Ibid.,* file 1210, p. 28.

redemarcation question was entrusted for consideration through diplomatic channels.

The Japanese government consciously postponed the solution of this matter to show to the Americans, who were considering coming to terms with them, that Japan was not striving to normalize relations with the U.S.S.R. Seeking to prevent a Soviet-Japanese rapprochement, the United States government in December 1939 tried to obtain an official confirmation from the Foreign Office that "a nonaggression pact was not part of the Japanese program of negotiations with the Soviet Union at the present time."

As the provisional fisheries agreement expired, the Japanese concerns intensified their pressure on the government for a settlement of the fisheries question—they realized that the Soviet fleet would prevent unrestricted fishing—and the Japanese government was compelled to deal with the railway issue. On December 31, 1939, an agreement was reached on the final payment by Manchukuo for the Chinese Eastern Railway on January 4, 1940, and on the same day the fisheries convention of 1928 was renewed for the year 1940.[62] In prolonging the old convention, provision was made for the substitution of a new convention, which was to be concluded in 1940,[63] but Japanese procrastination in the demarcation of the Mongolian-Manchurian frontier kept the Soviet government from signing a new fisheries convention.

With the conclusion of the Soviet-German nonaggression pact, British and American anti-Soviet feeling was heightened. The situation was particularly tense during the Soviet-Finnish war, when Great Britain and

[62] *Vneshnyaya politika SSSR*, vol. IV, p. 400.
[63] *Ibid.*, p. 478.

France considered armed intervention on Finland's behalf. The United States rendered Finland aid in arms and ammunition.

Pro-British and pro-American elements in Japan, which had considerable influence with the Abe and Yonai governments, vehemently opposed a Soviet-Japanese détente. They were supported in this by ultranationalists who called for the creation of a united anti-Soviet front. But the Japanese press was less hostile than before, and the *Kokumin,* alongside tendentious articles composed in the Foreign Office (through the efforts of Vice-Minister for Foreign Affairs Kishi and his assistant Ando) began to publish articles giving a realistic account of Soviet life. In mid-December 1939 the newspaper began a series of articles about the national policy of the U.S.S.R. under the general heading, "National in Form, Socialist in Content." Newspapers were filled increasingly with statements, including remarks made by Foreign Office spokesmen at press conferences, about the need to achieve good-neighborly relations with the U.S.S.R. and the importance for both sides of concluding a new long-term fisheries convention, *Hoshi* reviving the question of a nonaggression pact with the Soviet Union.

The possibility of a Soviet-Japanese rapprochement alarmed the United States. Ambassador Grew questioned his Soviet colleague about the state of Soviet-Japanese relations,[64] while American journalists inquired about the subject at the Japanese Foreign Office. To some extent Japanese talk of a rapprochement with the Soviet Union was an attempt to blackmail the United States into continued appeasement of Japan; at the same time increased trade with the Soviet Union was to serve

[64] Soviet Archives, 0146, file 1210, p. 30.

as a counterbalance to American economic and political pressure. A Soviet-Japanese détente, furthermore, would have freed large military forces stationed at the Soviet borders for use in China or for expansion in the South Pacific and French Indo-China.

Some newspapers were skeptical about the possibility of a Soviet-Japanese rapprochement. *Kokumin* asserted on December 4, 1939, that the position of friendship adopted by the U.S.S.R. toward Japan was a temporary phenomenon and that no serious compromise between Japan and the Soviet Union could take place under any circumstances. Yet the signing of a border agreement between the two powers on December 31 was hailed by most of the press as proof of improving Soviet-Japanese relations, as was the extension of the fisheries agreement. Foreign Minister Nomura told the Soviet ambassador that he agreed with Molotov's assertion that 1939 marked the beginning of better relations between the U.S.S.R. and Japan and that 1940 would witness further improvement.[65]

Germany favored at this time a stabilization of relations between the Soviet Union and Japan, so that the latter might deal more firmly with Great Britain and the United States. When Ambassador Smetanin on his arrival in Tokyo made the customary courtesy call on the German ambassador, Ott, who since his days as military attaché had close ties with the Japanese military, sought to convince him that they had changed their attitude toward the Soviet Union and favored the settlement of all outstanding issues, the conclusion of a commercial treaty, and the signing of a nonaggression pact.[66]

On November 27, 1939, on a visit to the Soviet Em-

---

[65] *Ibid.,* 0146, file 1219, pp. 162–163.
[66] *Ibid.,* p. 152.

bassy, Ott reiterated that "the Japanese, particularly the army, wanted to establish friendly relations with the U.S.S.R." He produced a copy of that morning's *Asahi* and read out excerpts from the editorial, which emphasized the necessity of removing the "unwanted tension" in Japanese-Soviet relations. Calling upon the Soviet Union to cooperate with Japan in the establishment of peace in the Far East, the newspaper hinted that if she did so, Japan would not adhere to an anti-Soviet course. Ott referred also to a statement by Shiratori, who, upon his return from Rome, had publicly propounded the idea of coming to terms with the U.S.S.R., and to a speech by Count Terauchi, recently back from Germany, who had adduced the signing of a nonaggression pact between the Soviet Union and Germany as an argument for improving Japanese relations with Russia. Ott hinted that the Japanese military expected such a détente to entail Soviet recognition of Manchukuo and the discontinuation of Soviet aid to the Chungking government.[67]

Ott used every opportunity—receptions, theater performances, luncheons and dinners—to tell Smetanin about the desire of circles close to the army to normalize and strengthen relations with the Soviet Union. On December 15 he took advantage of the visit of his wife to Mrs. Smetanin to have another talk with the Soviet representative. Reiterating that the military were urging the government to establish friendly relations with the U.S.S.R., he stressed the need to solve the fisheries question and conclude a Soviet-Japanese treaty of commerce.[68]

The inability of the Abe government to settle the

[67] *Ibid.*, pp. 53–53.
[68] *Ibid.*, pp. 70–71.

China question and to solve the economic and political problems plaguing Japan led to its downfall. While the military and ultranationalists, who wanted a "dynamic" foreign policy, clamored for a strong cabinet, headed by a dependable army man, a split in their ranks—some favored General Hata, others General Sugiyama or Terauchi—enabled the Court circles, which preferred the "status quo" (Lord Privy Seal Yuasa, former Premier Okada, and the Minister of the Imperial Household Matsudaira, with the support of Baron Harada and Prince Saionji) to secure the appointment of Admiral Yonai, former minister of the navy, as premier.[69]

Although the formation of the Yonai government in January 1940 appeared to strengthen the hand of the pro-British and pro-American groups in Tokyo, its attempt, two months later, to solve the China question by setting up a puppet central government under the collaborator Wang Ching-wei worsened Japanese relations with the Western powers, which interpreted this step as a move by Japan to put the whole of China under her control.

To mollify Western feelings, Arita, an adroit diplomat with a chameleonic streak in his character who had been reappointed foreign minister, revived his line of common opposition to the Comintern, having in mind, of course, the Soviet Union. Although he had assured Smetanin that the consequences of the signing on January 19 of the border agreement would be tantamount to the conclusion of a nonaggression pact and that since the summer of 1939 relations between the U.S.S.R. and Japan had been improving and that he would be glad to work for their continued improvement, and had stated two weeks later that "the atmosphere in relations

[69] *Istoriya voiny na Tikhom okeane,* vol. II, pp. 322–23.

between the two countries has changed" and that "this is a very convenient factor for establishing friendly relations in the future,"[70] he delayed the settlement of outstanding issues while waiting to see how the world situation would develop.[71]

In view of the power of the Soviet Union, which was not yet engaged in war, the Yonai government had to make the utmost use of the possibilities created by the war in Europe, but with the minimum of risk and expenditure. Hence the accent on diplomatic negotiations and on indirect pressure on Great Britain. As for the United States, Japan did not want relations with her to deteriorate further.

Japanese business circles did not agree with the wait-and-see attitude of the government toward the U.S.S.R. Interested in trade and in economic concessions, they began to press for stronger ties with the Soviet Union. Some had favored military and naval threats in the past, but the Soviet show of strength had dissuaded them from such tactics. On February 5, 1940, Vice-Admiral Sakonji Seizo, president of the North Sakhalin Petroleum Company, called on Smetanin and insisting that it was necessary to establish friendly relations between the two countries, offered to do his best to facilitate the resolution of outstanding issues. Noting that neither side had any aggressive designs, Saionji expressed confidence that an understanding could be achieved. On March 13 Ott urged Smetanin to meet the Japanese desire for friendly relations with the U.S.S.R. When the Soviet ambassador pointed to the delay of the Japanese authorities in the sale of goods as partial payment for the Chinese Eastern Railway and the disruption of the work of the

---

[70] Soviet Archives, 0146, file 1219, p. 166.
[71] *Ibid.*, file 1087, p. 6.

frontier commission, Ott asserted that a large part of the military and many ministers were well disposed toward the Soviet Union.[72]

Yet War Minister Hata, Vice-Minister of War Terauchi, General Muto, the chief of the Military Affairs Bureau of the Ministry of War, and General Itagaki continued to make hostile pronouncements. Hata told the Diet that the losses suffered by the Japanese at the hands of the Red Army had been "a tremendous lesson." "We have already launched appropriate corresponding measures," he declared. "The blood spilt on the fields of Nomonhan has by no means been shed in vain."[73]

Japanese newspapers and magazines, connected with the Foreign Ministry and the pro-British and pro-American circles, also renewed their anti-Soviet campaign. *The Japan Times* and *Nichi-Nichi* systematically printed provocative reports. By alleging, for example, that Soviet ships were being used to deliver cargo from American countries and Indonesia to Germany,[74] they tried to instigate the seizure of Soviet merchant vessels by British men-of-war and set the U.S.S.R. and Great Britain against each other.

At a meeting of the British-Japanese Society in Japan on March 29, Sir Robert Craigie made a speech in which he argued that Japan and Great Britain had a community of interest in the Far East. Referring to the necessity of "defense from outside destructive influences," Craigie stressed that "the methods could in some cases be different but that both sides were struggling to achieve the same purpose, and that was durable peace and preservation of our institutions."[75] The *Japan*

[72] *Ibid.*, file 1219, pp. 175, 185–86.
[73] *Ibid.*, p. 180.
[74] *Ibid.*, file 1219, p. 278.
[75] *Asahi*, April 19, 1940.

Times editorialized on April 1 that "it is fully possible that the British ambassador had in mind the Soviet Union when he was speaking about the outside destructive influences." Other papers interpreted the speech as the virtual adherence of Great Britain to the Anti-Comintern front. Taking note of Craigie's visit to the United States, they speculated that he went there to explain the true intentions of Japan in China in order "to change the American opinion in favor of Japan."[76]

Meanwhile the Soviet government found it necessary to complain about the fact that the Japanese did not live up to their professed desire to improve Soviet-Japanese relations. On February 28 Smetanin protested against Japanese violation of the agreement of December 31, 1939. As he pointed out to Foreign Minister Arita, the Ministry of the Commerce had delayed the issuance of licenses to implement the orders of the Soviet Trade Mission for goods to be furnished in payment for the Chinese Eastern Railway; the Bank of Korea had refused to transfer to the State Bank of the U.S.S.R. one-third of the sum due for the Chinese Eastern Railway as stipulated in the agreement; and the dispute with the Matsuo Dockyard Company had not been settled.[77]

On March 29 Molotov declared at the Sixth Session of the Supreme Soviet of the U.S.S.R. that the Soviet Union's relations with Japan did not give ground for much satisfaction.

Thus, despite the long talks between the Soviet-Mongolian and the Japanese-Manchurian delegates the important question of establishing the borderline in the territory which was the scene of a military conflict last year still remains unsolved. The Japanese authorities are continuing to put obstacles in the way

[76] *Asahi,* April 10, 1940.
[77] Soviet Archives, 0146, file 1219, p. 175.

of the normal utilization of the last monetary contribution which had been made by Japan for the use of the Chinese Eastern Railway. The attitude of the Japanese authorities toward the staff of the Soviet organs in Japan and Manchuria is absolutely abnormal in many cases. It is time that Japan understood at last that the Soviet Union will under no circumstance tolerate the violation of her interests. Only if this is understood can Soviet-Japanese relations develop satisfactorily.[78]

The speech of the head of the Soviet government received little coverage in the Japanese press, as the authorities instructed the newspapers not to comment about it.[79] The *Asahi* did publish on April 1 and 2 articles entitled "The U.S.S.R. Intensifies Independent Diplomacy" and "Firm Position of the U.S.S.R. with Regard to Japan."

A number of political and military leaders made threatening speeches. Viscount Inoue, addressing the Diet, demanded no less than the occupation of the Kamchatka peninsula, while Vice-Admiral Sakonji came out in favor of dispatching a division to capture North Sakhalin.[80] Slogans like "Let us create a solid front against the Soviet Union" appeared in the streets and squares of Tokyo at the beginning of April, and on April 16 the Kenkokukai, an ultranationalist society, put up posters pleading for "serious attention" to South Sakhalin and for "strengthening the military system in all its aspects."[81]

[78] Union of Soviet Socialist Republics, Verkhovnyi Sovet. *Shestaya sessiya Verkhovnogo Soveta SSSR. 29 marta—4 aprelya 1940 g. Stenograficheskii otchet* (Moscow, 1940), pp. 40–41.
[79] Soviet Archives, 0146, file 1219, p. 279.
[80] *Ibid.*, file 1219, p. 279.
[81] *Ibid.*

The April issue of *Trans-Pacific* magazine alleged that the Japanese fishing industry in northern waters was being harmed by an increase in the number of seals on the Commodore Islands and advocated a review of the 1911 Convention on the Protection of Seals, signed by Japan, Russia, Great Britain and the United States. It stated that Foreign Minister Arita intended to approach the signatory powers about the matter. The Japanese thus wished, on one hand, to obtain permission for the unlimited killing of seals and, on the other hand, to change the conditions of the Soviet-Japanese fisheries convention so as to remove the restrictions on fishing in coastal waters. At the same time their demands provided them with possible leverage in negotiations with the Soviet Union.

It was for the same purpose that the Japanese government began discussions about the organization of a new fishery company under government control. The concern was to have a capital of 120 million yen and was to be in charge of the entire fishing industry in Soviet, North Korean and oceanic waters. But private fishers objected to the venture, fearing that it would operate to their detriment.

The Japanese continued to sound out the Russians through the Germans, who, as noted before, then desired a Soviet-Japanese rapprochement to free Tokyo for a southward drive that would direct the attention of Great Britain and the United States away from Europe. When telling Smetanin on April 19 of the desire of the Japanese military to be on good terms with the U.S.S.R., Ott tried to find out, however, how seriously the Far Eastern borders of the Soviet Union were guarded, and the German Naval Attaché Wennecker hinted that the

Kwantung Army was preparing to revenge itself against the Soviet-Far Eastern Army.[82]

Although Foreign Minister Arita confided to Baron Harada on March 2 that there had been no progress at all in the solution of outstanding questions between Japan and the Soviet Union,[83] Great Britain and the United States continued to worry about a Soviet-Japanese rapprochement. On March 23 Craigie and Yoshida, the Japanese ambassador to Great Britain who was at the time in Tokyo, called on Harada, who later noted in his diary that Craigie had expressed anxiety at the possibility of Japanese-German-Soviet collaboration and had left greatly relieved when Harada had assured him that Japan would preserve a strictly neutral position with regard to the European war.[84]

Meanwhile, the advocates of a "dynamic" foreign policy became increasingly outspoken in their criticism of the government's inertia and demanded that Japan capture the "unsupervised" colonies. The process of making Japan a fascist state was in full swing. On June 3 a general assembly of the League of the Deputies of Parliament for the Conclusion of the Sacred War passed a resolution calling for the establishment of one "comprehensive" party.[85] An active role in this movement was played by Kuhara Fusanosuke, one of the most influential spokesmen for big business, and Prince Konoe, who represented the Court circles.

Though the Yonai cabinet announced "the deep interest of the Empire" in the Dutch East Indies and French Indo-China and Arita publicly spoke about Japa-

[82] *Ibid.*, file 1219, pp. 280, 283, 329; Hubertus Lupke, *Japans Ruszland politik von 1939 bis 1941* (Frankfurt am Main, 1962), 54–63.
[83] *Ibid.*, file 5/42, p. 4.
[84] *Ibid.*, file 1219, p. 6.
[85] *Asahi*, June 3, 1940.

nese claims regarding the South Seas, the military wanted a change in government, feeling that the Yonai administration was unsuitable for strengthening the ties with Germany and for effecting the southward expansion. When a group of officers of the General Staff wrote to the high command that the government had not done all it could "to react fittingly to the international situation that has arisen of late,"[86] Prince Kanin, chief of the General Staff, energetically supported their action. On July 8 Vice-Minister of War Anami told Lord Keeper of the Privy Seal Kido that in the opinion of the military the Yonai cabinet was not suitable for achieving agreement with Germany and Italy. "There is the danger of our being too late for action. To enable us to act properly in such extremely hard times, there is no other way out but to change the government."[87] On July 16 War Minister Hata resigned, thereby toppling the cabinet.

Meanwhile, the resolute stand of the U.S.S.R. and the Mongolian People's Republic had forced Japan to abandon her unfounded claims, and on June 9 agreement had been reached on the delineation of the disputed Mongolian-Manchukuoan frontier. Giving a positive appraisal of the agreement, the chairman of the Council of People's Commissars declared that Soviet relations with Japan had begun to normalize of late. "One can recognize that generally there are certain signs that the Japanese side is willing to improve relations with the Soviet Union." Yet he remarked that "the real political intentions" of "the ruling circles of Japan" and their actual attitude toward the Soviet Union remained unclear.[88]

[86] Soviet Archives, 436b, file 15, p. 171.
[87] *Istoriya voiny na Tikhom okeane,* vol. III, pp. 63–64.
[88] Union of Soviet Socialist Republics, Verkhovnyi Sovet, *Sed'maya sessiya Verkhovnogo Soveta SSSR. 1 avgusta—7 avgusta 1940 g. Stenograficheskii otchet* (Moscow, 1940), p. 30.

The conclusion of the border agreement was followed by the resumption of negotiations concerning a new fisheries convention. Japan wanted to prolong the 1928 convention unchanged for another ten years; the Soviet Union, on the other hand, pointed out in her proposals of June 20 that it was necessary to make certain modifications in the convention and in the documents appended thereto, taking into consideration changes in the situation that had occurred since 1928. At the same time the Soviet side insisted on retaining the auction system in the leasing of fishing grounds, while the Japanese wished to abandon it.[89]

As the fishery talks bogged down, Ambassador Togo, tired of the vacillation of his government and of Arita's reluctance to work for the settlement of Soviet-Japanese relations, took the initiative in trying to improve relations between the two powers and requested permission from his government, both by telegrams and through an embassy official he sent to Tokyo, to negotiate a neutrality pact with the Soviet Union.

In early July Togo approached Foreign Commissar Molotov about the conclusion of an agreement on the following terms:

1. Confirmation that the Basic Convention of 1925 would govern relations between the two countries, and the maintenance of peaceful and friendly relations and the territorial integrity of each other.
2. In the event that one of the parties is attacked by a third power or powers, the other party is to maintain neutrality throughout the entire conflict.
3. The agreement is to run for five years.

[89] Soviet Archives, 0146, file 1226, pp. 161–85; Lupke, 6163.

Molotov replied several days later that the Soviet government agreed in principle and remarked that it was in effect a proposal for a neutrality pact.[90] He told Togo that the Soviet Union consistently adhered to a policy of peace and reminded him that the Soviet government itself had repeatedly suggested to Japan the conclusion of a treaty formalizing peaceful relations between the two countries. In mid-August Molotov informed Togo that the U.S.S.R. would be willing to accept the Japanese proposal, if the first provision were excluded. He explained that the Soviet government could not leave the convention of 1925 as the basis of relations between the U.S.S.R. and Japan, because some of its articles were obsolete, while others had been violated by Japan. For example, the Treaty of Portsmouth, whose provisions were reaffirmed by the Basic Convention, stipulated that Russia and Japan both "completely and simultaneously evacuate Manchuria" and maintain only railway guards, not exceeding 15 per kilometer. Yet Japan had violated it unilaterally by pouring up to 500,000 troops into Northeastern China and completely occupying the territory. The occupation of Northeastern China and its alienation from Chinese sovereignty, furthermore, were in violation of Article III of the Treaty of Portsmouth, whereby Russia and Japan had committed themselves "to entirely and completely restore to the exclusive administration of China all parts of Manchuria now occupied by Russian and Japanese troops, or which are under their control."[91] Japanese violations of the Treaty of Portsmouth had by and large nullified it. For this

---

[90] *Ibid.*, 436b, collection 22, file 66, p. 16.
[91] *Sbornik dogovorov Rossii s drugimi gosudarstvami, 1856–1917* (Moscow, 1958), p. 338.

reason and in view of the radical changes which had taken place in both states since its conclusion, the Treaty of Portsmouth could no longer serve as the basis of relations between the Soviet Union and Japan, as provided by the convention of 1925. The latter had become obsolete in other respects. For example, Article VI of the Basic Convention provided for the granting of oil and coal concessions on North Sakhalin to Japanese subjects, but by 1940 the majority of these concessions had proven not viable and were merely the object of constant disputes and friction not only between those responsible for the concessions and the respective Soviet organs, but also between the governments of both countries. Since Japan's oil and coal concessions were not viable, the Soviet government suggested their liquidation in return for fair compensation for the investments made by the Japanese.[92]

Togo recommended to his government that the Soviet proposals be accepted, but Matsuoka Yosuke, who became foreign minister when the Yonai government resigned in July, instructed him to discontinue the discussions and return to Tokyo. The sudden recall of the ambassador, at the height of the important negotiations, was incomprehensible, and Molotov warned Japan in a speech to the Supreme Soviet that the settlement of outstanding issues between the U.S.S.R. and Japan was of equal importance for both countries. Togo tried to dispel the misgivings of the Soviet government by asserting that the negotiations, though started on his initiative, had been authorized by Tokyo.

The Konoe government, which had been formed on July 22, was dominated by representatives of the military and of monopolies connected with them, especially

[92] Soviet Archives, 06, collection 34, file 371, pp. 78–84.

interested in the continental policy, i.e. in widening the expansion in China and in South Asia. It consisted of people who had expended great effort in promoting the "exploitation" of Northeast China, notably War Minister General Tojo Hideki, who had made his career in the Kwantung Army, Foreign Minister Matsuoka, former president of the South Manchurian Railway, and his main adviser and intimate friend, the industrialist Ayukawa Gisuke, who was an advocate of collaboration with Germany and Italy. Great influence was exercised also by the president of the Planning Bureau, Minister without Portfolio Hoshino, who had worked in Northeast China, and by the Vice-Minister of Foreign Affairs Ohashi Chuichi, who had served as director of the Foreign Affairs Bureau of Manchukuo. The Konoe government was supported by the Imperial Rule Assistance Association, a transcendent nationalist party formed by Konoe to take the place of the old political parties.

On July 27 the government adopted a "Program of Measures Corresponding to the Changes in the International Situation," which called for cutting off assistance to Chiang Kai-shek and for the conclusion of the China Incident. It provided for Japanese acquisition of the South Pacific region—the lands east of India, north of Australia and the Dutch East Indies—and the establishment of a Greater East Asia Co-Prosperity Sphere. To overcome America and British resistance to this policy, the ties with Germany and Italy were to be strengthened to the extent of a military alliance. The program stipulated "to use military force at the most propitious moment" to conquer the above-mentioned territory. This meant the decision was taken to go to war with Great Britain and to prepare for possible hostilities with the United States. As for the U.S.S.R., the government desired "a speedy settlement of Soviet-Japanese relations" in order to avoid a two-front war.[93]

On August 1 the government published a declaration, in which it announced abstractly that "the foreign policy of Japan, whose ultimate purpose is the construction of a New Order and a Co-Prosperity Sphere in a Great East Asia, will be directed first and foremost towards a complete solution of the China problem and the development of the national destiny."[94] Similar vague aspirations were voiced by Matsuoka personally.

Leading newspapers, such as the *Nichi-Nichi, Hochi* and *Asahi,* expressed dissatisfaction with the nebulous phrases and ancient slogans of the government—the concepts of "Hakko ichiu" (the eight corners of the world under one roof) and "Kodo" (the Imperial Way), as well as with Matsuoka's declaration that "for the present, Japan will pursue a policy of non-interference with regard to the European war."[95] The vagueness of the foreign policy declarations was due to the complexity of the international situation: the war in China continued, the outcome of the conflict in Europe was not certain, and relations with the Soviet Union were not settled. There was disagreement as to whether or not Japan should sign a military alliance with Germany and Italy. At first the government was inclined not to bind Japan by a treaty of military alliance and to proclaim merely a community of interests between Germany, Italy and Japan in the construction of a new world order. Cautious statesmen tried to slow down the gradual movement of Japan toward open expansion in

[93] *Istoriya voiny na Tikhom okeane,* vol. III, pp. 66–67.
[94] *Asahi,* August 1, 1940.
[95] *Ibid.,* August 3, 1940.

the South Pacific. But the victories of the German army in Europe—the seizure of Holland, Belgium and France—raised the question of the fate of the colonies in the Pacific, first of all, French Indo-China and the Dutch East Indies. Japanese ultranationalists demanded that advantage be taken of the defeat of the "mother countries" to seize the unsupervised colonies.

Speaking on the third anniversary of the war against China, on July 7, War Minister Hata stated:

> The international situation is developing favorably for conducting our national policy. We must take advantage of this golden opportunity. If other countries put obstacles in the way of solving the China Incident, we should adopt a firm position toward them. . . .[96]

The former ambassador to Italy, Shiratori, insisted that the policy of noninterference in the war be revised and that, as he wrote in *Asahi,* Japan independently solve "the question of a new domination over the Dutch Indies and various other colonies of Great Britain and France."[97]

The idea of "the golden opportunity" was supported by numerous ultranationalist and fascist organizations, whose membership extended to the ranks of the government as well as of the army and navy. They included the Tohokai ("Eastern Society"), the Parliamentary League for Concluding the Sacred War, to which over half of the deputies of the Lower House belonged, the Federation for the Building of a Greater East Asia, and the All-Japan Youth League.[98] These extremist groups advocated the following measures: (1) abandonment of the policy of noninterference in the war; (2) substitu-

[96] Soviet Archives, 0146, file 1372, p. 104.
[97] *Asahi,* August 9, 1940.
[98] Soviet Archives, 0146, file 1371, p. 106.

tion for the "world status quo" of a "new order"; (3) reactivation and strengthening of the Berlin-Rome-Tokyo Axis; (4) southward expansion—the seizure of the Far Eastern possessions of the European powers, in particular French Indo-China and Indonesia; (5) discontinuance of the orientation towards the United States and Great Britain and, if necessary, war with them; (6) temporary settlement of the relations with the U.S.S.R. to safeguard Japan's northern frontiers and allow her to concentrate fully on the expansion southward.[99] As the *Asahi* chimed in on September 2: "Japan should endeavor to make Great Britain, the United States, France and Holland leave Asia forever. Asia should be governed by Asian states."

At the same time newspaper advocacy of a settlement with the Soviet Union mounted. Urging that "relations with the U.S.S.R. should be settled on the basis of a Soviet-Japanese nonaggression pact," the *Nichi-Nichi* argued: "In this way, Japan could achieve security of her northern frontier, which would allow her to conduct her policy of southward advance. This would also provide an opportunity to prepare for war against the United States." Willing to resort to force in order to expand southward, the *Nichi-Nichi* advocated the creation of "an East Asian economic sphere which would include not only Japan, Manchuria and China but also French Indo-China, Siam, and the Dutch Indies, which would strengthen the economic basis of the East Asian League."

In a talk with Smetanin on July 1, Sakonji asserted that there would soon be three blocs—the German-Italian, the British-American, and the Soviet blocs—which would determine world policy. He stated that

[99] *Ibid.*, file 1372, p. 108.

Japan was interested in solving the frontier question and the fisheries and North Sakhalin concession questions. The old position of the navy, favoring "passivity in the North and activity in the South," was gaining new support.[100]

Foreign Minister Matsuoka had served in St. Petersburg before the Revolution as second secretary of the Japanese embassy and had studied the Russian language. He had returned to Moscow in 1932 and had conferred with Litvinov concerning the Soviet Union's proposal for the conclusion of a nonaggression pact. During his first meeting with the Soviet ambassador on July 27, 1940, he sought, therefore, to show his familiarity with Russian customs, and spoke at length about the noble and good qualities of the Slavic soul and of the spiritual affinity between the Ainus and the Russians.[101] In a subsequent talk with Smetanin on August 3, Matsuoka discoursed at length about his efforts for the past 30 years to improve relations between Japan and Russia.[102]

On August 24 he again depicted himself as a champion of friendly ties with the U.S.S.R., asserting that he was doing his best to follow in the footsteps of Goto Shimpei, long-time advocate of a Russo-Japanese rapprochement. "After the Revolution in Russia, I did not change my conviction," Matsuoka declared, "and after Mr. Yurenev arrived in Japan, I actively worked for this." He asserted that in 1932 he had tried to obtain authority from the government to conclude the nonaggression pact proposed by the U.S.S.R. and that he had met with the Soviet ambassador in Tokyo at the

[100] *Ibid.*, file 1220, pp. 63–64.
[101] *Ibid.*
[102] *Ibid.*, pp. 110–11.

time allegedly "at the risk of his life." Asking Smetanin
to convey his views to Moscow, Matsuoka reiterated:
"I was an advocate of closer relations with the U.S.S.R.
even when all other countries were against it."[103]

Matsuoka received Smetanin in a room whose walls
were adorned with paintings by the Russian artists Il'ya
Repin, Vladimir Makovsky and Vasilii Perov. Speaking
constantly of his love for Russia and the Russian people and his "indifference to the forms of government in
Russia," he declared that he "simply liked the Russian
people who were close and understandable to him."
Referring to "the smashing of the Ministry for Foreign
Affairs," as he called his almost complete replacement
of the Japanese ambassadors and ministers after his appointment as foreign minister, Matsuoka labelled himself a "revolutionary." Yet he avoided taking any practical steps to solve the outstanding issues between the
Soviet Union and Japan.[104]

The appointment of Tatekawa Yoshitsugu as the new
ambassador to Moscow was hailed by the Japanese press
as marking perhaps a new era in the relations between
the two countries.[105] But the Soviet government was
fully aware of the extremely anti-Soviet position, the
lieutenant general had voiced in the past. The Minister
of the Imperial Household Matsudaira Tsuneo feared
that the Soviet government might not agree to the appointment of Tatekawa as ambassador because of his
anti-Soviet position in the League of Nations, but the
Soviet government understood that his rejection might
be used by anti-Soviet elements to block the possible
stabilization of relations between the two countries.

[103] *Ibid.,* p. 117.
[104] *Ibid.,* file 1376, pp. 29–30.
[105] *Ibid.,* file 1220, p. 160.

Although there was mounting public support for the relaxation of tensions between the Soviet Union and Japan and the newspaper *Hochi* reiterated on September 21 that "if Japan wants to advance southward, she must be free from any misgivings in the North," the Japanese government was reluctant to make any concessions or compromise. As the influential newspaper *Tsugai* wrote on September 21:

The majority of the Japanese people desires the improvement of relations with the U.S.S.R., but this does not mean to sacrifice important Japanese interests for the sake of Soviet-Japanese friendship. Giving up the fishing rights in the northern waters and the liquidation of the concessions on North Sakhalin, which constitute compensation for the Nikolayevsk Incident, would make even the dead turn in their graves.

As a symbol of the establishment of "new" relations with the U.S.S.R. in all fields, the Japanese decided in September 1940 to revive the Japanese-Soviet Society.[106] Hostile statements continued to appear in the Japanese press. On September 20, for example, the *Hokkaido Times* published an interview with General Koiso Kuniaki,[107] one-time minister for colonies, on his arrival at the town of Otomari on South Sakhalin. "Al-

---

[106] The Japanese-Soviet Society had been founded in 1926, after diplomatic relations had been established between Japan and the U.S.S.R. Its chairmen included Prince Kanin and the prominent industrialist Kurachi. In 1940 the society had a membership of 250, but its leaders—Matsuoka, Professor Yasuda, and the journalist Fuse, who had strong anti-Soviet views—hampered its efforts to spread propaganda about achievements of the U.S.S.R. and the need to improve Soviet-Japanese relations.

[107] Koiso was known for his arrogance in speech and action. He had recently been considered for the post of ambassador to the Dutch East Indies, but had talked himself out of the assignment by demanding that he be sent on a man-of-war with the authority to open fire in case of "extraordinary circumstances."

though it appears that we are considered champions of defense in the north and advance on the south," Koiso declared, "I personally consider myself a champion of the advance northward. Japan is a country which is based on the great idea of the 'eight corners [of the world] under one roof,' which extends to the north, and it is following along this road." Koiso criticized the local inhabitants, because "they show little interest in North Sakhalin, inadequate preparedness for the critical moment both from the point of view of language and resources," and advocated "instilling the Japanese spirit and culture in our closest opponent." But the majority of the Japanese newspapers increasingly called for better relations with the Soviet Union.

The objectives of Tatekawa's mission to Moscow reflected the fisheries, oil and coal interests. The commercial and industrial circles hoped to take advantage of the Russian desire to improve relations with Japan to gain economic concessions from the Soviet Union and purchase North Sakhalin from her. At the very least, they wanted an extension of their concession rights in North Sakhalin.

At a farewell luncheon for the ambassador, arranged by the Japanese-Soviet Society on September 26 and attended by the leaders of the fisheries, oil and coal concession companies and by the former Japanese ambassadors to Moscow, Tanaka and Ota, Tatekawa promised to work for better relations between the two countries and a settlement of outstanding problems.

In his talks with Smetanin, Matsuoka never failed to mention the special trust he placed in Tatekawa and contended that his appointment to Moscow was an important step toward improving Soviet-Japanese relations. "Mr. Tatekawa is one of my best acquaintances and will speak in the same terms as I," he declared on October 1, and stressed that Tatekawa, an advocate of closer relations with the U.S.S.R., was popular in the country. Matsuoka asserted that in appointing him he hoped "to turn a new page" in the relations between the two countries.[108]

The fact that Japan was at the same time engaged in negotiations with Germany and Italy concerning the conclusion of a military alliance disconcerted a number of Japanese statesmen. On September 20 Harada told Konoe that he was opposed to such a treaty because it imperiled relations between Japan and the United States and between Japan and the U.S.S.R. He remarked that it would be reasonable to find out first whether Japan could conclude a nonaggression pact with the Soviet Union. "If this should prove possible, it will be possible to conclude the treaty with Germany too. We can conclude the treaty with Germany, but the Soviet Union might refuse."[109]

Konoe favored signing a pact with Germany first, because Germany could then act as a "mediator" in the settlement of differences between the Soviet Union and Japan. He hinted that "Germany has concentrated large forces at the Soviet borders" and warned that in the event of a British victory, Great Britain together with the United States could emerge in the Far East. Besides, he remarked, Japan had initiated the negotiations regarding a new treaty with Germany when Matsuoka had broached the matter to Ott.[110] It was obvious that the Japanese government intended to use the alliance with Germany as a means of pressuring the Soviet Union into

[108] Soviet Archives, 0146, file 1220, pp. 161 and 166–67.
[109] *Ibid.*, file 5/42, pp. 43–44.
[110] *Ibid.*

giving in to the Japanese fisheries and concession demands and into discontinuing her aid to China.

The Tripartite Pact, which was concluded in September, was directed against the Western powers as well as the U.S.S.R. As Ambassador Ott, who was close to Japan's military leaders, telegraphed to Berlin on October 4: "The inherent purpose of the Tripartite Pact is to achieve a new distribution of forces in Europe and the Far East through the destruction of England's world domination. This objective might be obtained by rebuffing America and putting the Soviet Union out of action."[111]

Publicly the Japanese leaders asserted that the Tripartite Pact was not directed against the U.S.S.R., that, on the contrary, it was a vehicle for settling Soviet-Japanese relations. They made reference to Article V, which specifically stated that the pact did not affect the political relations between the respective signatories and the Soviet Union. Privately and secretly, however, they expressed a very different outlook. Thus on September 26, at a meeting of the Research Committee of the Privy Council, Matsuoka declared in response to a question that despite the nonaggression pact between Germany and the U.S.S.R. "Japan will render assistance to Germany in case of a Soviet-German war, while Germany will render assistance to Japan in case of a Russo-Japanese War."[112] He asserted that "an improvement in Russo-Japanese relations will be as desirable as before," and that the Japanese government did not "predetermine war against the Soviet Union," but he warned: "Even if we do witness an improvement in Russo-Japanese relations, this could hardly last more than three

[111] *Ibid.*, 436b, file 14, p. 171.
[112] *Ibid.*, file 17, p. 228; Lupke, 88–89.

years. We will have to reconsider relations between Japan, the Soviet Union, and Germany in two years."[113] He told the Privy Council frankly that he would consider it a correct policy for Germany to increase her threat against the U.S.S.R. so that Japan could take advantage of it for settling her relations with the Soviet Union.[114]

Nevertheless, in preparation for its southward thrust, the Japanese government decided to renew conversations with the U.S.S.R. at once concerning the improvement of Soviet-Japanese relations. In informing Smetanin on October 1 of the conclusion of the Tripartite Pact, Matsuoka stressed the concern of the signatories for peace and for a New Order. He asserted that the pact "far from being directed against the Soviet Union, pins hope on cooperation with the U.S.S.R. in building a new world order and achieving full understanding between Japan and the U.S.S.R.," and expressed the desire "to remove all causes of the unhappy state of affairs in the relations between the two countries." On October 8 Matsuoka reiterated that the Tripartite Pact was but the first step in a shift in Japanese foreign policy and repeated that he wanted "to open a new page in Soviet-Japanese relations."[115]

Protests were raised by extremists who complained that the Tripartite Pact had not produced any "positive results." General Araki told Baron Harada on October 15 that the government's policy toward the Soviet Union led him to believe that Premier Konoe had fallen under Communist influence and that the conclusion of a nonaggression pact with the Soviet Union "would affect not only the domestic affairs of the nation but also its

[113] *Ibid.*, pp. 228–229.
[114] *Ibid.*, p. 231.
[115] *Ibid.*, file 1220, pp. 169, 190.

ideology." Admiral Yamamoto Isoroku, the commander-in-chief of the navy, also expressed doubt to Harada that day that a nonaggression pact with the Soviet Union would be of benefit to Japan.[116]

Nonetheless, the Japanese government went ahead with its plans, and on October 30 Ambassador Tatekawa made a new proposal to the Soviet government for a nonaggression pact on the lines of the Soviet-German pact of 1939.

The draft agreement, communicated by Tatekawa to the Foreign Commissariat, provided that both sides undertake (1) to refrain from aggressive action toward each other, (2) not to give assistance to a third power if the latter finds itself in a state of war with one of the contracting parties, (3) to maintain close contact with each other and consult each other on all questions affecting the interests of both parties, (4) not to participate in any grouping of powers openly or publicly directed against the other, and (5) to solve all disputes and conflicts exclusively by peaceful means. The agreement was to be valid for 10 years.[117]

Tatekawa added that this was a new proposal and that the talks begun by Togo on the question of a neutrality pact would be considered terminated and not used as a basis for discussion. As for the various outstanding issues between Japan and the U.S.S.R., the Japanese government proposed that they be solved after the pact was concluded.[118]

Foreign Commissar Molotov replied that the outstanding issues must be settled before a nonaggression pact could be signed. He recalled that the Soviet government had indicated this to Togo.

[116] *Ibid.*, file 436b, file 5/44, pp. 5–6.
[117] *Ibid.*, file 26, pp. 46–47.
[118] *Ibid.*, p. 13.

On November 18 the Soviet government detailed its views concerning the draft agreement proposed by Japan. It informed Tatekawa that it would be more expedient to conclude a neutrality pact, since Soviet public opinion would link the conclusion of a non-aggression pact with the return to the Soviet Union of territories lost in the Far East, namely South Sakhalin and the Kuril Islands.[119] In the belief that Japan would hardly agree to such conditions, the Soviet government suggested the signing of a neutrality pact instead, with the understanding that the Japanese oil and coal concessions would be liquidated.

The Soviet draft agreement of a neutrality pact provided that (1) peaceful and friendly relations and mutual respect for territorial integrity would be preserved, and (2) in case one of the contracting parties became the object of military action on the part of one or several third powers, the other contracting party would observe neutrality during the entire period of the conflict. The treaty was to be concluded for a period of five years and prolonged automatically for another five years if not denounced one year prior to expiration.[120] A protocol stipulating the liquidation of the Japanese oil and coal concessions in North Sakhalin and the transfer of the property of these concessions to the U.S.S.R. was to be signed simultaneously with the neutrality pact. The Soviet government expressed its willingness to compensate the concessionaires and in addition to supply Japan with 100,000 tons of Sakhalin oil over a period of five years on ordinary commercial terms.[121]

Tatekawa replied on November 21 that his govern-

[119] *Ibid.*, p. 27.
[120] *Ibid.*, pp. 47–50.
[121] *Ibid.*, pp. 48–50.

ment was willing to discuss the neutrality treaty draft, but that the draft protocol was absolutely unacceptable. Instead the Japanese government proposed to purchase North Sakhalin from the Soviet Union in order "to put an end to the disputes between the U.S.S.R. and Japan." But the Russians referred Tatekawa to Molotov's speech at the sixth session of the Supreme Soviet on March 29, 1940, in which he had derided those who were willing to buy what was not for sale.[122]

On December 19 Vice-Minister for Foreign Affairs Ohashi told Smetanin that the Japanese government was striving to improve relations with the Soviet Union and was conducting negotiations in Moscow, but that "the position of the Soviet authorities was not understandable." He wantonly accused the Soviet organs on North Sakhalin of unlawful actions with regard to the oil and coal concessions and asserted that the Mongolian representatives in the border commission adhered to "insincere and arbitrary positions" which prevented the successful conclusion of the work of the commission. Ohashi attempted to blame the U.S.S.R. for the border incidents provoked by Japanese-Manchurian units on the Soviet-Manchurian frontier in early November, and protested that the "unlawful actions" of the Soviet side were not conducive to the conduct of negotiations for the settlement of relations between the two powers.[123]

These and other charges by Ohashi, some of them pure fabrications, others distortions of fact, were made in order to create an atmosphere of anxiety during the Soviet-Japanese negotiations to compel the Soviet government to meet the Japanese demands. But neither such tactics nor the conclusion of the Tripartite Pact

[122] *Ibid.*, 436b, file 26, p. 33.
[123] *Ibid.*, 0146, file 1376, p. 77.

intimidated the U.S.S.R., and the Japanese government, in view of the firm position of the Soviet side, had to abandon the idea of a new fisheries convention that preserved the provisions of the 1928 convention, and suggested the conclusion of an agreement similar to that concluded in 1940. The Soviet government agreed, but demanded a change in the manner of payment, substituting payment in yens at the rate of exchange set by the State Bank of the U.S.S.R. in place of payment by bonds, the Soviet state having sustained serious losses under the old arrangement as the result of drops in the exchange rate of the yen.

On December 30 Tatekawa told Molotov that the Japanese government agreed to make the Matsuo Dockyard Company return to the Soviet Union the advance payment for the ships and to pay 300,000 yen for damages, but that it refused to change the manner of payment for the leases, though it was willing to increase the amount by 10 percent. Molotov countered that a 10 percent increase would not solve the problem. Producing data concerning the exchange rate of the yen and fisheries profits for the past 10 years, he showed that the exchange rate of the yen had dropped over three times, while the profit of the Japanese businessmen had increased almost eightfold.[124]

On January 20, 1941, a protocol prolonging the fisheries convention of 1928 until December 31, 1941, was signed, the Japanese government agreeing to increase lease payments for fishing lots by 20 percent. A binational commission was to be formed to give further consideration to a new fisheries convention.[125]

While the United States, to safeguard her rear in the

[124] *Ibid.*, file 1220, pp. 181, 191–95.
[125] *Vneshnyaya politika SSSR*, vol. IV, pp. 540–41; Lupke, 62–63.

event of war with Germany, was trying to wreck the German-Japanese alliance by appeasing Japan, Japanese close to the Germans, such as Oshima, the former ambassador to Berlin, worked for a Soviet-Japanese-German rapprochement. At a luncheon given by Ambassador Ott on January 8, 1941, Oshima told Smetanin that "he personally is an ardent advocate of the idea of a rapprochement between Japan and the U.S.S.R. and wishes that a nonaggression pact between the U.S.S.R. and Japan be concluded." He asserted that all prominent military leaders wished "to establish friendly relations" with the Soviet Union, anti-Soviet feelings being limited to junior officers on the Soviet-Manchurian border and such military figures as General Araki, Ugaki and Koiso, who were "under the influence of political and business circles, propounding moderation," i.e. the circles that wished to continue the former orientation towards the United States and Great Britain and struggle against the Soviet Union.[126] When Smetanin remarked that the preservation of the Treaty of Portsmouth, which was reminiscent in the minds of the Soviet people of the Treaty of Versailles, constituted an obstacle to the improvement of relations between the two countries, Oshima said that he personally regarded the Portsmouth Treaty as an impending factor, but that its annulment would produce a "burst of indignation" in Japan. "It is possible to retain its forms while introducing certain amendments," he added.[127]

On February 3 a meeting of the Liaison Committee, encompassing representatives of the government and the military, approved at Matsuoka's behest a set of principles for conducting negotiations with Germany, Italy

[126] Soviet Archives, 0146, file 1376, pp. 82–83.
[127] *Ibid.*

and the Soviet Union, which contained a concrete plan for a treaty with the U.S.S.R.[128]

On February 12 Matsuoka told Smetanin that he planned to go to Berlin and Rome via Moscow and that he wanted to exchange opinions with the Soviet leaders, indicating that he "could talk in Moscow in greater detail if the trade and fisheries agreement were concluded by that time." He stressed that Japan had made some concessions, in particular it had agreed to the status of the trade mission in Tokyo, though this had produced "a violent storm" in the Privy Council. Complaining that he had to overcome the opposition of such men as Home Minister Hiranuma Kiichiro, Justice Minister Yanagawa Heisuke, and General Araki in his attempt to achieve a rapprochement with the Soviet Union, Matsuoka expressed his desire for a "heart-to-heart" talk with the Soviet leaders, for he believed that only in personal meetings could statesmen "confide their secrets to each other depending on time, place, and the problem involved."[129]

On March 12 Matsuoka left for Europe, promising to solve the cardinal problems of Japan's foreign policy by his "new diplomacy." The press called his mission "historic" and compared it to the Komura mission, which had negotiated the Treaty of Portsmouth.[130]

Two days later, on March 14, officials of various ministries and government leaders convened a conference to discuss the economic development of the Kuril Islands which, as the Domei News Agency noted, was of "great strategic importance in the defense system of Japan." Allegedly addressing itself to such problems as

---

[128] *Istoriya voiny na Tikhom okeane*, vol. III, pp. 211–12.
[129] Soviet Archives, 0146, file 1376, pp. 112–14 and 205.
[130] *Ibid.*, p. 208.

land reclamation and the agricultural and mining resources of the archipelago, the conference set up a permanent council for the development of the Kuril Islands under the chairmanship of Count Ogasawara, with General Araki, Arima Yoriyasu and Baron Sakamoto as advisers.[131] In view of the well-known anti-Soviet and pro-fascist views of these men, and the emphasis on the strategic importance of the islands, their "development" bore an anti-Soviet character. This was followed in April by the consolidation of the fishery companies operating in the Kuril region and the fishing companies operating in Soviet waters into one concern.[132]

On March 24 during his sojourn in Moscow, Matsuoka proposed the conclusion of a Soviet-Japanese non-aggression pact. In response, the Soviet side reiterated that a neutrality pact would be more appropriate.

Matsuoka's journey to Moscow and Berlin alarmed the United States and Great Britain, which feared that an agreement with the U.S.S.R. might trigger a Japanese drive southward. Matsuoka tried to reassure the American ambassador in Moscow, Laurence Steinhardt, by telling him on March 24 that Japan would "under no circumstances attack Singapore or any American, British or Dutch possessions." Declaring that Japan had no territorial claims, he asserted that she was ready to join the United States in guaranteeing the territorial integrity or independence of the Philippine Islands. Matsuoka said that Japan would not go to war against the United States and "should a conflict take place, this would be the result of action on the part of the United States."[133] When Matsuoka reached Berlin several days later, he

---

[131] *Ibid.*, pp. 213–14.
[132] *Ibid.*, pp. 220–21.
[133] *Ibid.*, 436b, collection 11, file 25, pp. 74–75.

made promises of a very different character to the Germans.

In a number of talks Matsuoka had with Hitler and Ribbentrop, the possibility of war between Germany and the Soviet Union was mentioned. Ribbentrop told Matsuoka on March 27:

> Germany has troops in the east which are ready at any time to invade Russia, and if Russia takes a position hostile to Germany, then the Führer will rout Russia. There is complete confidence in Germany that a war with Russia would end in complete victory for Germany and an ultimate defeat of the Russian armies and the overthrow of her state system. The Führer is convinced that the U.S.S.R. will cease to exist as a great power after the first month of the war.

Ribbentrop repeated the idea several times in his talk with Matsuoka and said that "a conflict with Russia is possible at any time." Matsuoka remarked that "Japan will always be a loyal ally, which will dedicate itself entirely to the common cause and will not be indifferent to it."[134] Thus he virtually promised to give assistance to Germany in the event of a Soviet-German war and not honor the pact he was about to conclude with the U.S.S.R. "No Japanese prime minister or minister for foreign affairs will be able to force Japan to remain neutral in case of a conflict between Russia and Germany," he declared. "In that event circumstances will compel Japan to attack Russia on the side of Germany. No neutrality pact will help in this case."[135]

Stopping in Moscow on his way back from Berlin to Tokyo, Matsuoka called on Molotov on April 8, and reiterated his proposals for a nonaggression pact and the

---

[134] Paul Schmidt, *Statist auf diplomatischer Bühne 1923–45* (Bonn, 1950), pp. 509–10.
[135] Raginsky and Rozenblit, p. 255.

purchase of North Sakhalin. Molotov categorically rejected the proposals. He repeated that the Soviet government would be willing to conclude a neutrality
pact if Japan would give up her concessions on North
Sakhalin.[136]

The same day Matsuoka told Ambassador Steinhardt
that he had made no commitments either in Berlin or in
Rome, that Japan had not pledged herself to enter the
war against the United States, though the situation could
change should the United States declare war on Germany. Matsuoka expressed the wish that President
Roosevelt would help Japan terminate the war in China
by informing Chiang Kai-shek that the United States
would not render assistance to China, if the Koumintang
refused a "just and equitable peace."[137]

The British ambassador handed to Matsuoka on April
12 a letter from Prime Minister Churchill, in which the
latter tried to impress on him that Japanese hope of German assistance in a war against Great Britain was unreal,
that the American economy was superior to that of
Japan, and that in the event of war, Japan would not be
able to overcome the naval superiority of the two
English-speaking nations regardless of the conflict in
Europe, and that Japan, therefore, should seek to maintain amicable relations with Great Britain.[138]

Meanwhile Matsuoka's negotiations with Molotov on
April 9 and 11 had brought no agreement.[139] Matsuoka
sought the conclusion of a nonaggression pact, while
wishing to postpone the settlement of the concessions
question; Molotov, on the other hand, wanted a neu-

[136] Soviet Archives, 06, file 383, pp. 8, 10, 26, 27, 54, 55; Nihon gaiko
hyakunen shoshi, p. 181.
[137] Soviet Archives, fund 436b, file 21, pp. 47–48.
[138] Ibid., pp. 170–78.
[139] Nakamura Kikuo, Showa jidai no seijishi (Tokyo, 1956).

trality pact and the inclusion of a provision for the liquidation of the concessions in the pact itself or in an attached document. Matsuoka promised to make every effort to win over the Japanese government and public opinion to relinquishing the concessions on North Sakhalin. The Soviet government in turn suggested that he give a written obligation to solve the question of the concessions on North Sakhalin in a matter of several months. After Matsuoka talked to Stalin personally on the 12th, agreement was reached and on April 13 a neutrality pact was signed.

The Neutrality Pact consisted of four articles. Article I provided for the maintenance of peaceful and friendly relations between the two powers and mutual respect for each other's territorial integrity and inviolability. Article II stipulated that in case either of them became the object of attack by one or several third powers, the other would observe neutrality throughout the entire conflict. Article III stated that the pact would run for five years and would be extended automatically for another five, if not denounced one year prior to expiration. Article IV provided for prompt ratification and for the exchange of ratifications in Tokyo.[140]

At the time of the signing of the Neutrality Pact, Matsuoka gave a written obligation to solve the question of the liquidation of the North Sakhalin concessions within several months.[141]

While the Soviet Union signed the Neutrality Pact in an attempt to preserve peace in the Far East, Japan had a different purpose. Matsuoka merely bought time until the outbreak of war between Germany and the U.S.S.R. might provide the opportunity for a Japanese attack on

[140] *Vneshnyaya politika SSSR,* vol. IV, pp. 549–551.
[141] *Ibid.,* vol. V, pp. 362–63.

the latter. The Japanese army regarded the pact as a tactical maneuver on the part of the government. At a secret meeting of military commanders at the end of April, General Umezu Yoshijiro, the chief-of-staff of the Kwantung Army, called the pact "a genuinely diplomatic step from the point of view of strengthening the alliance of the three powers," and urged "by no means to relax efforts in preparing for military operations" against the U.S.S.R. in order to obtain "a practical result from this treaty in the future." Umezu demanded that the intensification of preparations for war with the Soviet Union be continued at the same time as the establishment of friendly relations with Russia."[142]

The Kwantung Army had a plan of operations against the U.S.S.R., which entailed the conquest of the Maritime Region, the occupation of such cities as Vladivostok and Blagoveshchensk and the capture of North Sakhalin and Kamchatka.[143] While the true intentions of Japan may be gleaned from this, the Neutrality Pact nonetheless restrained the Japanese militarists to a certain extent and thereby diminished the threat of a two-front war for the Soviet Union. Thus its conclusion was a victory for Soviet diplomacy.

The Neutrality Pact aroused little enthusiasm in Japan. Noting that it was not a pact of mutual assistance, the press commented that despite its signing, the rate of armament production must not be slowed down. *Nichi-Nichi* reflected that its conclusion "was prompted by the necessity of the present time," *Hochi* commenting that "Japan, being on the brink of war with the United States, needs the pact more than the Soviet Union." Agreeing that the pact guaranteed Japan's security, the

---

[142] Soviet Archives, 436b, file 68, pp. 220–21.
[143] Raginsky and Rozenblit, p. 249.

newspapers depicted its conclusion as the failure of the United States and Great Britain to sow discord between the U.S.S.R. and Japan.

Home Minister Hiranuma, who was one of the most reactionary and thickheaded anti-Soviet figures, suppressed further press comments about the treaty. The Privy Council tried to delay its ratification and agreed to it "with pain in their hearts" only after Matsuoka returned from Moscow.[144]

The conclusion of the Neutrality Pact cleared the way for renewed efforts to sign a new fisheries convention. Negotiations had begun on February 12, prior to Matsuoka's departure for Europe. The head of the Japanese delegation, Counselor Nishi Haruhiko, had proposed on February 19 that the new convention, to be concluded for a period of five years, formalize the former lease contracts, i.e. virtually eliminate the auctioning system. The Japanese government agreed in general to a change in the method of payment for the leased lots, but proposed to make a lump sum payment in yen of the total average of all previous payments due for the last three years in place of all other kinds of payments,[145] which would have brought the Soviet Union far less revenue than in the past. As Deputy Foreign Commissar Solomon Lozovskyy had pointed out, Nishi proposed the stabilization of all the lots and the reduction of payments by more than 1 million yen per year, in spite of the fact that Japanese catches of fish and crabs had increased sharply compared with the prerevolutionary period.[146]

Lozovskyy had declared that it was impossible to abandon the auction principle, because natural changes in

---

[144] The treaty was ratified on April 25; ratifications were exchanged on May 21. (Soviet Archives, 0146, file 1376, pp. 230–57.)
[145] Soviet Archives, 0146, file 1220, pp. 161–62.
[146] *Ibid.*

the course of river channels might place the fishery lots in estuaries where fishing was prohibited, because it seemed reasonable to terminate leases on fishing grounds that had not been exploited for some time, and because some areas might have to be closed for strategic reasons. In his words: "The economic importance of fishing lots is subject to change, prices on the world market are subject to change, the whole situation is subject to change, and for these reasons the principle of auctioning which takes into account all these circumstances must be preserved." He added that the method of payment for the leased lots suggested by the Japanese side was not acceptable either. To Nishi's objection that the Japanese had a right to fish in the Far Eastern waters of the U.S.S.R., Lozovsky had reported that Japanese rights derived from the convention and the lease contracts—"with a fisheries convention and lease lots the Japanese subjects will have certain rights, while without a convention there will be no rights."[147]

While Nishi and Lozovsky had been conferring about a new fisheries convention, Ambassador Tatekawa had opened talks with Anastas Mikoyan, the people's commissar for foreign trade, on February 18. But the treaty drafts which Tatekawa had presented on that day and in revised form on March 27, had not provided for most-favored-nation treatment with regard to customs duties and other matters and had been rejected by the Soviet side as a basis for negotiation, so that the talks concerning a treaty of commerce had ground to a halt too.

With the conclusion of the Neutrality Pact in mid-April, the fisheries and trade negotiations were resumed. Linking the fisheries and trade agreements with the liqui-

[147] *Ibid.*, p. 171.

dation of the North Sakhalin concessions, the Soviets succeeded on May 31 in obtaining a more specific commitment from Matsuoka, namely that Japan would give up the concession within six months from the date of signature of the Neutrality Pact. In return, the Soviets modified their stand on the auction system and expressed willingness to extend some of the Japanese leases without bidding, but the progress in the fishery talks and the initialing of a commercial treaty draft on June 12 came to naught when Germany, Japan's Axis partner, suddenly invaded the Soviet Union on June 22.[148]

[148] Soviet Archives, 0146, file 200, p. 121; file 1121, pp. 151–53; file 1376, pp. 181–83 and 336–37.

4

Japan and the United States:
The Policy of Collision

The German seizure of Denmark and the Netherlands, the fall of France and the enormous difficulties
facing Britain whetted the appetite of the Japanese
aggressors. The influential press more and more
openly called on the government to take advantage of
the situation for the realization of far-reaching plans
of aggrandizement. However, the Japanese leaders,
who intended to extend their sphere of expansion at
the expense of the colonial powers, still feared to
start an open war.

While concentrating on solving the China Question, the Yonai government, which guided Japan during the first half of 1940, planned expansion in the
South Pacific. Yet the government and its supporters
among the "moderate" elements at the court and a
large section of the financial-industrial circles, as well
as the leaders of the long-established political parties,
assessed Japan's military, financial, economic and po-

198

litical position more soberly than the military-ultranationalist elements. They were aware of the difficulties they would have in carrying out their plan, saw the growing displeasure of the United States, and realized they would not get effective aid from Germany and Italy. The might of the Soviet Union, which was not involved in war, also aroused their apprehensions.

The Yonai government, therefore, pursued a policy of making the utmost use of the possibilities created by the war in Europe with the least risk and expenditure. It stressed diplomatic negotiations and a gradual increase in pressure on Great Britain, while adopting a wait-and-see attitude towards the Soviet Union and the United States.

The Konoe government, which took office in July 1940, after military opposition had toppled the Yonai administration, was more forceful. It labored for the conclusion of a military alliance with Germany and Italy and the establishment of a Greater East Asia Co-Prosperity Sphere, even at the risk of war with the United States. The Tripartite Pact, which was signed on September 27, sought to coordinate the actions of the three aggressive powers for the attainment of world hegemony.

In encouraging a Japanese attack on Singapore in order to bring England to her knees, the Germans tried to dispel Japanese misgiving about a war with the United States. Foreign Minister Ribbentrop told Ambassador Oshima on February 23, 1941, that the capture of Great Britain's Far Eastern bastion without a declaration of war would be "the best way to keep America out of the conflict."[1]

[1] DGFP, vol. XII, doc. 4.

Oshima replied that preparations for the seizure of Singapore would be completed by about the end of May, but that a conflict with the United States could not be ruled out. When he informed Ribbentrop that Japanese plans envisaged also the seizure of Hongkong and the Philippines, the German foreign minister suggested that the Philippine "project" be postponed, for he knew of the impending attack on the U.S.S.R. and was eager, therefore, to keep the United States out of the conflict until the Soviet-German war was over.[2] The following month Ribbentrop reiterated to Matsuoka, during his visit to Berlin, that "the capture of Singapore would perhaps be most likely to keep America out of the war, because the United States could scarcely risk sending its fleet into Japanese waters." He argued that Roosevelt would find himself in a difficult position if Japan captured Singapore in a single determined attack and that if, despite everything, he would want to declare war on Japan, the prospect of seeing the Philippines issue settled in favor of Japan would probably restrain him from doing so.[3] Should the United States nonetheless open hostilities in response to the Japanese seizure of Singapore, Hitler personally assured Matsuoka, Germany would side with Japan, "for the strength of the allies in the Tripartite Pact lay in their acting in common."[4] But there was general agreement that war with the United States should be avoided if possible; Germany and Japan preferred to deal with their adversaries one by one.

Meanwhile the long-standing rivalry of the imperialist

[2] *Ibid.*
[3] *Ibid.*, vol. XII, doc. 218.
[4] *Ibid.*, doc. 266.

powers had grown ever more acute. American capitalists could not reconcile themselves to the gradual subordination by Japan of China, a potentially vast market for the United States, nor could they agree to Japanese seizure of Southeast Asia, a major source of strategic raw materials. But while some American leaders realized that war with Japan was inevitable, others, linked with business concerns that had lucrative dealings with Japan, tried to avoid a collision by appeasing Japan.

The deterioration in America's relations with Germany directly affected her Far Eastern policy. Faced with the growing menace of Germany in the Atlantic, the United States endeavored to break up the Japanese-German alliance by coming to terms with Japan. Not only did she feel that some concessions at China's expense might postpone an American clash with Japan, but that Japanese expansion in Southeast Asia was for the purpose of securing the resources for war against the Soviet Union. Japan herself was not in a position to strike at once. In August 1940 the Japanese naval command informed the government that it would require at least eight months to prepare for war against the United States and Britain.[5] Negotiations with the United States would give her time to arm, at the same time that they would camouflage her designs. It was the mutual desire to delay an armed conflict that gave rise to the confidential talks that were begun between the two governments in the spring of 1941.

On April 16 Secretary of State Cordell Hull proposed an agreement based on the following four provisions: (1) respect for the territorial integrity and

[5] Hattori Takushiro, *Dai-Toa senso zenshi* (Tokyo, 1953), vol. I, p. 171.

sovereignty of all nations; (2) support of the principle of noninterference in the internal affairs of other countries; (3) support of the principle of equality, including equality of commercial opportunity; and (4) nondisturbance of the *status quo* in the Pacific.[6]

When Ribbentrop, who had not been informed by the Japanese of their negotiations with Washington, learned about them from German intelligence sources, he summoned Oshima on May 3, and, visibly angered, showed him the draft agreement proposed by Hull, commenting indignantly that he could not understand the intentions of the Japanese government.[7] Oshima, to whom Ribbentrop had talked "as a friend," had not known about the negotiations and was deeply embarrassed. The German military attaché in Tokyo speculated two days later in a telegram concerning rumors of a visit by Matsuoka to Washington, reported by Oshima, that such a visit might nullify the results achieved during Matsuoka's stay in Germany and Italy and raise the question of Oshima's resignation, which would "spell the complete collapse" of the main line of German foreign policy.[8]

On May 5 Ott called on Matsuoka and insisted on being informed about Japanese-American relations.

---

[6] FRUS: *Japan, 1931–1941*, vol. II (Washington, 1943), p. 407. Hull's proposal was rather vague. A more specific plan for an understanding between the United States and Japan was advanced by two American Catholic priests, Bishop James E. Walsh and Father James M. Drought, with the support of influential American financiers. But although the document provided for American recognition of Manchukuo, the signing of a new trade agreement with massive credits for Japan, and American support in merging the Chiang Kai-shek and Wang Ching-wei governments, the Japanese military balked at the stipulation that Japanese troops evacuate China proper and demanded that the "China problem" be settled without foreign interference.

[7] Soviet Archives, 436b, 10, file 21, p. 2.

[8] *Ibid.*, 23, file 70, pp. 50–51.

Realizing that the Nazis knew of the talks with the United States, Matsuoka gave Ott the gist of the American proposals and the draft agreement and a copy of the oral reply that Nomura was to make, assuring him that he would oppose any decisions incompatible with the Tripartite Pact.[9]

That day and again on the 6th, Ott warned Matsuoka against seeking an agreement with the United States, which sought to wrest Japan away from the Axis and prevent her from taking advantage of Britain's weakened position and implementing her plans in Greater East Asia.[10] Matsuoka agreed, but pointed out that not only business circles but also senior naval officers were taking the American proposals seriously. He said he would try to compel the United States to keep out of the European war, but was not sure he would be able to manage it as the United States was moving rapidly towards involvement in the war. He told Ott that he would like to have Ribbentrop's opinion of the American proposal as soon as possible.[11]

On May 9 Ribbentrop showed Oshima a telegram from Ott, giving the draft of Japan's reply to the United States. He said that as far as he could judge, Japan had initiated the negotiations. Recalling Matsuoka's promise to enter into the war against the Soviet Union if war broke out between Germany and the latter and his assurances of Japan's intention to attack Singapore, he contended that an agreement

---

[9] DGFP, vol. XII, doc. 454. Nomura had been instructed to intimidate Hull by telling him that Japan was confident that Germany and Italy would defeat Great Britain and her allies and that Japan would remain faithful to her commitments under the Tripartite Pact. (*Ibid.*, doc. 455)
[10] *Ibid.*, docs. 456 and 466.
[11] *Ibid.*, doc. 464.

with the United States would be senseless and dangerous for Japan.[12]

On May 9 and 10 Ott called on Matsuoka in an attempt to obtain the text of the American proposals, but Matsuoka confined himself only to general comments about the proposals, though he promised to delay sending a reply to the Americans until hearing from Ribbentrop about the matter.[13] He said that he wanted to obtain American assurances that the United States really did not intend to enter the European war and would induce Chiang Kai-shek to start direct negotiations with Japan without American participation; only after such assurances were received would Japan be prepared to begin scrutinizing the American proposals in detail.[14] He repeated that he would not engage in negotiations "detrimental to the Tripartite Pact, the new order in Greater East Asia and the interest of his allies."

German attempts to delay, if not prevent, Japanese-American talks were thwarted as President Roosevelt threatened that the United States would begin patrolling the high seas and organizing convoys of American vessels, if Japanese-American talks did not get under way.[15]

On May 12 Ambassador Nomura presented to Secretary of State Hull not the preliminary questions, mentioned by Matsuoka, but the complete draft of an agreement covering all the fundamental aspects of the relations between the two countries.[16] Pressure

[12] Soviet Archives, 436b, file 48, pp. 45–46.
[13] DGFP, vol. XII, docs. 480 and 484.
[14] *Ibid.*, 483.
[15] *Ibid.*, 488.
[16] For the text of the Japanese reply on May 12, see FRUS, *Japan 1931–1941*, vol. II, pp. 420–25.

from Germany and the Japanese military had brought a number of additions and amendments: (1) Japan declared her intention to honor her military commitments under the Tripartite Pact; (2) she rejected all the proposed terms for a peace settlement with China and intended to dictate terms herself; (3) in the question of Japanese expansion in the Southwestern Pacific, provision was made for a number of cases when, depending on the situation and on the action of other countries, Japan would be compelled to resort to armed force.

The new draft sought to insure Japanese control over China and various regions in Southeast Asia. It demanded recognition of the three "Konoe principles," proclaimed on December 22, 1938, which implied the "independence" of Manchukuo, "economic cooperation" between Japan, Manchukuo and China, and the conclusion of an agreement for "joint defense against Communism." There was no mention of the Open Door, which was the basic channel for American imperialist penetration into the colonies, dependent countries and markets of other countries.

Although the draft had already been transmitted, Ott called on Matsuoka, accompanied by the Italian Ambassador Mario Indelli, and handed him a long telegram from Ribbentrop expounding the German attitude regarding the Japanese talks with the United States. Warning that the defeat of Germany and Italy would signify the collapse of Japan as well, Ribbentrop contended that the purpose of the American proposal was to give Roosevelt a tactical advantage for entering the war by showing the American people that he had done everything in his power to preserve peace. Arguing that it was important for Roosevelt to reach an agreement which would guarantee Japan's nonparticipation in the war on the side of the Axis, Ribbentrop proposed that Japan reply that such steps by the United States as the patrolling of the high seas and the organization of convoys would force Japan to enter the war in conformity with the Tripartite Pact. If the United States halted all acts that might provoke an armed conflict, the Japanese government would study the details of the American proposal.[17]

Ott sharply criticized the reply made before the receipt of the Ribbentrop cable. He complained that there was not "even the mildest criticism of America's unneutral conduct" in her interference in the European war and asserted that the text showed that Japan had abandoned the New Order envisaged by the Tripartite Pact. Matsuoka brushed aside Ott's accusations and repeated that domestic considerations had compelled him to send a reply without waiting for the German views. He asked Germany to trust him, promising to keep in mind the interests of Germany and Italy, and reiterating that Japan would side with Germany in the event of war between the latter and the Soviet Union. Matsuoka declared he would be "extremely grateful to the German government for timely information on Germany's intentions so that he could take a position accordingly."[18]

On May 14 Ribbentrop personally expressed his dissatisfaction with the Japanese reply to the United States proposal to Ambassador Oshima in Rome. He

---

[17] DGFP, vol. XII, doc. 496. The Germans sought to prevent an agreement between Japan and the United States, for such an agreement would have weakened Germany's position in Europe by depriving her in effect of the support of her Japanese ally.

[18] *Ibid.*, doc. 512.

resented that Matsuoka had acted without first getting his views, and declared that the Japanese draft agreement might automatically deprive the Tripartite Pact of all significance.[19]

The next day Ribbentrop instructed Ott to call on Matsuoka again and tell him that his independent reply to the United States was unacceptable to the German government; inasmuch as the negotiations were being conducted in secret, very few people could have exerted pressure on Matsuoka and his excuse that he had been forced to act precipitatedly was untenable.[20] Ott duly conveyed this to Matsuoka on May 17, and told him that Germany believed the best way to prevent American participation in the war was for Japan to refuse to negotiate with the United States. An objective of the Tripartite Pact was to prevent third powers from entering the war; any treaty between a pact member and a third power weakened the Axis alliance. Realizing, however, that Japan would not abandon her negotiations with the United States, Ott insisted again on the inclusion of an American commitment not to interfere in the war between the Axis countries and Great Britain and of the reaffirmation of Japan's commitments under the Tripartite Pact. Ott demanded that Germany be kept fully informed about the course of the negotiations and be told immediately of the American reply. For Japan to reach an agreement with the United States without consulting Germany would be a violation of the Tripartite Pact.[21]

Matsuoka replied that he had told the British and

[19] Soviet Archives, 436b, 10, file 21, pp. 215–16.
[20] DGFP, vol. XII, doc. 518.
[21] *Ibid.*, docs. 518, 537.

American ambassadors on May 15 that the introduction of the American convoy system might be regarded as an indirect attack on Japan's allies and that Japan would have to honor her obligations under the Tripartite Pact,[22] that he had intimated in his message to Hull that he would not let the Tripartite Pact be affected, and had upheld this viewpoint at a secret meeting of the cabinet and in conversation with members of the government. As Ott described Matsuoka's attitude in his notes of the conversation:

> He regarded the prospects of Japanese-American negotiations with extreme skepticism and counted as before on America entering the war soon. His motive in negotiating with the U.S.A. was purely to delay or if possible to prevent the United States from entering the war, and in addition also to eliminate an increase in the present American aid to England.[23]

Matsuoka promised to inform Germany and Italy at once about the American reply and to "consult them as far as possible," but noted that Japan could not await the opinion of her Axis partners in every case, especially if a quick statement were absolutely necessary.

On May 17 Weizsäcker summoned Oshima and in a long talk conveyed his government's extreme anxiety over the outcome of the Japanese-American negotia-

---

[22] *Ibid.*, doc. 516.

[23] *Ibid.*, doc. 537. Ott believed that Matsuoka went back on his promises because of pressure from pro-British circles at court (Minister of the Imperial Household Matsudaira Tsuneo), industrialists and capitalists (Minister Without Portfolio Ogura), influential naval officers, among them Admiral Nomura Kichisaburo, the Japanese ambassador to the United States, and some members of the Army Command and Home Minister Hiranuma Kuchiro, who wanted to win time in order to secure freedom of action against the Soviet Union. The neutralization of Japan would have seriously affected German plans of using her against Great Britain, the United States, and the U.S.S.R.

tions. On May 20 Oshima reported to Matsuoka that he had come to the conclusion that "Germany suspects that while Japan is seeking to prevent American participation in the war she is, at the same time, trying to evade honoring her pledge to enter the war." It was very unpleasant to feel, he wrote, that "Germany's interests have been betrayed." "It will be very bad if Japan loses the trust of Germany and Italy, who will be the leading force in Europe," Oshima stated and warned: "I fear that double-faced diplomacy of this kind will lead Japan to complete international isolation in the course of the critical period that might set in after the war." He argued that an agreement with the United States would prevent a radical settlement of the "China problem" and deprive Japan of the "convenient opportunity for territorial expansion southward and the possibility of attacking Singapore." It would mean "the abandonment by Japan of her great mission of establishing a New Order in Greater East Asia."[24]

On June 8 Nomura communicated the American reply to Tokyo. The Americans considered that they could, with reservations, accept the three "Konoe principles" relative to "defense against Communism" and economic cooperation between Japan and China, but they refused to recognize Japanese supremacy in China and the restriction of the interests of other countries. On June 21 Hull handed to Nomura another document, elaborating the American position, and took the opportunity to make an oral statement, in which he sharply criticized Matsuoka and his supporters for their readiness to fight on the side of Hitler, should the United States become involved in the European war.

[24] Soviet Archives, fund 436b, 10, file 21, pp. 217–18.

The German invasion of the Soviet Union on June 22 sparked an acute conflict among the Japanese leaders. Matsuoka favored an immediate attack on the U.S.S.R., while Konoe held that the deflection of the Soviet Union's attention to the defense of her western frontiers gave Japan a free hand to expand southwards. Feeling that Germany had betrayed Japan in going to war with the Soviet Union without so much as notifying Tokyo in advance while insisting that Japan attack the British possessions in the Far East, Konoe and his supporters in the government argued that the situation had to be utilized to settle Japan's differences with the United States and that an attack on the U.S.S.R. should be postponed until a more propitious time. Japan's cardinal task, Konoe argued, was to settle her relations with the United States and clear the road for Japanese expansion in China and Southeast Asia. Her membership in the Tripartite Pact hindered the attainment of final victory in China by threatening the involvement of the United States in the war, and should, therefore, be dissolved. Naval leaders supported Konoe's view, Navy Chief-of-Staff Osami Nagano recommending to the Emperor Japan's renunciation of the pact on the ground that "the diplomatic relations between Japan and the United States cannot be regulated as long as such an alliance exists."[25] In a compromise decision on June 23, top army and navy leaders agreed that military operations would be conducted simultaneously in the north and south in accordance with changes in the international situation.[26]

[25] *Ibid.*, file 22, p. 47.
[26] *Gendai shiryo,* vol. II. p. 176. Protocol of interrogation No. 17 of March 6, 1942. Evidence by Ozaki, adviser to Konoe. When the Soviet ambassador queried Matsuoka that day about Japan's attitude toward the

At an imperial conference on July 2, attended by top-ranking Japanese statesmen and military leaders in the presence of the emperor, a program of "National Policies of the Empire in view of the Changing Situation" was adopted. Emphasizing that Japan would adhere firmly to the policy of building the Greater East Asia Co-Prosperity Sphere and continue her attempts to settle the China Incident, it noted that "this will involve taking steps to advance south, and, depending on changes in the situation, will involve a settlement of the Northern Problem as well."

Although our attitude to the war between Germany and the Soviet Union is founded on the spirit of the Tripartite Pact [the conferees agreed], we shall not intervene in it for the time being and shall preserve our independent position, at the same time secretly completing military preparations against the Soviet Union. In the meantime, diplomatic negotiations must be conducted with the utmost caution. If the war between Germany and the Soviet Union takes a course favorable to the Empire, we shall, by resorting to armed force, settle the Northern Problem and ensure stability in the north.

The program gave preference to the south, however, and here too diplomatic negotiations were to be accompanied by preparations for war.[27]

Soviet-German war, Matsuoka evaded giving a direct reply, but stressed that the Tripartite Pact was the foundation of Japan's foreign policy and in the event the two agreements came into conflict the Neutrality Pact would lose force. By this statement Matsuoka nullified the Soviet-Japanese Neutrality Pact. The desire of Matsuoka and Togo to attack the U.S.S.R. without further delay was not supported by the other ministers, however, and the Japanese sat back to see how the German campaign in Russia developed.

[27] *Istoriya voiny na Tikhom okeane,* vol. III, pp. 379–80.

When Ott was informed of the decisions of the conference he attached special significance to Japanese preparations for operations against the U.S.S.R. and drew the conclusion that Japanese participation in the war against the Soviet Union was inevitable.

Meanwhile the American counterproposals, dated June 21, had been received in Tokyo. The United States objected to Japan's claims to economic supremacy in China and in the Western Pacific as well as to the presence of Japanese troops in China. The latter objection was not formulated in categorical terms, however, the implication being that the prolonged Japanese military presence in China would not be opposed. President Roosevelt undertook to suggest that China negotiate peace "on a basis mutually advantageous and acceptable" to both sides, if the Japanese terms were in line with the principles of good-neighborly, friendly relations and respect for sovereignty and territorial rights. The possibility was left open for "further discussion of the question of co-operative defense against communistic activities, including the stationing of Japanese troops in Chinese territory, and the question of economic cooperation between Japan and China." The Americans expressed willingness to discuss United States recognition of Manchoukuo and the neutralization of the Philippines; they offered to restore normal trade and economic relations with Japan. In exchange they demanded the restoration of "equal opportunity in trade relations" and Japan's assurances that she was not bound by any obligations to take steps that would come into conflict or infringe upon the fundamental aims of "the present agreement."[28]

The American counterproposal was an attempt by the United States to neutralize the Tripartite Pact vis-à-vis herself. It showed that the United States was not absolutely committed to uphold the territorial integrity and independence of China, but was

[28] Soviet Archives, 236b, 10, file 21, pp. 284–86.

prepared to make a deal with Japan at Chinese expense. The readiness to negotiate "cooperative defense against communistic activities" was aimed against the U.S.S.R. and made it plain that the American government did not object to aggression against the Soviet Union or to the suppression of the national liberation movement in China and other Asian countries. On the other hand, Washington's unwillingness to relinquish American interests in China and the South Pacific remained an obstacle to a Japanese-American agreement.

At the Liaison Conference on July 10 Matsuoka, pressured by the Germans, urged that the negotiations with the United States be broken off. That night Konoe summoned Matsuoka and the war and navy ministers to work out a common position. After coordinating their views with the army and navy commands, they proposed at the Liaison Conference of July 12 to accept the American proposal as a basis for negotiation, provided the United States clearly understood that (1) Japan's attitude toward the war in Europe was determined by treaty commitments and the interests of self-defense; (2) the China Question had to be settled on the basis of the Konoe "three principles" without American interference; and (3) Japan reserved the rights, if necessary, to employ armed force in the Pacific.

Fearing a conflict with the military, Matsuoka raised no objections, but under the pretext of illness delayed the reply to the United States. His "illness" did not prevent him from meeting Ott the same day and informing him that he planned to send first a telegram rejecting Hull's verbal statement and then the Japanese counterproposals. Konoe intervened on

July 14, demanding that the rejection and the counterproposals be sent simultaneously, lest the former
be interpreted in the United States to mean that Japan intended to terminate the negotiations.[29] But
Matsuoka defied the premier's instructions and that
day sent only the telegram rejecting the Hull statement. He ordered Yamamoto Kumaichi, chief of
the Bureau of European and Asian Affairs, to inform
Ott of the contents of the Japanese proposal before
sending it to the United States. When Terasaki Hi-
denari, the chief of the Bureau of American Affairs,
learned of the matter, however, he went to Vice-
Minister Ohashi on his own authority and persuaded
him to sanction the dispatch of the Japanese counterproposal by telegraph to the United States.[30]

Konoe and the military were furious at Matsuoka's
arbitrary conduct and his open support of German
policy. On July 16 Konoe handed in his resignation
and two days later formed a new cabinet without
Matsuoka. In his place as foreign minister he appointed Admiral Toyoda Teijiro, who held that a
clash with the United States had to be avoided,
though he reassured Ott on July 20 that he would
continue Matsuoka's policy and "further strengthen
the close alliance between Japan, Germany and Italy"
and move forward toward their common objectives.[31]

The Japanese occupation of southern Indochina at
the end of July 1941 worsened relations with the
United States and Great Britain. On July 26 the
latter countries and the authorities of the Dutch East
Indies froze Japanese assets. On August 1 the United

[29] *Ibid.*, pp. 412–13.
[30] *Istoriya voiny na Tikhom okeane*, vol. III, pp. 220–21.
[31] Soviet Archives, 426b, 10, file 21, pp. 420–421.

States placed an embargo on the export to Japan of a long list of strategic goods. In retaliation Japan seized control of British and American property in China. In early August Japan presented Thailand with a note, demanding territory for military bases and the right to control the output of tin, rubber and rice, an action which evoked American and British protests. The American oil embargo inclined the Japanese navy to favor the commencement of hostilities before Japan's oil reserves became exhausted; it calculated that it had enough oil for about two years, after which it would be paralyzed. But Konoe was opposed to embarking on another war before the conflict in China was settled. Assessing the war potential of the United States more correctly than the military, he tried to reach agreement with her for the joint domination of the peoples of Asia and the Pacific basin.

The Imperial Conference of September 6 adopted a set of "Principles for Implementing the State Policy of the Empire." Japan would demand of the United States and Great Britain that they (1) not interfere in her attempts to settle the China Incident; (2) undertake no action which might threaten Japanese security; and (3) insure Japan with the necessary resources. In turn she was prepared to withdraw her troops from Indochina "after a lasting and just peace was established" and to guarantee the neutrality of the Philippines.

Although the conferees agreed to resort to war only if no prospects of achieving their demands could be seen by mid-October,[32] they realized that it would be next to impossible to bring the United States around to their view by peaceful means, particularly in such

[32] *Ibid.*, p. 454.

a short time. Though they favored attaining Japan's objectives primarily through diplomacy, the military preparations that were to be completed towards the close of the negotiations undermined their significance and created a situation in which war was becoming inevitable, particularly as the imperial court and big business were becoming increasingly receptive to the position of the military.[33]

As October came without significant progress in the negotiations, the Japanese army increased its pressure on the government. General Tojo Hideki and his supporters categorically opposed the withdrawal of Japanese troops from China and demanded the discontinuation of the talks with the United States. Unable to come to terms with the Americans, who had rebuffed his proposal for a personal meeting with Roosevelt, Konoe quit the political stage, unwilling to take the responsibility for beginning the Pacific War. He recommended that Tojo be appointed premier to carry out his own policy.

When Tojo formed a new cabinet on October 18, the German government sought Oshima's opinion about the change in administration. Oshima replied indirectly: "At the time the Tripartite Pact was signed the Japanese government was sure that the Greater East Asia Co-Prosperity Sphere could be created only by advancing southwards sword in hand. This action had been prepared."[34] To ensure that Japan remain loyal to the Axis cause and to obstruct her negotiations with the United States, Germany informed Japan that month of her desire to renew the

---

[33] *Istoriya voiny na Tikhom okeane,* vol. III. pp. 233–234.
[34] Soviet Archives, 436b, 23, file 70, p. 84.

Anti-Comintern Pact.[35] As long as there was hope of reaching an agreement with the United States, the Japanese government did not want to complicate matters by reaffirming the pact, but on November 5 an imperial conference decided to begin hostilities in early December if the negotiations with the United States were not concluded successfully by midnight, November 30.[36] A secret order, dated November 8, scheduled the outbreak of war for December 8, Japan time.[37] Ambassador Nomura was instructed to complete the negotiations by November 25. He was warned that "the success or failure of the present negotiations will tremendously influence the destiny of the Japanese Empire."[38]

Any hope that Tokyo might have had of a successful outcome of the negotiations faded, however, when Hull declared that until Japan clarified her attitude toward Germany and Italy and firmly stated her intention to pursue a peaceful policy, there could be no question of the cessation of American aid to the Chungking government. Tokyo turned to Berlin to ascertain Germany's position in the event of war between Japan and the United States, and after being reassured by Ribbentrop on November 21 that Germany would duly declare war on the United States,[39] gave its consent to the renewal of the Anti-Comintern Pact for another five years.

The Anti-Comintern Pact was renewed with much pomp in Berlin on November 25. The next day Hull

[35] *Ibid.*, pp. 143–44.
[36] *Ibid.*, 436b, 22, file 67, pp. 73–74.
[37] *Ibid.*, 436b, 10, file 21, p. 559.
[38] *Ibid.*, pp. 533–37.
[39] International Military Tribunal of the Far East (hereafter cited as IMTFE), Record of Proceedings, pp. 24643–44.

handed to Nomura and Kurusu his reply to the Japanese proposals. It contained more demands than had ever been presented by the United States to Japan and, though not accompanied by threats, was in effect an ultimatum. At a meeting with the Japanese envoys Roosevelt showed no desire to modify the note.[40]

The Imperial Conference of December 1 approved the date for the outbreak of hostilities, but decided to continue the negotiations with the United States in order to preserve the element of surprise.[41] On December 6 Nomura received the final reply from Japan to the United States. It was a very long telegram and took the Japanese longer to decipher than the Americans, who had broken the Japanese code and were reading the dispatches between the Foreign Office and its representatives. By the time that Nomura and Kurusu called on the American Secretary of State the following day, the Japanese navy had sunk the bulk of the American fleet at Pearl Harbor, attacked the British possessions in the Far East and launched the Pacific War. On December 11 Germany and Italy declared war on the United States, asserting that America had "violated" her neutrality and had engaged in open hostilities against Germany, thereby creating a state of war between their countries.

That day Japan, Germany, and Italy signed a new agreement, supplementing the Tripartite Pact. They pledged themselves to conduct the war against the United States jointly until victory, with all means at

[40] William L. Langer and S. Everett Gleason, *The Undeclared War, 1941* (New York, 1953), p. 905.
[41] Soviet Archives, 436b, 11, file 22, p. 8.

their disposal; not to conclude a separate armistice or peace without full, mutual agreement; and after the victorious conclusion of the war to collaborate closely in the establishment of a New Order.[42]

[42] Hearings, part 35, pp. 691–92.

Epilogue

Japan's attack against the possessions of the United States and Great Britain was a corollary of her aggression in East and Southeast Asia and of her attempt to gain control over the peoples of China, India, Burma, Indonesia and Indo-China. Her desire to seize also a substantial part of Soviet territory strengthened her collaboration with Nazi Germany, which had invaded the U.S.S.R.

The German-Japanese-Italian treaties of September 27, 1940, and December 11, 1941, were buttressed on January 18, 1942, by a military agreement which sought to "insure effective cooperation between the three powers with the aim of destroying the armed forces of the enemy as quickly as possible." The military agreement divided the war effort into zones of operation. Japan was assigned the waters east of longitude 70° E. and Soviet territory as far west as the Ural Mountains. Germany and Italy were to operate in the waters west of longitude 70° E. and in Soviet territory as far east as and including the Ural Mountains. Japan undertook to destroy the key bases and land, naval and air forces of Great Britain, the United States and the Netherlands in the Pacific and Indian Oceans and to occupy their possessions in Greater East Asia. Germany and Italy were to annihilate the key bases, armed forces and merchant ships of Great Britain and the United States in the Middle East, the Mediterranean and the Atlantic Ocean. The agreement provided also for broad collaboration in the conduct of economic warfare, the exchange of military, economic and technological information, and the establishment of air and sea communication between the Axis powers.[1]

In January 1943 Germany, Italy and Japan signed a general agreement on economic and financial collaboration during the war. In a secret protocol they gave themselves priority of treatment over third parties in the economic blocs which they hoped to set up upon victory.[2] Trade agreements, signed soon afterwards, spelled out the nature of mutual assistance. Japan, for example, pledged to supply Germany's aircraft and tank industries with Thai rubber.

Japan rendered her European partners great assistance by diverting substantial American, British and Soviet forces from the European theater of operations. In 1942 Japan pinned down nearly 40 Soviet divisions in the Far East by keeping over a million troops—about one third of her army, half of her air force and two-thirds of her tank forces—along the borders of the U.S.S.R. In contravention of her obligations under the Neutrality Pact, Japan supplied Germany with secret information about the Soviet Union's economic, political and military position, gathered by her diplomatic and military representatives in the U.S.S.R., and obstructed the Soviet war

[1] Soviet Archives, 436b, file 14, pp. 282–85.
[2] IMTFE, exhibit 50, 3520; Proceedings, p. 34044.

effort by provoking frontier incidents and by hindering the transportation of food supplies to the Russian Far East. In the period from August 1941 to December 1944 Japanese warships detained 178 merchant vessels; 18 were seized or sunk in 1941–45.[3]

Japan did not respond to Germany's insistence that she enter the war against the U.S.S.R. Like Germany she was compelled, after initial successes, to go over to the defense of the territories she had seized. An attack on the Soviet Union would have necessitated the redeployment of Japanese forces from China and the South Pacific to the north, a risk that the Japanese High Command was not prepared to take.

As Soviet victories at Kursk and Belgorod and Anglo-American successes in the Mediterranean brought Germany's defeat into sight, Japan sought to help Germany by mediating an end to the Soviet-German war. But the Soviet government rejected a Japanese proposal, made in September 1943, to send a special mission to Moscow,[4] rejoining that "in the existing war situation the Soviet Government rules out all possibility of an armistice or peace with Germany or her satellites in Europe."[5] When another Japanese attempt, a year later, to send a special mission to Moscow and Berlin to restore amicable relations between the Soviet Union and Germany (and thereby permit Germany to throw all her forces against the British and Americans) was rebuffed by the Soviet government,[6] the Japanese leaders began to think of

[3] L.N. Kutakov, *Istoriya sovetsko-yaponskikh diplomaticheskikhotnoshenii* (Moscow, 1962), pp. 374–76.
[4] Soviet Archives, 06, file 431, pp. 47–50.
[5] *Ibid.*, 0146, file 26, p. 8.
[6] Shigemitsu, *Japan and Her Destiny*, p. 296; Japan Foreign Office, *Shusen shiroku* (Historical documents on the ending of the war) (Tokyo, 1952), pp. 157, 165–66.

negotiating peace with the United States and Great Britain through the mediation of other countries. It was their hope that the United States and Great Britain would not wish to see Japan utterly defeated, but would want to use her as a counterweight to Soviet influence in the Far East as well as national liberation movements in Asia.

But although peace feelers were initiated through neutral Sweden in the autumn of 1944[7] and the Chiang Kai-shek government was approached at about the same time through Mao Pin, an official of Wang Ching-wei's puppet government who was on good terms with high Kuomintang officials,[8] the Japanese government did not fully grasp the seriousness of the situation and failed to act with sufficient determination. While the seizure of Okinawa by the Americans in June enabled the United States Air Corps to bomb Japanese towns systematically, the Allied forces were unable to blockade Japan completely until the Soviet Union's entry into the Pacific War, and the Japanese were confident that they could resist the Americans and the British for a long time. In fact, American and British military planners thought the same; Churchill expected the war against Japan to last until 1947.[9]

The denunciation of the Neutrality Pact by the U.S.S.R. on April 5, 1945, was a heavy blow for Japanese diplomacy, which had hoped to take advantage of the contradictions existing among the Allied powers to secure a peace which would leave Japan in possession of some of the territories she had

[7] Shigemitsu, *Showa no doran*, pp. 262–63.
[8] *Shusen shiroku*, p. 246.
[9] Winston S. Churchill, *The Second World War*, vol. VI (London, 1954), p. 141.

conquered. Yet the Japanese military continued to ignore the realities of the situation. They went on propounding the thesis that the day of national salvation
would come when the Japanese would destroy the
enemy as he set foot on Japanese soil. The military
did not turn their back on diplomatic maneuvers, but
their objectives were unrealistic. The Army sought
to avert the Soviet Union's entry into the Pacific
War on the Allied side; the Navy wanted to trade
Japanese cruisers and other armaments for Soviet oil
and aircraft.

Although Foreign Minister Togo realized that Japan could not continue the war and had lost all
military, economic and diplomatic bargaining power,
the government failed to reverse Japanese policy
fundamentally and continued to look for a magic key
that would save Japan from the inexorably approach-
ing catastrophe. Regarding the Soviet Union's alliance
with the United States and Great Britain as a marriage
of convenience, the Japanese decided on May 14 to
try to win her over by economic and territorial concessions now that the war with Germany had ended
and, if this failed, to seek her mediation in a negotiated peace with the United States and Great Brit-
tain.[10] In doing so, they lost sight of the Soviet Union's
determination to stamp out the fires of war and help
free the subjected peoples of Asia.

As noted, the Japanese had already made a peace feeler
through Sweden. In a proposal transmitted through
Widar Bagge, the Swedish minister to Japan, upon his
return to Europe to the United States Ambassador to
Sweden Herschel V. Johnson, they had stipulated
that the peace terms provide for the preservation of

[10] *Shusen shiroku,* p. 330.

Japanese control over Korea and Taiwan.[11] Johnson retorted that this would be unacceptable, the Allies having clearly stated in the Cairo Declaration that Taiwan would be returned to China and that Korea's independence would be restored.[12]

Another attempt to end the war without loss of empire was made through the Swedish banker Per Jacobsson, adviser of the Bank of International Settlements, who was on friendly terms with the staff of the United States Consulate in Basle, Switzerland. Again the Japanese stipulated retention of Taiwan and Korea; they proposed an international administration for Manchuria, and sought assurance that they could keep their Emperor and their constitution.[13] Allen W. Dulles of the OSS, who dealt with the Japanese peace overture, replied that the United States wished to preserve the monarchy, but that since other countries—the U.S.S.R., France and China—did not, she could not make a written statement to this effect; she could merely voice her understanding that the Imperial regime would be maintained if Japan surrendered, though the constitution would have to be amended. Dulles said nothing about the Japanese claims to Korea and Taiwan.[14]

Rebuffed by the Americans, who were getting ready for the Potsdam Conference,[15] the Japanese renewed their efforts to secure Soviet mediation, although they did not state so outright at first, when asking for permission to send a special envoy to Moscow;[16] in

[11] *Ibid.,* pp. 238, 235.
[12] *Ibid.,* p. 248.
[13] *Ibid.,* pp. 301–302.
[14] *Ibid.*
[15] *Ibid.,* p. 424.
[16] Soviet Archives, 436b, file 21, pp. 36–37.

fact, they reiterated that as long as the United States and Great Britain insisted on unconditional surrender, they would have no choice but to continue the war. On July 13 Ambassador Sato handed to Deputy Foreign Minister Lozovsky a letter in which he conveyed the Emperor's desire to send Prince Konoe as his official representative; appended to the letter was a message from the Emperor himself, stating in general terms his desire "to put an end to the war as quickly as possible."[17] When the Soviet government replied on July 18 that "the considerations stated in the message from the Emperor of Japan are general and contain no specific proposals" and that the purpose of Prince Konoe's mission was not clear,[18] Sato informed Lozovsky on July 25 that the purpose of the Konoe mission was to request the Soviet government to act as an intermediary to help end the war.[19]

The following day, on July 26, the Potsdam Declaration of the United States, Great Britain and China was proclaimed. It called upon Japan to surrender her armed forces unconditionally, warning that further resistance would lead to her swift and total defeat, to the inevitable destruction of her large cities and the annihilation of her armed forces. It stated the basic political principles that were to be applied to Japan upon surrender: fulfillment of the terms of the Cairo Declaration, limiting Japanese sovereignty to Honshu, Shikoku, Kyushu, Hokkaido and to minor islands, to be determined by the Allies; the disarmament of Japan and the uprooting of militarism; the

---

[17] *Istoriya voiny na Tikhom okeane*, vol. IV, p. 188.
[18] Soviet Archives, 06, file 897, p. 7.
[19] *Shusen shiroku*, p. 443.

punishment of war criminals and the occupation of Japan until the implementation of the fundamental objectives of the declaration.[20]

When the Japanese did not accept the demand for surrender, the United States, which had been informed by the U.S.S.R. at Potsdam of the Japanese request for Soviet mediation and of Soviet determination to enter the war in conformity with the Yalta agreement, dropped atomic bombs on Hiroshima and Nagasaki on August 6 and 9 respectively.[21] Meanwhile, on the afternoon of August 8, Foreign Minister Molotov notified Ambassador Sato that the Soviet government subscribed to the Potsdam Declaration and in order "to hasten peace, spare the people further sacrifice and suffering and enable the Japanese people to deliver themselves from the dangers and destruction which Germany had experienced after her refusal to surrender unconditionally" declared that as of August 9 the Soviet Union would consider herself in a state of war with Japan.[22] The Soviet entry into the Pacific war put an end to Japanese hopes of further resistance and shattered Japanese attempts to save Japanese imperialism from defeat and surrender by securing a compromise peace with the United States and Great Britain.

Japanese diplomacy had been unable to assess correctly the policy of the great powers in the anti-fascist coalition. The anti-Communism of the Axis powers had softened the opposition of the capitalist governments to German and Japanese aggression so long as there had been hope that the Soviet Union

[20] *Pravda*, July 27, 1945.
[21] Joseph L. Marx, *Nagasaki. The Necessary Bomb?* (New York: Macmillan, 1971), pp. 62–63.
[22] *Vneshnyaya politika SSSR, vol. III*, pp. 362–63.

would be the main victim, but once their own vital interests were threatened, the capitalist states joined with the U.S.S.R. in common opposition to the Axis powers. Japanese diplomacy failed in particular to comprehend the fact that imperialist deals and backstage bargains were alien to the Soviet Union, which was determined to crush the aggressors and liberate the peoples of Europe and Asia from fascist bondage. Steeped in the ideas of the "Imperial Way" and "the eight corners [of the world] under one roof," which envisioned Japanese world supremacy, Japanese diplomacy, after serving the aggressive, predatory policy of Japanese imperialism for many decades, was unable to adapt itself to changing conditions and effect a retreat with minimum losses. Before and during the Pacific War, Japan and Germany proved unable to attain their aims, not so much because their diplomatic apparatus was inefficient, but because their objectives were adventurist and so excessive as to be unrealizable.

The Second World War brought havoc not only to the victims of fascist aggression, but to the peoples of Germany, Italy and Japan themselves. Japan suffered 6½ million casualties.[23] The damage to her economy amounted to 65 billion yen,[24] not counting the military expenditures, totalling 56 billion yen.[25] One quarter of all dwellings were destroyed by air raids. The lack of food during the war and the nervous tension and emotional strain caused by the constant air alert undermined the nation's health, increasing rates of illness and death by 70 to 80 per cent.[26]

[23] *The World Almanac and Book of Facts* (New York, 1949), p. 326.
[24] Annex to *Istoriya voiny na Tikhom okeane,* part IV, p. 310.
[25] *The World Almanac and Book of Facts,* p. 317.
[26] *Nihon tokei nenkan 1945* (Tokyo, 1946), pp. 150, 152, 251.

The history of Japanese policy on the eve of the Pacific War shows the cost and futility of resorting to force in international relations. It is a lesson that must be taken to heart especially now, when thermonuclear war could spell an end to mankind. The risks inherent in an adventurist foreign policy of aggression are heightened by the interdependence of international relations in the postwar world. Any "local" conflict affects the world at large. The old Soviet thesis that "peace is indivisible" is relevant today, when any clash anywhere can plunge humanity into the abyss of total war. The time for reckless gambles and bluffs is past, and the only realistic policy for any nation to pursue is a policy of peace and international cooperation.

Bibliography

UNPUBLISHED SOURCES

People's Republic of China, Ministry of Foreign Affairs, Press Department. Archives.
Union of Soviet Socialist Republics, Ministry of Foreign Affairs. Foreign Policy Archives.

PUBLISHED SOURCES

Adamov, E. A. and L. N. Kutakov. "Angliiskiye fal'sifikatory istorii: Dokumenty Britanskoi Vneshnei Politiki, 1919–1939, III seriia" (The English falsifiers of history: the Documents on British Foreign Policy, 1919–1939, Third Series), *Izvestiya Akademii Nauk SSSR. Seriya istorii i filosofii,* vol. VII (Moscow, 1950), No. 2.

Amerasia, 1938–1941.

Asahi Shinbun, 1938–1945.

Bisson, T. A. *Japan's War Economy.* New York: Macmillan, 1945.

Chen, Bo-da. *Chan Kai-shi—vrag kitaiskogo naroda* (Chiang Kai-shek—enemy of the Chinese people). Moscow: Izdatel'stvo inostrannoi literatury, 1950.

China Economist.

Churchill, Winston S. *The Second World War.* Boston: Houghton Mifflin, 1948–1953. 6 vols.

Craig, William. *The Fall of Japan.* New York: Dell, 1968.

Craigie, Sir Robert. *Behind the Japanese Mask.* New York: Hutchinson, 1945.

Friedman, Irving S. *British Relations with China 1931–1939.* New York: Institute of Pacific Relations, 1940.

Gaiko jiho, 1938–1941.

Gol'dberg, D. I. *Vneshnyaya politika Yaponii (Sentyabr' 1939 g.–Dekabr' 1941 g.)* (The foreign policy of Japan [September 1939–December 1941]). Moscow: Izdatel'stvo vostochnoi literatury, 1959.

Great Britain, Foreign Office. *Documents on British Foreign Policy, 1919–1939.* London: His Majesty's Stationery Office, 1946.

Great Britain, Parliament. *Parliamentary Debates. House of Commons.* Fifth Series.

Grew, Joseph C. *Ten Years in Japan.* New York: Simon and Schuster, 1944.

Hattori, Takushiro. *Dai-Toa senso zenshi* (A complete history of the Greater East Asia War). Tokyo: Masu Shobo, 1953. 4 vols.

International Military Tribunal for the Far East. Record of Proceedings. 1946–1948.

Istoriya Velikoi Otechestvennoi voiny Sovetskogo Soyuza 1941–1945 (History of the Great Patriotic War of the Soviet Union 1941–1945). Moscow: Voyenizdat, 1961. 3 vols.

Istoriya voiny na Tikhom okeane (History of the war in the Pacific). Russian translation of *Taiheiyo senso-shi,* compiled by the Rekishi-gaku Kenkyu-kai.

Moscow: Izdatel'stvo inostrannoi literatury, 1957–1958. 5 vols.

Izvestiya. 1938–1945.

Japan, Foreign Office. *Nihon gaiko hyakunen shoshi* (Brief history of a century of Japanese diplomacy). Tokyo, 1958.

————. *Shusen shiroku* (Historical record of the ending of the war). Tokyo: Shinbun Gekkansha, 1952.

Kaizo. 1938.

Kajima, Morinosuke. *Saikin Nihon no kokusai-teki chi-i* (The international situation in contemporary Japan). Tokyo, 1938.

Kiyosawa, Kiyoshi. *Nihon gaiko-shi* (History of Japanese foreign policy). Tokyo, 1943. 2 vols.

Konoe Fumimaro. *Heiwa e no doryoku* (My efforts toward peace). Tokyo: Nippon Dempo Tsushinsha, 1946.

Kutakov, L. N. *Istoriya sovetsko-yaponskikh diplomaticheskikh otnoshenii* (History of Soviet-Japanese diplomatic relations). Moscow: Izdatel'stvo mezhdunarodnykh otnoshenii, 1962.

————. "Iz istorii podgotovki 'dal'nevostochnogo Myunkhena' (Yapono-angliiskiye otnosheniya nakanune vtoroi mirovoi voiny)" (The making of the "Far Eastern Munich" [Anglo-Japanese relations on the eve of the Second World War]), in *Mezhimperialisticheskiye protivorechiya na pervom etape obshchego krizisa kapitalizma.* Moscow: Sotsegiz, 1959.

————. "Vosstanovleniye istoricheskikh prav" (The restoration of historical rights), *Izvestiya Akademii Nauk SSSR. Seriya istorii i filosofii,* vol. V (1951), No. 5, pp. 562–66.

Langer, William L. and S. Everett. *The Challenge to Isolation, 1937–1940.* New York: Harper, 1952.
———. *The Undeclared War, 1941.* New York: Harper, 1953.
Luk'yanova, M. I. *Yaponskiye monopolii vo vremya vtoroi mirovoi voiny* (The Japanese monopolies during the Second World War). Moscow: Izdatel'stvo Akademii Nauk SSSR, 1953.
Lupke, Hubertus. *Japans Ruszlandpolitik von 1939 bis 1941* (Japan's Russia policy from 1939 until 1941). Frankfurt am Main: Alfred Metzner Verlag, 1962.
Marx, Joseph L. *Nagasaki. The Necessary Bomb?* New York: Macmillan, 1971.
Nakamura, Kikuo. *Showa jidai no seijishi* (Political history of the Showa Period). Tokyo, 1956.
New York Times. 1938–1945.
Nihon tokei nenkan 1945 (Statistical annual of Japan 1945). Tokyo, 1946.
Pravda. 1937–1945.
Raginskii, M. Yu. and S. Ya. Rozenblit. *Mezhdunarodnyi protsess glavnykh yaponskikh voyennykh prestupnikov* (The international trial of the main Japanese war criminals). Moscow: Publishing House of the Academy of Sciences of the U.S.S.R., 1950.
Roth, Andrew. *Dilemma in Japan.* Boston: Little, Brown, 1945.
Royal Institute of International Affairs. *Japan in Defeat: A Report by a Chatham Study Group.* London, 1945.
Sasa, Hiro. *Taikoku Nihon no shorai* (The future of a strong Japan). Tokyo, 1935.
Sbornik dogovorov Rossii s drugimi gosudarstvami 1856–1917 (Collection of treaties between Russia

and other states). Compiled by I. V. Koz'menko, edited by E. A. Adamov. Moscow: Gosudarstvennoye izdatel'stvo politicheskoi literatury, 1952.

Schmidt, Paul. *Statist auf diplomatischer Bühne 1923–45* (Supernumerary on the diplomatic stage 1923–45). Bonn: Athenäum, 1950.

Shigemitsu, Mamoru. *Japan and Her Destiny.* New York: Dutton, 1958.

——. *Showa no doran* (Showa upheaval). Tokyo, 1952.

Sladkovskii, M. I. *Ocherki razvitiya vneshneekonomicheskikh otnoshenii Kitaya* (Essays on the development by China of economic relations with other countries). Moscow: Vneshtorgizdat, 1953.

Sommer, Theo. *Deutschland und Japan zwischen den Mächten 1935–1940* (Germany and Japan between the powers 1935–1940). Tübingen: J. C. B. Mohr (Paul Siebeck), 1962.

Togo, Shigenori. *The Cause of Japan.* New York: Simon and Schuster, 1956.

——. *Jidai no ichimen* (An aspect of the times). Tokyo: Kaizosha, 1952.

Trans-Pacific. 1938.

Tsuji, Masanobu. *Nomonhan.* Tokyo, 1947.

Union of Soviet Socialist Republics, Ministry of Foreign Affairs. *Dokumenty i materialy kanuna vtoroi mirovoi voiny* (Documents and materials relating to the eve of the Second World War). Moscow: Gospolitizdat, 1948.

——. *Vneshnyaya politika SSSR. Sbornik dokumentov* (Foreign Policy of the U.S.S.R. Collected Documents), vols. IV and V (Moscow, 1945).

——. *Vneshnyaya politika Sovetskogo Soyuza, 1948 god. Dokumenty i materialy* (Foreign policy of the Soviet Union, 1948. Documents and materials). Part I (Moscow, 1950).

Union of Soviet Socialist Republics, Verkhovnyi Sovet. *Sed'maya sessiya Verkhovnogo Soveta SSSR. 1 avgusta–7 avgusta 1940 g. Stenograficheskii otchet* (Seventh session of the Supreme Soviet of the U.S.S.R. August 1–August 7, 1940. Stenographic record). Moscow: Gospolitizdat, 1940.

——. *Shestaya sessiya Verkhovnogo Soveta SSSR. 29 marta–4 aprelya 1940 g. Stenograficheskii otchet* (Sixth session of the Supreme Soviet of the U.S.S.R. March 29–April 4, 1940. Stenographic record). Moscow: Gospolitizdat, 1940.

——. *Tret'ya sessiya Verkhovnogo Soveta SSSR. 25–31 maya 1939 g. Stenograficheskii otchet* (Third session of the Supreme Soviet of the U.S.S.R. May 25–31, 1939. Stenographic record). Moscow: Gospolitizdat, 1939.

United States Congress, Joint Committee on the Investigation of the Pearl Harbor Attack. *Hearings before the Joint Committee on the Investigation of the Pearl Harbor Attack.* Washington: U.S. Government Printing Office, 1946. 39 parts.

United States Department of State. *Documents on German Foreign Policy 1918–1945.* Series D. Washington: U.S. Government Printing Office, 1949.

——. *Foreign Relations of the United States. Diplomatic Papers.* Vols. for 1938 and 1939. Washington: U.S. Government Printing Office, 1955.

——. *Report of the Mission on Japanese Combines.* Part I. Washington: U.S. Government Printing Office, 1946.

United States Strategic Bombing Survey, *Japan's*

Struggle to End the War. Washington: U.S. Government Printing Office, 1946.

The World Almanac and Book of Facts. New York: Press, 1949.

Zhukov, E. M. (ed.). *Mezhdunarodnye otnosheniya na Dal'nem Vostoke (1840–1949)* (International relations in the Far East [1840–1949]). Moscow: Gosudarstvennoye izdatel'stvo politicheskoi literatury, 1956.

Zhukov, Marshal G. K. *Vospominaniya i razmyshleniya* (Memoirs and reminiscences). Moscow: Novosti, 1969.

Index

238

THE DIPLOMATIC PRESS, INC.

1102 BETTON ROAD, TALLAHASSEE, FLORIDA 32303, U.S.A.

Satow, Sir Ernest. *Korea and Manchuria between Russia and Japan 1895–1904. The Observations of Sir Ernest Satow, British Minister and Plenipotentiary to Japan and China.* Selected and edited with a historical introduction by George Alexander Lensen. First published 1966; second printing 1968. 300 pp., collotype frontispiece, cloth. ISBN 910512-01-9. $12.50.
". . . a welcome addition to primary source material for the study of Far Eastern diplomatic history."—*The Journal of Asian Studies.*
". . . full of interesting and illuminating views from a diplomat of experience and wisdom. . ."—*The American Historical Review*

D'Anethan, Baron Albert. *The d'Anethan Dispatches from Japan 1894–1910. The Observations of Baron Albert d'Anethan, Belgian Minister Plenipotentiary and Dean of the Diplomatic Corps.* Translated and edited with a historical introduction by George Alexander Lensen. 1967. 272 pp., collotype frontispiece, cloth. ISBN 910512-02-7. $15.00.
"A companion volume to . . . Sir Ernest Satow . . . Masterfully selected excerpts of heretofore unpublished official dispatches . . ."— *Historische Zeitschrift*
"Valuable to students in East Asian international relations. . ."—*Choice*

Lensen, George Alexander. *The Russo-Chinese War.* 1967. 315 pp., collotype frontispiece, maps, extensive bibliography, cloth. ISBN 910512-03-05 $15.00.
"The first full-length treatment of Sino-Russian hostilities in Manchuria during the Boxer Rebellion of 1900. . . . Lensen writes clearly, vividly, and with full mastery of his subject."—*Choice*

Will, John Baxter. *Trading Under Sail off Japan 1860–1899. The Recollections of Captain John Baxter Will, Sailing-Master and Pilot.* Edited with a historical introduction by George Alexander Lensen. 1968, 190 pp., lavishly printed and illustrated, cloth. ISBN 910512-04-3. $12.50.
". . . this extremely interesting story . . . ranks with the few which, while not perhaps of the type to keep young children from play, should keep most men 'in the chimney corner.' "—*The Japan Times*

Lensen, George Alexander (comp.). *Japanese Diplomatic and Consular Officials in Russia. A Handbook of Japanese Representatives in Russia from 1874 to 1968.* 1968. 230 pp., hard-cover. ISBN 910512-05-1. $15.00.
"A useful handbook for every serious student of the relations between Japan and the U.S.S.R."—*Narody Azii i Afriki*

Lensen, George Alexander (comp.). *Russian Diplomatic and Consular Officials in East Asia. A Handbook of the representatives of Tsarist Russia and the Provisional Government in China, Japan and Korea from 1858 to 1924 and of Soviet Representatives in Japan from 1925 to 1958.* 1968. 294 pp., hard-cover. ISBN 910512–06–X. $15.00.

"The two handbooks are essential reference works for every library of East Asian or Russian history; for specialists in the field of Russian-East Asian Relations where the author is known as a distinguished pioneering scholar, they will be indispensable companions."—*Pacific Affairs*

Westwood, J.N. *Witnesses of Tsushima.* 1970. xiv, 321 pp., plus 38 illustrations. Cloth. ISBN 910512–08–06. $15.00.

"Dr. Westwood, by interweaving his own narrative with eyewitness accounts and the official reports both Russian and Japanese gives us a far more accurate version of the famous Russian voyage out of Kronstadt to the Straits of Tsushima and the subsequent battle than has been available heretofore."—*Journal of Asian Studies*

Lensen, George Alexander. *Japanese Recognition of the U.S.S.R.; Soviet-Japanese Relations 1921–1930.* 1970. 425 pp. illustrated, cloth. ISBN 910512–09–4. $15.00.

"The book is a careful detailed treatment of an important period in Russo-Japanese relations. It will be of special interest to diplomatic and economic historians and of more general interest to those concerned with Japan's position in East Asia or the Soviet Union's relations there."
—*Choice*

McNally, Raymond T. *Chaadayev and his Friends. An Intellectual History of Peter Chaadayev and his Russian Contemporaries.* 1971, 315 pp. frontispiece, imitation leather. ISBN 910512–11–6. $15.00.

A new and highly readable interpretation of the place of Peter Chaadayev (1794–1856), the first Russian Westernizer and a unique thinker, in intellectual history, based on research in Soviet archives.

Poutiatine, Countess Olga. *War and Revolution. Excerpts from the Letters and Diaries of the Countess Olga Poutiatine.* Translated and edited by George Alexander Lensen. 1971, 111 pp. illustrated, cloth. ISBN 910512–12–4. $12.50.

A moving eyewitness account of the Russian Revolution and of conditions in Russian and Anglo-Russian military hospitals during the First World War by the granddaughter of the Russian admiral who competed with Commodore Perry in the opening of Japan.

Sansom, Lady Katharine. *Sir George Sansom and Japan. A Memoir.* 1971, 183 pp., illustrated, cloth. ISBN 910512–13–2. $15.00.

The diplomatic and scholarly life of Sir George Sansom, foremost Western authority on Japan, mirrored in the letters and diary entries of his wife and himself, with unforgettable thumbnail sketches of leading diplomatic, political, military and literary figures n Japan from 1928 to 1950.

Kutakov, Leonid N. *Japanese Foreign Policy on the Eve of the Pacific War.* Edited with a foreword by George Alexander Lensen. 1972. About 250 pp., frontispiece, cloth. ISBN 910512–15–9. $15.00.

An analysis on the basis of unpublished Soviet archival material by a Russian diplomat historian, currently under-secretary-general for political and Security Council affairs of the United Nations.

Lensen, George Alexander. *The Strange Neutrality: Soviet-Japanese Relations during the Second World War, 1941–1945.* 1972. About 320 pp., illustrated, cloth. ISBN 910512–14–0. $15.00.
A study based on unpublished Japanese archival material as well as Soviet sources.

Vishwanathan, Savitri. *Japan's Relations with the U.S.S.R. since 1945. An Indian View.* 1973. About 275 pp., illustrated, cloth. ISBN 910512–16–7. $15.00
A detailed survey, based primarily on Japanese source material.

*   *   *

Lensen, George Alexander, *Faces of Japan: A Photographic Study.* 154 large collotype reproductions, beautifully printed in a limited edition. 1968. 312 pp., cloth. ISBN 910512–07–8. $30.00
Candid portraits of Japanese of all walks of life at work and at play. "A terrifically beautiful book."—Wilson Hicks

Lensen, George Alexander. *April in Russia: A Photographic Study.* 100 large collotype reproductions, beautifully printed in a limited edition. 1970. 208 pp., cloth. ISBN 910512–10–8. $40.00.
"An enlightening educational tool as well as an artistic, almost poetic, addition to personal libraries."—*Tallahassee Democrat*
". . . this historian has the soul of a poet and the eye of an artist." —*Novoye Russkoye Slovo*